Women's Spiritual Autobiography in Colonial Spanish America

Women's Spiritual Autobiography in Colonial Spanish America

Kristine Ibsen

University Press of Florida
Gainesville · Tallahassee · Tampa · Boca Raton
Pensacola · Orlando · Miami · Jacksonville

Copyright 1999 by the Board of Regents of the State of Florida
Printed in the United States of America on acid-free paper
All rights reserved

04 03 02 01 00 99 6 5 4 3 2 1

Library of Congress Cataloging-in-Publication Data

Ibsen, Kristine, 1961-
Women's spiritual autobiography in colonial Spanish America / Kristine Ibsen.
p. cm.
Includes bibliographical references (p.   ) and index.
ISBN 0-8130-1727-0 (alk. paper)
1. Nuns—South America Biography. 2. Spiritual biography—South America—History and criticism. 3. Autobiography—Religious aspects—Christianity. 4. Autobiography—Women authors—History and criticism. 5. Spanish American literature—Women authors. 6. Spanish A   an literature—18th century—History and criticism. I. Titl
BX4225.I37 1999
271'.900228—dc21 99-39580

The University Press of Florida is the scholarly publishing agency for the State University System of Florida, comprising Florida A & M University, Florida Atlantic University, Florida International University, Florida State University, University of Central Florida, University of Florida, University of North Florida, University of South Florida, and University of West Florida.

University Press of Florida
15 Northwest 15th Street
Gainesville, FL 32611-2079
http://www.upf.com

Contents

Preface   vii

Principal Authors Discussed   xi

Introduction—Multiple Heroines: Women's Spiritual Autobiography in Colonial Spanish America   1

1. Body and Soul: Self-Representation as Confessional Discourse   19

2. Immaculate Conceptions: Madre Castillo Wrestles with the Truth   48

3. Cloisters of the Soul: Spiritual Autobiography and the Hagiographic Tradition   62

4. Geography of the Sacred: Sebastiana Josefa de la Santísima Trinidad and the Hagiographic Representation of the Body   85

5. The Hiding Places of My Power: Visionary Authority and Mystic Space   97

6. The Unimprisoned Mind: Úrsula Suárez and the Self-Fashioning Heroine   121

Epilogue: And the Rest Is Silence—*Reply to Sor Filotea* and Other Random Thoughts   137

Notes   141

Bibliography   183

Index   199

Preface

This book studies women's personal narrative in colonial Spanish America, focusing in particular on the spiritual autobiography of the viceregal period. In Spanish America, women's autobiography is rooted in the hagiographic tradition of *vitae,* in which, at the request of a confessor, nuns wrote about their spiritual lives in an autobiographical form. Although not intended for publication, these personal histories, or *vidas,* often circulated informally among other religious women; in fact, they were often written with this audience in mind. Simultaneously written for the nuns' male confessor(s) and female peers, such texts illustrate a fascinating exercise in double-voiced discourse.[1]

Through an examination of the autobiographical writings of María de San José (Mexico, 1656–1719); Úrsula Suárez (Chile, 1666–1749); Gerónima del Espíritu Santo (Colombia, 1669–1727); Francisca Josefa de Castillo (Colombia, 1671–1742); María Manuela de Santa Ana (Peru, 1695–1793); Sebastiana Josefa de la Santísima Trinidad (Mexico, 1709–1757); María Marcela (Mexico, 1719–?); and María Coleta de San José (Mexico, ?–1776), the nature of female self-representation is addressed from the perspective of two fundamental and interrelated issues. First, to what degree did the expectations of the intended and implied audiences shape these texts? Second, what were the discursive strategies employed by each author to accommodate these conflicting demands? By selecting a form of discourse that hinges on the explicit mediation of an intended (actual) reader, this study examines the influence of the reader as representative of the dominant culture in the narrative construction of self. To placate their readers and at the same time assert their own identities, whether for themselves or for future potential readers, these authors developed certain linguistic stratagems that subtly undermined such power relations and challenged the official ideology that denied women access to the public sphere.

What follows is both a synthesis of original archival work and an extension of, and dialogue with, the work of other scholars. It is the product of several years' research at the Benson Collection at the University of Texas, the National Library and General Archives of the Nation in Mexico City, the John Carter Brown Library at Brown University, and the Bancroft Library at the University of California, Berkeley. Altogether, I have examined twelve unpublished manuscripts, ten published autobiographies, and twenty-one published biographies and collective biographies that incorporate the writings of religious women in colonial Spanish America, as well as numerous supplementary materials (confession manuals, rules and regulations, pastoral declarations, funeral sermons) from the viceregal period. By placing these works in their historical context, I have examined the textual self not only in terms of the discursive strategies themselves but also in the way these strategies incorporated and questioned prevailing social, rhetorical, and cultural structures.

Of the eight women whose work forms the foundation of this book, three (María Coleta de San José, María Marcela, and Sebastiana Josefa de la Santísima Trinidad) have not been published, and a fourth (María de San José) has had only the first volume of her life story in print, although a second volume of translated selections is in preparation. To my knowledge, María Coleta de San José has not been mentioned in any other study. The life stories of the four remaining authors (Úrsula Suárez, Francisca Josefa Castillo, Gerónima del Espíritu Santo, and María Manuela de Santa Ana) have been transcribed in their entirety. Unless otherwise indicated, all translations are my own, with the original Spanish text indicated in the notes. In general, spellings of the original texts have been standardized and syntactical and grammatical idiosyncrasies preserved. For these translations I have referred primarily to the *Diccionario de autoridades* of the Real Academia Española (1726) and Sebastián de Covarrubias Orozco's *Tesoro de la lengua castellana o española* (1611). Contemporary dictionaries consulted include María Moliner's *Diccionario del uso del español* (1966), Martín Alonso's *Enciclopedia del idioma* (1958), the *Diccionario de mejicanismos* compiled by Francisco J. Santamaría (1959), the Larousse *Gran diccionario español-inglés* (1993), and the Oxford *Spanish Dictionary* (1994). Published translations are indicated with the page number of the original followed by the page number of the translated text.

One final technical note: after considerable thought and discussion with religious women at Notre Dame, I have decided not to preface authors' names with the titles "Sor" and "Sister" except at the beginnings of individual chapters. As one of my colleagues aptly expressed it, "sister" is "a title presented to the world"; here, in a discussion of women's intimate spiritual writings and inner lives, the title "only seems to get in the way."

My omission of the titles should in no way detract from the profound respect I have for these exceptional women.

I would like to thank all the friends and colleagues who have offered encouragement and advice during the preparation of this book; I am particularly indebted to Stacey Schlau, Sherry Velasco, and Encarnación Juárez for their attentive readings and helpful comments. Julia Douthwaite and José Anadón read and commented on earlier drafts of the manuscript. Frederick Luciani contributed critical insights on the sections dealing with Sebastiana Josefa de la Santísima Trinidad. Susan Fernandez and Gillian Hillis at the University Press of Florida deserve special thanks. Acknowledgment and thanks are also due the Institute for Scholarship in the Liberal Arts at the University of Notre Dame, especially Robert Burke, Christopher Fox, Kenneth García, and Jennifer Warlick.

Portions of chapter 4 were published in the *Colonial Latin American Review* 7, no. 2 (1998) and are reprinted here with permission of CARFAX Publishing Limited, Abingdon, United Kingdom. Extracts from Francisca Josefa Castillo *Su vida* (1968) appear by permission of the Biblioteca Luis Ángel Arango of the Banco de la República, Bogotá, Colombia. Excerpts from Úrsula Suárez *Relación autobiográfica* (1984) appear courtesy of the Universidad de Concepción (Chile) and the Academia Chilena de la Historia. The final stage of this project was made possible by a fellowship from the National Endowment for the Humanities, an independent federal agency.

Principal Authors Discussed

Chile

Ursula Suárez y Escobar (1666–1749)

Colombia

Francisca Josefa de la Concepción
(Francisca Josefa Castillo Toledo Guevara, 1671–1742)

Gerónima del Espíritu Santo
(Gerónima Nava y Saavedra, 1669–1727)

Mexico

María Coleta de San José (?–1776)

María de San José
(Juana Palacios Berruecos, 1656–1719)

María Marcela
(María Marcela González, 1719–?)

Sebastiana Josefa de la Santísima Trinidad
(Sebastiana Josefa Maya Marín Samaniego, 1709–1757)

Peru

María Manuela de Santa Ana
(María Manuela Hurtado de Mendoza, 1695–1793)

Introduction

Multiple Heroines

Women's Spiritual Autobiography in Colonial Spanish America

> How unpleasant it is to be locked out; and ... how ... worse perhaps to be locked in.
>
> Virginia Woolf

Gender hierarchies in viceregal Spanish-American society were legitimated and maintained through a complex system of symbolic representations expressed in social, political, scientific, and religious discourses. The belief in the God-given inferiority of women and in women's subordinate position did not begin with Christianity, but it became more pronounced with the consolidation of an institutional power structure in which religious women were completely dependent on male clerics, since only priests could perform mass, give communion, and hear confession. Discursive practices in Counter-Reformation Spain were in fact so "thoroughly masculinist," observes George Mariscal, "that it is difficult for modern readers to imagine the extent of its consequences in the social realm" (*Contradictory Subjects* 55).[1] Like most of the Western world, in both learned and popular sectors of Spain and Spanish America man was associated with the soul, spirit, and reason, and woman with the body, carnality, and sinfulness.[2] Inherently transgressive, the woman's body was believed to require constant surveillance. This surveillance was not limited to the physical enclosure of women but also encompassed their voices and thoughts, since women's speech and women's bodies had been inextricably associated since antiquity.[3] As Peter Stallybrass notes in his study of seventeenth-century England, notions of space, voice, and chastity often crossed borders and combined, so that a woman who was a "whore of her tongue" could well be perceived as more dangerous than one who was a "whore of her body" (126–27). In his treatise *On Wifely Duties* (1415–16), Italian humanist Francesco Barbaro conjures a similar, albeit less flamboyant, turn of phrase that he attributes to Plutarch: "the speech of a noble woman can be no less dangerous than the nakedness of her limbs" (ctd. Kohl 123–24).

As early as the thirteenth century these restrictions were extended to control women's movement. Limitations were particularly severe for religious women: in 1215 nuns could not go outside the cloister without the bishop's permission; beginning in 1293, regular reviews by male clerics became obligatory, and from 1545 on nuns were forbidden to leave the convent except under extraordinary circumstances.[4] Convent life was strictly regulated: women were required to follow a rigid schedule that dictated their activities for every hour of the day. Meetings with family members and other visitors were effected behind bars in the *locutorio* [locutory or receiving room] and monitored by other nuns. Black-veiled doorkeepers, the *porteras* and *torneras,* controlled visitors and messages between the convent and the outside world; *rederas* [grille attendants] and *escuchas* [literally, "listeners"] accompanied nuns in the locutory and were responsible for listening to the conversations between nuns and their visitors. During visits either a drape had to be pulled over the bars or the nun was required to cloak her face with a veil, although this rule was relaxed in some orders. Under normal circumstances even priests' access to the convent was limited. Communion was given through a *cratícula,* or *comulgatorio,* a small opening next to the lower choir, and the confessional was similarly situated in the wall dividing the church from the convent.[5]

During the reign of Isabel la Católica in the late fifteenth and early sixteenth centuries, Spain had appeared to be moving toward a relatively humanistic form of religious practice under the patronage of Cardinal Francisco Ximénez Cisneros (1436–1517).[6] An ardent defender of mystic experience, Cisneros initiated several monastic reforms including the translation and distribution of previously inaccessible devotional and mystic works as well as portions of the Scriptures.[7] Ironically, it was precisely this expansion of the printed word that led to the first *Índices* and catalogs of books prohibited by the Inquisition in Spain (Valdés: [1551], 1559; Quiroga: 1583–84; Sandoval: 1612; Zapata: 1632; Sotomayor: 1640; Valladares-Marín: 1707; Pérez de Prado: 1747; Rubín de Cevallos: 1790, 1805).[8] Reaffirming a rigid model of clerical authority and practice, individual spiritual expression was once again discouraged. Vernacular translations of spiritual treatises, including those of Pedro de Alcántara and Luis de León, were now forbidden reading; even Spanish translations of the Bible were proscribed beginning in 1492. Discouraged and ultimately prohibited from learning Latin, most women were rendered unable to participate in the language of the Church by this ban on texts in the vernacular.[9] Women's participation in the Church was further circumscribed in reaction to the *alumbrado,* or Illuminist movement. Although recent investigation seems to suggest that the basic precepts of this movement were not heretical (indeed, the *alumbrados* counted among their supporters Juan de la Cruz and Ignacio de Loyola), the personalized worship of the movement was perceived as a serious threat to the hierarchy of the Catholic Church. The discovery that many of these groups were led by women made it particularly suspect.[10] In this way, the repressive environment of the Counter Reformation effectively silenced any voices—both male and female—of personal religious experience.

* * *

In the Americas, the establishment of convents paralleled the consolidation and expansion of colonial rule. The most populated viceroyalties were New Spain (Mexico), with six million inhabitants, and Peru, which initially encompassed most of South America and included a million and a half subjects (Sebastián 29). It was in these regions that convents were first founded and where they proliferated most rapidly.[11] The first convent to be founded in Spanish America was La Concepción in Mexico City, established in 1540, five years after the viceroyalty of New Spain was formalized. It was followed in Peru by La Encarnación in Lima (1561). Six orders were represented throughout Mexico and Peru: the Augustinians, Conceptionists, Discalced Carmelites, Dominicans, and Franciscans (Capuchines, Clarissan Urbanists). A third region in which convent culture thrived was the northern part of the Peruvian viceroyalty, which would later become New Granada (Colombia), with the establishment of the Franciscan convent of Santa Clara in Tunja in 1573, followed by convents in the Augustinian, Conceptionist, Discalced Carmelite, and Dominican orders. By the eighteenth century, the Conceptionists, Dominicans, Franciscans, and Discalced Carmelites had expanded into Chile, Cuba, the Dominican Republic, Ecuador, Guatemala, Puerto Rico, and Venezuela; the Franciscans also had two convents in the Philippines and one in Buenos Aires, where the Dominicans had founded the first convent in the relatively late year of 1745 (Muriel *Las mujeres de hispanoamérica* 252–69; Fraschina 9). Other orders represented in Spanish America included the Hieronymites and Bridgettines (Mexico), the Company of Mary (Mexico, Colombia, Argentina), the Cistercians and the Mercedarians (Peru).

Since full status as a choir or black-veiled nun required a dowry and literacy, this option was accessible only to women from privileged classes.

A secondary level of white-veiled or lay nuns (*legas*), from families of lower social status with lesser dowries, could participate in most activities but had no vote in convent elections and could not hold administrative positions. White-veiled nuns also included cooks, musicians, and skilled laborers. Women who for one reason or another were unable to enter convents could be accommodated in the less formal setting of the *recogimiento,* a holding place for disenfranchised women: aristocratic spinsters, indigent widows, orphans, and daughters of families that did not have the economic means to support them and whose only other option would likely have been—and in some cases had been—prostitution. Women could also be placed in convents for criminal or aberrant behavior: for example, a husband could place his wife under the care of nuns if he suspected her of adultery. Conversely, some women seeking refuge from abusive husbands found a place in these communities of women. Recogimientos for women of high moral character were limited to criollas and mestizas and distinguished from "corrective" recogimientos, although in some orders, "redeemed" or "rescued" women were admitted as white-veiled nuns with minimal dowries (Lavrin "In Search" 40, 56; Guernica 78–79; Burns 146).[12] Working-class and non-white women were usually relegated to work as slaves or servants, although in Peru light-skinned mestizas and mulattas were sometimes admitted as *donadas,* servants who wore the nun's habit and supervised other servants and slaves below them (Arenal and Schlau *Untold Sisters* 297).[13]

Convents were thus rarely an option for women of lower social ranking; many, moreover, required proof of "limpieza de sangre" [purity of blood], although in reality the racial situation in New Spain was considerably more fluid than most elite families would have liked to admit.[14] A rumor of questionable lineage nearly prevents Mexican nun María Marcela from professing (41–42), and the testimony of witnesses for the entrance of María Francisca González Carrillo into the Convent of Santa Brígida (Mexico City) in 1778 underscores the importance of lineage in such cases even in the late eighteenth century. Witnesses were required to testify that the professant's parents and grandparents "have been, and were, Spaniards, Old Christians, untainted by any bad race, with no mixed blood whatsoever from Moors, Jews, apostates, recent converts to our holy Catholic faith, nor from mulattos" (*Declaración de Doña María Francisca* 521).[15] Although documents included the concept of religious purity, with "Old Christians" more privileged than those recently converted to Catholicism, the primary purpose of such documentation in the colonies, according to Ann Miriam Gallagher, was to ensure racial homogeneity (152). Evidence seems to suggest, however, that in practice social rank often played a more important role than racial purity, and that an indigenous heritage was more tolerated than African blood. In Mexico, four mestiza descendants of Moctezuma took their vows in the Convent of Santa Clara; and in Peru a generous donation of 20,000 pesos was apparently sufficient for nuns to bend the rules and admit one and possibly two illegitimate mestiza daughters of Alonso de Alvarado to the Convent of la Encarnación in Lima.[16] In Buenos Aires, in contrast, the controversial case of Antonia González, accused by her sisters of having mulatto blood and of being the daughter of a tailor, continued for over fifteen years (Fraschina 14).

In sixteenth-century Cuzco, convents willing to admit non-Spanish women were encouraged by local secular authorities to consolidate Spanish control over an unyielding native population by separating young indigenous and mestizo women from the influence of their mothers (Burns 27–51).[17] With a similar logic, although beginning much later, convents for descendants of indigenous nobility were founded in New Spain by Spanish authorities to ensure a division between native and criollo populations (Arenal and Schlau 355). The first such convent, Corpus Christi, was founded in 1724 in Mexico City, followed by Nuestra Señora de Cosamaluapán in Valladolid (now Morelia) (1737), and Nuestra Señora de los Ángeles in Oaxaca (1782); a fourth convent was proposed for Puebla beginning in 1779 but was never completed. The convents in Morelia and Oaxaca were supported by Purepecha and Zapotec leaders desirous of the prestige that such institutions could bring to their communities; in these convents women were required to document the purity of their native American lineage. In eighteenth-century Peru, the Convent of Copacabana was founded for the daughters of Quechua nobles (Muriel *Las mujeres* 132–33, 135, 138–41, 257, 261; Gallagher 172). Indigenous elites had not only cultural but economic reasons to maintain the purity of their lineage: in New Spain they were afforded many privileges including the right to maintain their lands and continue to receive tributes from their subjects. As convent records seem to confirm, by the eighteenth century indigenous nobility no longer enjoyed the same prosperity as they had in the early years of colonial rule; nonetheless, they still belonged to an elite minority with the economic means to educate their daughters. Indigenous women entering these convents had to be able to read and write in Spanish as well as possess some training in Latin, mathematics, music, and other basic skills such as embroidery and cooking (Muriel *Las indias caciques* 29, 31, 56).

Clearly, the placement of daughters in convents during the viceregal period was one way to ensure hierarchies of race and class. Since the high sum required for marriage dowries often precluded even families from the dominant class from making suitable matches for all their daughters, the convent was considered preferable to marriage to men of "mixed blood" (McKnight 85; Colmenares 294; Muriel *Las mujeres* 30). Often, families whose daughters were sent to the convent belonged to the ranks of the lower aristocracy or to the merchant class: many autobiographies recount a family fortune in decline (María de San José, Francisca Josefa Castillo, Úrsula Suárez, María Marcela, and María Anna Águeda de San Ignacio), financially unable to provide adequate marriage dowries for all their daughters. Although the average marriage dowry for criollo families was 4,000 to 5,000 pesos, competition for conspicuously high dowries led to a regular increase in these sums ranging anywhere from 12,000 to 20,000 pesos or more. In 1686, in the viceroyalty of Peru, Pedro de Torres provided his only daughter, María, with the astronomically high dowry of 84,258 pesos plus another 20,000 as the sole heir to his estate to ensure her marriage into a family of the highest social category. And that same year, Antonio Alfonso de Irarrázaval took the extraordinary step of placing five of his six daughters into convents just so the sixth could bring a dowry of 50,000 pesos to her marriage; all this during a time in which the economy was in decline and the average working-class Spanish immigrant earned around 300 pesos a year (Ramón 74; Burns 36, 80). Although the 2,000 to 3,000 pesos required for profession as a black-veiled nun were not easily obtained, families faced with the alternatives of marrying into another class or raising funds for a suitable marriage viewed the convent as an attractive and affordable option. Indeed, religious life was often embraced by young women in Spanish America as one of the few available outlets for autonomy and dignity. Furthermore, if they belonged to the upper class, the convent could provide them with an authority inadmissible in marriage. It was, in fact, often privileged women who supported the development of convents in the New World. In Mexico City alone, eighteen of twenty-two convents were founded by secular women who either financed the costs themselves or encouraged others to make donations, and records of books published in Mexico City and Puebla demonstrate that it was also often wealthy widows who published spiritual biographies and other devotional works written by women (Lavrin "In Search of the Colonial Woman" 47; Burns 100–101, 110, 118, 123; Medina *La imprenta en México, La imprenta en la Puebla de los Ángeles*). By the end of the eighteenth century, there were some sixty-three convents in New Spain alone, and by 1746, Kathryn Burns reports, the Spanish Crown began to strictly limit the number of new convents founded, while the issue of excessive numbers of religious in the Americas was "discussed at the highest levels" (Muriel "Los conventos de monjas" 12, 20; Burns 189).

Spanish authorities had reason for concern: although convents in the colonies followed the same tenets as their counterparts in Spain, different historical circumstances determined the nature of convent life. Contemplative ideals were respected; the prohibition of owning property usually was not. This was due in part to the requirement that convents in the New World be self-sustaining: by the beginning of the seventeenth century even the reformed Discalced Carmelite order required dowries for admittance. Although reformed orders retained their vows of poverty and criticized the way of life in less restricted communities, with such a significant percentage of Spanish-American elites sending their daughters to convents, many women who took vows did so less for a religious vocation than for convenience; dressing, eating, and socializing in the manner to which they were accustomed (Arenal and Schlau *Untold Sisters* 9, 339).[18] In larger convents, ample cells were typically divided into sitting room, bedroom, servant quarters, kitchen, and private bath (Reyna 17). The Convent of Santa Clara in Querétaro was like a city in miniature, with streets, plazas, and gardens; each professed nun received a pound and a quarter of mutton and four and a half pounds of bacon a day (Lavrin "Vida conventual" 52). Mexican María Ana de la Encarnación (1571–1657) recalls a cleric who berated the "pampered chocolate-drinking criollas" of certain convents (44).[19] The problem of indulging in sweets was apparently of such concern that when María went on to found the Convent of Santa Teresa la Nueva (also known as the Convent of San José) in Mexico, not drinking chocolate was added as a fifth element to the conventional vows of poverty, chastity, obedience, and cloister (Viñuales 199). Chocolate was not the only indulgence afforded cloistered women: nuns were even allowed to smoke or take snuff in some of the less austere orders.

The situation was further complicated in that most women had at their disposal two or more slaves or servants. In fact, professed nuns made up only a fraction of the population living in Spanish-American convents. Chilean Úrsula Suárez complains that at one time there were eleven other women in her cell, "playing around even when I was not in the mood" (196–97).[20] More telling still, in his biography of the Colombian nun Gerónima del Espíritu Santo, Juan de Olmos betrays the lifestyle in the convent, as well as his own class bias, by enumerating the "martyrdom" his subject was forced to endure due to incompetent and undependable servants: "Our Gerónima was beset by bodily torments, destitute and alone, and worst of all, she did not even have a servant" (39); "Aside from many seriously unpleasant incidents, her servants—that is, when she had them, I know how low-lifes like that can be—never attended her punctually, and did nothing according to her wishes. . . . She bore all this with great patience" (44).[21]

Some women may have spent more time enjoying themselves than engaging in spiritual contemplation; many more, however, directed their energies toward more constructive ends. In reality, the Spanish-American convent formed an integral and active part of the community: nuns managed water resources, provided education for girls and young women, administered loans, and contributed economic support for the rebuilding of neighborhoods after natural disasters.[22] Viñuales reports cases of religious women serving as bricklayers for construction work, which they performed—legend has it—with their faces masked by veils (214). Convents were, moreover, important centers for cultural activity in the colonies, providing opportunities for some of the most talented musicians, artists, and writers in Spanish America (Gutiérrez and Maeder 128–30; Guernica 95). Nuns themselves translated, copied, and distributed devotional works and musical texts, collaborated (without credit) with theologians and Church dignitaries, kept archives of historical records, and wrote collective biographies (Arenal and Schlau "Leyendo yo y escribiendo ella" 215). Creativity extended to the domestic arts, as many nuns contributed to the expenses of the convent by selling products such as sweets and embroidered garments, and it was frequently the sisters themselves who dressed and adorned the statues of the saints. As Viñuales suggests and the *vidas* document, in some orders nuns were even able to give a kind of unofficial confession, as they listened to penitents and offered advice from behind the walls of the *portería* [entryway or gatehouse] or *locutorio* (Viñuales 200; Suárez 231).

Although ultimately subject to ecclesiastical authority, most internal affairs of the convent were handled by the women themselves. In most orders, administrative positions were determined democratically, with three-year terms, and the average black-veiled nun would likely hold several positions during her lifetime. Evidence suggests that intelligent women often advanced rapidly through the ranks to high levels of convent administration, although internal political struggles for these positions complicated life and sometimes resulted in bitter acrimony and, in the case of Úrsula Suárez, extreme punishment, as will be discussed in chapter 6.[23] Normally, half a nun's dowry would immediately go to the convent and the remainder was administered by the nun until her death. Women who had been granted inheritances were permitted to administer their lands and finances personally (Reyna 12, 33; Armancanqui 106). Chilean historian Juan de Guernica records as many as twenty-six shops and private businesses rented out in a single year by the Clarissan convent of Nuestra Señora de la Victoria in Santiago (131). In addition, in many convents professed women received monthly stipends plus money for clothing expenses, although these funds were usually handled by a male administrator, the *mayordomo* (Reyna 34).[24] Some women supplemented their incomes through the system of *devociones,* whereby friendly and sometimes amorous male sponsors provided gifts and money in exchange for periodic visits and prayers on their behalf. Úrsula Suárez, who insists that she "accidentally" became involved with "two or three" *devotos* whom she sought out of self-interest and not love (164, 176), explains to a jealous Christ that she must continue meeting men to maintain her standard of living: "thanks to him I am dressed and fed" (178).[25] Not surprisingly, *devociones* were strongly opposed by ecclesiastical authorities, who passed a series of measures to abolish the practice.[26] Obedience to ecclesiastical and canonical authorities was, however, not only regularly questioned but actively disputed by nuns in Spanish America. Indeed, proposed reforms by bishops were continually frustrated by nuns who wished to defend their way of life (Lavrin "De su puño y letra" 48–50; Martín 206–42); and the desire for independence from canonical jurisdiction in the viceroyalty of Peru led to prolonged court battles, violence, and even riots such as those in the Convent of Santa Clara in Santiago (1656) and the Convent of Santa Catalina in Quito (1679) (Martín 245–79).

* * *

While learning to write in the colonies, as in Spain, was contested by some authorities (Arbiol y Diez 490) and higher education prohibited, economically privileged women in Spanish America could study reading, writing, elementary mathematics, music, religion, and domestic skills in convents and *colegios. Beaterios,* voluntary associations of pious lay women supervised by the secular Church, and *amigas,* schools improvised by and held in the homes of educated women for the instruction of girls from privileged families, also contributed to the education of women in the colonies (Lavrin "In Search" 40; Muriel *Cultura femenina* 37).[27] Later, if a young woman's family could afford it, she might be granted a private teacher to continue her education and learn Castilian and Latin grammar (Muriel *Cultura femenina* 19).[28]

Most convents and *beaterios* had their own libraries. Josefina Muriel's study of conventual reading in colonial Mexico counts fifty-three volumes of mystical treatises in a single convent and twenty-two in the holdings of a private library ("Lo que leían las mujeres" 165). Moreover, unlike their sisters in peninsular Spain, nuns in the Americas usually had access—albeit limited—to Scripture and to mystic writings, which they could creatively integrate into their own texts (Achury cxvii; Muriel *Cultura femenina* 20, 22).[29] While Teresa de Jesús was forced by her confessor to burn her *Meditaciones sobre el Cantar de los cantares* and Luis de León imprisoned for more than three years for his vernacular translation, Spanish-American authors regularly paraphrased the Song of Songs in their devotional writings[30] and powerful bishops such as Manuel Fernández de Santa Cruz, Juan de Palafox y Mendoza, and Ángel Maldonado encouraged visionary experience.[31] Indeed, the complaint of many confessors and women's own admission of a fascination with forbidden novels and comedies suggest that even secular texts were generally tolerated in the colonies (Leonard *Baroque Times in Old Mexico* 98). And a single book could go a long way: because of the relative scarcity and high cost of books in the colonies, it was common practice to share books with friends and friends of friends (Muriel *Cultura femenina* 21). More important, perhaps, were women's writings that were copied and circulated informally in manuscript form. In many cases, these handwritten reproductions are the only copies of women's unpublished autobiographical writings that have survived.[32]

* * *

The privileged position of experiential knowledge during the Renaissance, along with the increasing limitation of women's access to and expression of greater theological issues, led to a more personalized relation to religion and knowledge in general. Women were instructed by their confessors to analyze every thought, action, and dream as part of their daily routine; and because they were ostensibly unable to analyze their own thoughts, they were ordered to write them down. Two steps, the methodic "account" or "examination of conscience," and the more clearly organized version that would be presented in confession, were combined and codified in letters and notebooks in which religious women wrote the history of their visionary experiences in a journal-like form and with little or no framing chronology. Following this epistolary account, the confessor could request a penitential confession (*confesión general*), usually, although not always, framed as a retrospective life story, the *vida*, to determine whether these revelations were an act of God or the work of the devil.[33] At this point the author would need to edit her papers and shape them into a coherent life story, usually marked by predestination from an early age. The specifics of the mechanism depended on the individual confessor. The letters of María Coleta de San José, for example, spanned some four hundred pages and twenty-four years without ever being converted into a *vida;* and Gerónima del Espíritu Santo's autobiographical narrative occurs almost exclusively in the visionary sphere, although it is usually preceded by a short mention of daily routine. While not conforming to modern notions of autobiography, these narratives may nonetheless be framed in a wider sense of *the process* of an "autobiographical impulse" where the truth is secondary to the ideal self that the writing subject wishes to present.[34]

Dozens of biographies of religious women, usually written by confessors from the subjects' own writings, were published in the seventeenth and eighteenth centuries and were used to fill the void left by prohibited devotional literature. In Mexico alone, Asunción Lavrin and Josefina Muriel have identified some 121 books published using women's life writings.[35] Although biographies were also written about saintly men, there are some key differences between these works and those about women. With few exceptions, the men who were singled out for biographical treatment had distinguished themselves in some way, as founders of monasteries and *colegios*, church leaders, or missionaries. Bodily mortification is mentioned but rarely a central theme of the text, and visionary experiences are conspicuously absent in most of these biographies. Most important, unlike biographies about women, studies of male subjects do not typically integrate autobiographical writings, and any mention of discourse on demand would be the exception and not the rule. In contrast, because a nun could not write her life story unless sanctioned or obligated to do so by a male religious authority, women's life stories, even in their original autobiographical manuscripts, are always mediated by the presence of their confessors. Moreover, although archives demonstrate the existence of exceptional women who participated in many facets of public life in colonial Spanish America, biographies of women actually confirmed gender hierarchies since the women selected for these texts were often chosen not so much for their accomplishments as for their extreme asceticism and heroic virtue.[36] It should be noted that the ultimate purpose for many biographies was to further the cause of beatification of the subject, and heroic virtue was one of the few attributes of sainthood open to cloistered women. In fact, as will be further discussed in chapter 3, many women's own writings seek to fit their lives into saintly models by downplaying or silencing altogether participation in any activity that could be conceived as worldly. Even secular chronology is consciously displaced in the *vida* by the liturgical calendar so that the writing subject could integrate her life with the lives of the saints (Myers introduction, *Word from New Spain* 20).[37]

* * *

Because gender representation is always associated with class relations, gender ideology is also inextricably bound with political and economic factors. If women were venerated in biographies it was primarily in an abstract and commodified sense: women's inclusion in the discursive order had no bearing on their position in the public sphere. In Counter-Reformation Spain as in Spanish America, the saintly woman's life story and personal visionary experiences had been appropriated for the confessor's own advancement, for the glory of his order and of the Catholic Church. In some cases, confessors were encouraged by their superiors to gather more material from the women whose souls they guided: Manuel Fernández de Santa Cruz, bishop of Puebla, offered compensation for subordinates who could coerce their spiritual daughters to write ever more detailed relations of their lives; María de San José was reportedly pressed by her confessor to write twenty-three hours a day to satisfy the zealous bishop's demands (Santander y Torres "Al lector"). In viceregal Spanish America these biographies took on yet another, more political agenda: if the New World could produce saintly men and women, it was proof of God's favor toward the colonies. Such arguments counteracted the peninsular contention that criollos were inferior by virtue of their contact with other races and, specifically, because of the excessive *freedom of their women* (Pagden 81–83), an attitude that had barred them from most high-ranking positions in viceregal society.[38]

In the opening chapter of his collective biography/chronicle, *Parayso Occidental* (1683), Carlos Sigüenza y Góngora traces women's honor in New Spain back to pre-Hispanic cultures, citing the example of virtuous women cloistered in Mexica temples (1–5). Appropriating a similar symbolic function, the Convent of Santa Catalina in Cuzco was housed in a former *acllahuasi,* the house of the chosen virgins of the sun (Burns 112).[39] And alluding to the indigenous convent of Corpus Christi, Joseph Eugenio Valdés, biographer for Sebastiana Josefa de la Santísima Trinidad, contrasts the relics of saintly bodies in the Old World with the pristine living treasures of the Americas: "In Mexico there is a shrine in which not just relics of bodies but whole bodies may be venerated" (100).[40] One of the arguments Spaniards had made for the exclusion of criollos from positions of power had to do with the physical environment into which they had been born which, the Spaniards said, led to wickedness and material ostentation. To counter this argument, criollo intellectuals had to "acquire, define, and defend a separate identity that took some account . . . of the *land* where they had been born" (Pagden 84). Sebastiana Josefa is thus described by Valdés as a precious stone (298) and a bounteous lode (3); Felipe Setagolo refers to Rosa of Lima as the "new mine" of Peru, and the title of Agustín de la Madre de Dios's collective biography alludes to the "hidden treasure" and "rich mine of models and virtues" of the Discalced Carmelites in Mexico.[41]

As Diego Lemus, biographer of María de Jesús Tomelín, observed, implicitly contradicting the conventional view of the criollos as materialistic: "and so in this way not only can New Spain pay tribute to the old with its precious metals, but also by enriching it with the gold of such celestial models; and for this [Old Spain] is more indebted to us than for our other riches, since moral edification is more precious than opulence" ("Al lector").[42] As Jean Franco points out, women's writings literally served as raw material that could be mined by male clerics; and not just for biographies but also for confessional manuals, sermons, and other devotional works (4).[43] Nearly every spiritual biography published in Spanish America was written about *and by* men and women born in the Americas.

Although the Jesuit hierarchy had initially shared the same biases as other orders toward criollos, by the time of their expulsion in 1767 the Jesuits had become the center not only of the criollos' nationalist aspirations but a powerful intellectual elite (see Rama 31–47). The order's founder, Ignacio de Loyola (1491–1556), was probably the most important Spanish saint during the Counter-Reformation, and his influence in the lives of religious women was further developed in the confessional. Intelligent women seem to have been drawn to Jesuit confessors even though, as Ross notes, Jesuit orthodox Counter-Reformation morality led to a "puritanical and sometimes misogynist attitude toward women" (103). Jesuit intellectual culture, with its emphasis on learning and the Ignatian method of visual meditation, resonates in the works of many female authors. Indeed, the examination of conscience itself, basis for written confessions, was first advocated by the Jesuit order as a daily practice (Stockman 137).[44]

While colonial *vidas* may have been written with criollo political interests, the language, structure, and even certain images usually derived from Spanish models. Nonetheless, this was an exercise based less on the class identification of the colonized with the imperial power than on the immediate need for writers—both male and female—to legitimize and consolidate their positions within a Church hierarchy controlled by Spain. At the same time, the unverifiable nature of visionary experience and the hybridity of the *vida* genre itself gave women a margin of flexibility from which to speak. If, as Mikhail Bakhtin suggests, each language also implies an ideological system, then the rhetorical hybridity of the *vida* also had the potential to challenge the hegemonic discourse of Counter-Reformation Spain.[45] Bakhtin distinguishes between "hidden" and "open" "polemical blows" that put another's discourse on the same theme into question. While the open polemic includes the strategies of academic discourse and parody (rarely accessible to women), the hidden polemic exercises its influence outside the text (*Problems of Dostoevsky's Poetics* 195–96). Hierarchy is further challenged by the combination of a personalized and sometimes even conversational tone with a baroque-influenced abstruseness of language that deliberately plays with double meanings of words, pronominal references, and temporal referents.

* * *

Situated outside representation by dominant ideology, a woman attempting to tell her story may, as Virginia Woolf suggests, "think back through her mother" to discover woman's command of language against language's command of woman (79). Whether conforming to the expectations of their confessors or deviating from the norm, religious women seek to establish a voice of authority by framing the authorization of writing within the experiences of female precursors who had successfully negotiated the delicate balance between expression and obedience. Although Octavio Paz's affirmation that literature *published* in colonial society was a closed system by and for men (69/45) is to some extent true, *in practice* women read—and were read by—both men and women.[46] In addition to informally circulated manuscripts, there were also published devotional works, chronicles, collective biographies, and even biographies written by women in viceregal Spanish America. Medina lists sixty-eight books by women published between 1640 and 1800 in New Spain alone, including ten editions of devotional works by Sor Juana Inés de la Cruz, and sixteen editions of *Estaciones de la pasión del Señor* and *Cadena de oro* by Spanish nun María de la Antigua (1566–1617). Between 1686 and 1730, there were also at least seventeen editions of Sor Juana's poetry and theater published in Spain. *La mística ciudad de Dios* (1670), by Spanish visionary María de Jesús de Ágreda, was so popular that seventy-two editions in Spanish were published in Europe and one in Mexico; a shorter version had twenty-seven additional printings, seven in Mexico, even though the book was eventually prohibited by the Inquisition in 1713 (Muriel *Cultura femenina* 315; Márquez 93).[47]

Visionary experiences allowed women to circumvent patriarchal authority by asserting a direct relation to God. Nonetheless, and although Christ continued to be the ultimate authority, the growing corpus of women's spiritual autobiography provided authors in the seventeenth and eighteenth centuries with an alternative lineage from which to draw. Female saints were often invoked directly to defend the actions of the writing subject and, particularly, as a rhetorical strategy to justify the act of writing.[48] María Coleta de San José has a vision of Christ in which he urges her to write; however, it is not until Teresa de Jesús (1515–1582) appears that she is able to sufficiently mitigate her anxiety and complete her task: "I felt that Santa Teresa had appeared before me with a compelling force . . . and I seemed to understand, or she told me, that just as clearly as she had told her confessors what happened to her, that I should do the same" (carta 3, folio 119).[49] In contrast to biblical tradition, in which women's testimony of the Resurrection is dismissed by the disciples as "an idle tale" until Christ himself reveals the truth to "foolish men" (Luke 24.10, 25), María doubts Christ's word and trusts that of Teresa.

Beatified in 1614 and canonized in 1622, only forty years after her death, Teresa de Jesús's success in eluding Inquisitorial authority and almost unprecedented road to sanctification make her autobiography, *El libro de la vida* (1588), the most frequently cited model for women's personal narrative in Spanish America.[50] Indeed, although Teresa reiterates a fear of being read in chapters dealing with her mystic visions and spiritual life which could be used against her (X.8, 188–89/61–62), she specifically designates the chapters about her life as a "sinner" to serve as an example to others: "I beseech [you] for the love of the Lord, that what I have thus far said concerning my wicked life and sins be published (I give this permission, here and now, to all my confessors, of whom he who will receive this is one. If they like, they can publish it now, during my lifetime, so I may no longer deceive the world and those who think there is some good in me)" (X.7, 187–88/60–61).[51] She further designates the final section, which deals with the foundation of the convent of San José, as one she would like to see passed on to future generations (XXXVI.28, 434–35/260). Teresa's exploration of her inner self was unusual during a historical moment in which the relatively new recognition of subjecthood and human agency came into conflict with the Counter-Reformation attempt to reassert control over expressions of individualism. Because such singularity was associated with demonic deception, the examination of conscience was used as a way to persuade individuals to exercise self-control. Nonetheless, the defensive strategy used by Teresa and emulated by her descendants was, as Allison Weber notes, "to embrace stereotypes of female ignorance, timidity, or physical weakness but disassociate herself from the double-edged myth of woman as seducible/seductive" (*Teresa of Ávila* 36). Teresa conceded women's powerlessness precisely to defend the legitimacy of her own spiritual and discursive authority (39, 49–50).

* * *

Paul had ordained: "Let your women keep silence in the churches, for it is not permitted unto them to speak; but they are commanded to be under obedience, as also saith the law. And if they will learn anything, let them ask their husbands at home" (I Corinthians 14.34–37); while the pastoral Epistles cautioned: "Let the woman learn in silence with all subjection. But I suffer not a woman to teach, nor to usurp authority over the man, but to be in silence. For Adam was first formed, then Eve. And Adam was not deceived, but the woman being deceived was in the transgression" (I Timothy 2.11–14). Such biblical precedents were used as justification for "holy ignorance" and illiteracy for religious women (Arenal and Schlau *Untold Sisters* 7). Indeed, because women were thought to be easily deceived by visionary experiences, they were discouraged from speaking out publicly in any form. In his widely distributed *Instrucción de la mujer cristiana* (1524), Spanish humanist Juan Luis Vives advocated teaching women to read, provided this activity was strictly monitored (33–34); however, he reiterated women's moral and intellectual inferiority when it came to a more active participation in the Church: "since woman is by nature a diseased animal and her judgment not entirely secure, and because she can be deceived easily, as was demonstrated by our mother Eve, who for very little reason allowed herself to be fooled and persuaded by the devil: for all these reasons and for others not expressed, it is not well that she be allowed to teach" (26–27).[52] Although ostensibly supporting women's virtues, such defenses ultimately maintained social order by relying on stereotypical notions of gender ideology. Internalizing these misogynous notions of women's intellectual inferiority and moral weakness had, as historian Gerda Lerner notes, a "devastating effect on women's minds" (47). Nonetheless, because the promise of sexual equality in salvation hinged on the acceptance of this code of social inferiority, women often voluntarily chose to reproduce structural gender relations through their own agency as a means of asserting discursive authority.

While not specifically directed to questions of gender ideology, Louis Althusser's theories of how subjects are attracted to or "interpellated" into cultural discourses (162) are useful in understanding the mechanisms through which women embraced even misogynous images of the female experience. According to Althusser, individuals consider their existence as part of a vast network of coercive ideological systems of representation that offer images or subjectivities through a mechanism of recognition (136–37, 162).[53] Because the writing subject understands that she must play the part assigned her in this discourse on demand, she must represent herself as her reader sees her: she converts herself into a commodity for both the reader's personal consumption and the wider institutional needs and expectations of the religious and social orders. The language of power, as we will see, is a language of seduction: as such, women risk becoming accomplices in their own oppression as they choose to play these designated roles. In many ways the construction of female subjectivity within the limitations of the confessional frame required the author to strategically situate herself in a discursive position that permitted access to power while satisfying the demands of her reader/confessor(s). Drawing on Wendy Hollway's analysis of the Foucauldian notion of power, Teresa de Lauretis defines this kind of position as an "investment," somewhere between "an emotional commitment and a vested interest, in the relative power (satisfaction, reward, payoff) . . . that position promises (but does not necessarily fulfill)" (16). Although the writing subject may frame her narrative of self-representation within a limited set of models, she exercises agency through a process of negotiation between subject positions in the textual construction of her life story.

Asked to assume center stage in her narration, the female subject of the *vida* was afforded the uncommon privilege of inscribing herself as an active agent, as heroine of her own life story and not merely as an objectified other. Nonetheless, as a text mediated by the authority of the confessor, her entrance into center stage is always problematic, because, as Sidonie Smith affirms, she must cast herself in the role he assigns, constructing herself symbolically as "an other intimately related to him as the image of what he is not, and therefore as an essential reminder of what he is" (48). In the chapters that follow, the female subject in colonial Spanish America will tacitly be associated with what de Lauretis has termed the "engendered subject," a subject who defines herself according to her culture's gender codes but who may simultaneously question this encoding. De Lauretis asserts that the construction of gender is therefore the *product* and the *process* of both representation and self-representation (9). On the one hand, by (re)presenting themselves as theatrical spectacle, authors may ironically perpetuate a system that subordinates them for the more immediate reward of achieving limited power and recognition within it. On the other hand, recognizing these strategies as a conscious negotiation of discursive authority or at the very least of justification for the act of writing expands the concept of agency for a writing subject conventionally perceived as disempowered by the discursive hegemony of power-knowledge (de Lauretis 16).

Gender is here defined as a means by which cultures and societies produce structures of sexual difference, a means, as Joan Wallach Scott notes, by which hierarchies of power, of domination and subordination, are constructed (2–5). As Michel Foucault observes, conventional power relations between author and reader are inverted in confessional discourse, since the reader/confessor implicitly exerts control over the writer/confessant. The confessional nature of such texts, combined with woman's unstable relation to authority and public discourse, leads her to situate herself in a subordinate position to her addressee. Nonetheless, while discursive *authority* resides in the confessor, *power* may be exercised "from innumerable points, in the interplay of non-egalitarian and mobile relations. . . . Where there is power, there is resistance. . . . These points of resistance are present everywhere in the power network" (*History of Sexuality* 61–62, 94–96). To evaluate spiritual autobiography as a study of *processes* and *systems* allows us to retain the notion of agency as the writing subject attempts to transcend the limitations imposed on her discourse by strategically situating herself in a position that permits access to power while satisfying the demands of both her real and implied readers.

In *The Madwoman in the Attic,* Sandra Gilbert and Susan Gubar allude to the activation of "multiple heroines," each embodying "alternative possibilities of selfhood for women" (564). This book is about such multiple heroines, about multiple subject positions and multiple models of representation, about power and authority, about the strategies that women used to simultaneously reinforce their position and subtly subvert hierarchies of discursive authority. Whether conforming to hagiographic models or deviating from the norm, this study proposes to show that women were able to express themselves and establish their own informal network of reading and writing to promote a type of discourse in which the female voice, mediated and monitored, but nonetheless her own, had an authority higher than that of the erudite elite from which she was barred.

1

Body and Soul

Self-Representation as Confessional Discourse

> By believing from the heart you are made righteous; by confessing with your lips you are saved.
>
> Romans 10.8–10

From its inception, confession functioned as an instrument of social control that reinforced the hierarchies of power from which class and gender distinctions derive. Within the Church, it secured the purity of those who received the consecrated Body of Christ during communion. In civil society, the threat of exclusion from the community helped reaffirm social order. Since women's bodies could ostensibly be in their places while their minds had been transported to forbidden spheres, the Church sought to channel and control expression by promoting a contemplative spiritual model and encouraging its presentation during private auricular confession. Although penitential exercises and public confession were retained well into the seventeenth century in monastic communities of Spain and Spanish America, a canon of the first council of Toledo in 398 indicates that private confession and the role of the priest was recognized early in Spain, especially for cloistered women (Lea I.179).[1] Following the codification of the sacrament of penance by the Fourth Lateran Council in 1215, the penitent's repentance could in principle atone for sin prior to confession, but it was only through the priest's absolution that the soul could be alleviated of the burden of guilt. Following the Council of Trent (1545–63), confession was universally prescribed as antecedent review (Lea II.413), further consolidating the power of the confessor. Nuns were obligated to confess at least once a month with an additional biannual review by special confessors appointed by the bishop; in practice, however, frequency of confession depended on the religious order. Once a week seems to be the most common prescription, although the Jesuits recommended a daily examination of conscience as corollary to confession with a priest to achieve perfection (Lea I.268, 271, 304–5; Stockman 137). While penitents were urged to avoid digressions, the need to make a complete confession was essential and priests were urged not to absolve penitents who did not come to the confessional adequately prepared (Lea I.348–49; Tentler 86, 109–10). To order one's thoughts, some scholars recommended daily reviews of conscience; and indeed, the Dominican theologian Jacopo Passavanti recommended bringing written notes to the confessional (Zimmerman 123–24). In practice, however, confession sometimes was incomplete because the priest simply did not have the time or patience to devote to each of his spiritual wards. In fact, some confession manuals stipulate that the priest has the right to cut a confession short if he deems fit (Lea I.350–53). In this situation lay another advantage to supplementing the confession with written documents, although in principle absolution could only be granted orally. Spanish theologians such as Pedro Soto and Francisco Suárez advocated the validity of written confession and absolution, but this position was never officially recognized by Church hierarchy.[2]

The confessional box, with its divider between penitent and priest, came into prominence beginning in the mid-sixteenth century, creating a further division between the penitent and the confessor, who became a disembodied voice behind a grille so narrowly barred that "a pea could not be squeezed through" (Tambling 68–69). According to Lea, by the beginning of the seventeenth century the confessional box was almost universally accepted (Lea I.394–95); however, it appears that in many parts of Spanish America the box was either not available, misconstructed, or misused. In María de San José's chronicle of an incident during which Fernández de Santa Cruz violently dismisses her, she recounts that she was at his feet and not at his side in the confessional (*Word* 182). Úrsula Suárez also refers to two separate incidents in which she was at the confessor's feet (189, 195), as well as another episode in which she was tempted to lift the cloth divider to look at the priest (207). A certain Madre Robledo caused a scandal in the convent of San Jerónimo in Mexico when she shut the door to the confessional (Reyna 30).[3]

* * *

Beginning in the sixteenth century, theology moved from an emphasis on the seven deadly sins to the Ten Commandments, underlining the importance of obedience and thereby the power of patriarchal authority. Christ's surrender to the will of the Father hinged on his obedience: "Although he was Son, he learned to *obey through suffering;* but having been made perfect, he became for *all who obey him the source of eternal salvation*" (Hebrews 5.8–10, emphasis added; see also *Philippians* 2.6–11). An imitation of Christ's perfection, obedience was a most highly prized virtue. Excessive pride (*soberbia*), in contrast, was associated with the devil and widely held to be responsible for his fall (Cross and Livingstone 475). Because of woman's inherent vulnerability toward sin, the precept of obedience was specifically fostered by official Church doctrine as a means of containing dangerous manifestations of individuality in general and female singularity in particular. Pride was emphasized as an element that could lead to condemnation of the soul. This doctrine, channeled through the direct influence of the confessor, ensured the male authority upon which ecclesiastical social hierarchies depended: an emphasis on obedience was also crucial to imperial rule in the colonies. The ultimate power of forgiveness, the "keys to the kingdom of heaven," were entrusted only to the Church and its male representatives.

As Beatriz Pastor notes, the relatively permissive attitude of civil authorities in Spanish America toward previously unsanctioned relations was met with an increasingly intolerant and repressive attitude in some sectors of the Church. The greater the danger of falling into temptation, the greater the power of the confessor to ensure the salvation of his spiritual wards (192–93, 195).[4] For religious women, the orders of the confessor were not to be questioned (Núñez de Miranda *Plática doctrinal* 6; *Cartilla de la doctrina religiosa* 12). The confessor's authority lay in his position as instrument of Christ's power in the world, the intercessor between God and man; but as spiritual mentor, he was also associated with God the Father. Women's autobiographical narrations further suggest that the confessor often took the place of the biological father, particularly if the father had died or was incapacitated. Antonio Núñez de Miranda, confessor to Sor Juana Inés de la Cruz (1651–1695), described the function of the confessor as a "Divine Oracle" who could "cure" souls (*Distribución de las obras ordinarias* 55), a claim Sor Juana privately disputed.[5] Joseph Sánchez de Castro, biographer of Antonia de la Madre de Dios (1662–1742), proudly reports that "not a single one of her acts originated from her own will, because all her natural and prenatural practices were performed by order of antecedent or concomitant obedience to her confessors" (224).[6] And in a letter to her confessor, Antonia, unlike Juana, willingly confirms her acceptance of his privileged position: "I have realized that the Lord God wishes me to be very faithful to you, and with good reason, since *you are in His place*" (Sánchez de Castro 79, emphasis added).[7] María de San José concurs, recalling for her confessor's benefit Christ's admonition to venerate him "*like a saint who is in His place,* and blindly obey all you command and order me to do" (III.97, emphasis added).[8] In short, the confessor, with the power of absolution, held his spiritual ward's eternal destiny in his hands. As father figure, teacher, judge, and physician of the soul, the confessor occupied the place of Christ and had "unlimited discretion" (Lea II.187).[9] The priest should be obeyed, some argued, even when morally corrupt: "One does not have to look at the vices and faults there are in the priest," counseled Juan Luis de Cerda, "but at the jurisdiction and authority that he has" (235r, ctd. Perry 70).

* * *

Writing was a special kind of confession because the act itself could be construed as a violation of authority; to value one's writing, moreover, could be interpreted as excessive pride. A woman could not admit to writing on her own initiative: from a strategic perspective, it was necessary to justify this act by framing it as the will of God and her confessor. Nonetheless, an awareness of future readers who could include other women (reading the work in manuscript form or in future published biographies) and Inquisitorial examiners, the dual requirements of confession and defense, led to what Weber describes as an "autobiographical double-bind" in which the author's task is "to develop a rhetorical strategy which will allow her to comply with the demands of her addressees, and at the same time communicate a sense of identity independent from the authority they represent" ("Paradoxes of Humility" 211).[10] María de San José suffers insecurity in the act of writing itself, since she does not, she says, know how to write: "I have written this with great fear of losing my soul by writing these things . . . I do no more than obey at the price of great difficulty since I do not know how to write well and for the great anguish I suffer in this" (II.101).[11] In other passages, however, María cleverly holds demonic powers responsible for any shortcomings her account may have: "this . . . part . . . is very poorly written because when I wrote it I was with those three demons whose assistants savagely hindered me, allowing me to write only with unspeakable difficulty and very poorly" (II.14).[12]

The rhetoric of humility, as Ernst Robert Curtius notes, is neither gender specific nor, indeed, a specifically Christian affectation. Authors regularly justify their uneducated and rude speech, lack of talent, and fear of writing; expressions of self-deprecation and of obedience to a higher authority were rhetorical formulae inherited from antiquity (83–85). In confessional discourse, moreover, all penitents—male and female—were encouraged to humble themselves before their spiritual director. In a 1921 adaptation of

Giovanni Battista Scaramelli's seventeenth-century manual, *The Method of Spiritual Direction*, P. J. Stockman recommends that *even if no sin has been committed* the penitent debase him- or herself as a "vile slave of the devil"; a "traitor and a perjurer"; an "ungrateful wretch" and a deicide, "for he contributed to the Savior's death and . . . is more guilty than they who crucified Him" (129–30). Nonetheless, in most cases, when men use expressions of self-deprecation, they are deferring to their readers in a formal sense only; whereas when a woman uses the same set of symbols, she is reaffirming a lowly status already assigned her.[13]

Some confessors forced nuns to write and rewrite their confessions to test their obedience or to subdue excessive pride, playing the anxiety of authorship against the vow to obey. Manuel Fernández de Santa Cruz, the bishop of Puebla, was himself involved in the cruel treatment of María de San José, forced to write twenty-three hours a day only to have her papers burned (Santander y Torres 164). Úrsula Suárez's confessor told her that her papers had been burned only to later admit he had them in his possession, a treatment she describes as inhumane and terrible (136–37). There were several cases in which the process was repeated each time a new spiritual advisor was engaged or an earlier version destroyed. In this way the definitive text often incorporated fragments from various previous versions written for different confessors. This circumstance affected the discursive configuration of the *vida* in at least two important ways. First, as Weber points out, a "particularly polymorphous" textual self is created as the "phantoms of earlier addressees," with whom the author would have had a varying degree of authority and intimacy, each leave a mark in her narrative (*Teresa of Ávila* 66–67). Second, the current addressee could obviously identify with earlier confessors; in fact, the original second-person narration is often maintained in successive versions of the life story. Moreover, as Jennifer Eich points out, women's descriptions of both men on earth and male figures in the visionary realm were understood *allegorically* as "emblematic representations" of obstacles women would have to overcome in their quest for spiritual perfection (71). As a result, even the most suggestive scenarios of mastery and domination could be imaginatively pursued without violating the distance between confessor and penitent.

Because women could not engage in theological discourse, it was important to stress that access to knowledge was through the affective and not the intellectual realm. Religious women could protect themselves from clues that would belie forbidden readings by integrating other texts within their work without citation, claiming that God had given them this information. Thus, although intellectual activity by women was viewed with suspicion, they could assert some measure of authority through the affective realm in their capacities as mediators for Christ. María Marcela, for example, is careful to distance herself from the process of interpretative mental activity: "I swear . . . that when I say that I 'contemplate' and I 'think,' that I am speaking of the past, because in the present I neither contemplate nor think because I can no longer do so, and I only see God with a simple vision totally possessed by the glory of the Lord" (75).[14] Teresa de Jesús distinguishes between "intellectual" visions, in which the presence of Christ is sensed but not visualized (literally, "intelligible," conceivable but not visible); "imaginary" visions (the "eyes of the soul"), provoked through fantasy; and corporeal visions (the "eyes of the body"), which refer to the physical vision of this world (*Libro de la vida* XXVIII:4, 336–37, 179–80). Thus, mental process was not abandoned altogether: the mind was distinguished from intellect.[15] In this way, when María Marcela asserts that her visions are "intellectual," she is in reality protecting herself from the dangers of corporeal visions: "Everything and anything I declare, I saw with my mind, because with my eyes . . . I have never seen anything" (153).[16] In a similar vein, María Manuela de Santa Ana asserts that her visions are the product of the heart and not the mind: "The light did not come to me through the mind; the fire of love and the infinite [wisdom] that God revealed to me was transmitted only by the love with which my heart was inflamed." She further discredits herself by requiring her confessor to assess whether she may "see" it or not because she is unable to interpret her visions without his guidance: "Do not fail to let me know if I may see all I believed [to see]. . . . My father, I do not know how to explain myself because I am a poor brute" (folio 14, *Esquela* 250).[17] Contemplative and visionary activity ensured a dependent relationship between the nun and her confessor since ultimately he controlled the space as interpretative authority. It was necessary, therefore, for authors to carefully negotiate a discursive space for themselves without openly challenging this authority. Even Gerónima del Espíritu Santo, who presents Christ at her feet and clearly has no doubts as to the validity of her claims, intellectually defers to her confessor: "Whatever you will see through my writing, is what has been imprinted upon me, careful to not leave out a single thing, nor having pondered nor exaggerated what I have said, and with the grace of God, no point has strayed from the dictates of truth, nor does it seem to me that I have said anything in error. And because I am a poor ignorant woman and my sex is so base, I say of almost everything that 'it seemed to me' and with great pleasure I submit [my writings] to be corrected in accord with your understanding" (99).[18] Here, as in other examples, the repeated use of "me parece" [it seems to me] was a way in which women authors could protect themselves from accusations of *excessive pride,* even though the passage leaves little doubt that she does not believe to have erred.

The rhetorical strategy of using language to cloak potentially precarious narrative interpretations is also exploited by Francisca Josefa Castillo. Many times she is careful to distinguish her visions as "dreams"; in other cases, she qualifies her interpretation with phrases such as "a mi modo de explicarme"; "yo entendí," and "me parecía" [in my way of explaining myself; I understood; it seemed to me]. However, she clearly differentiates between dreams and visionary experience and sometimes bypasses the confessor altogether in passages such as that when she feels the presence of Ignacio de Loyola: "I did not see the saint, but it *seemed to me* he was present in my soul," or sees an image of Christ on the altar come to life: "It *seemed as if* I had seen him (and this was not a dream) . . . and yearning with all my heart for Our Lord in this, his holy image . . . he sweated from the severity of my sorrows . . . and *I understood* that this was a sign that he accompanied me in my trials and tribulations" (*Su vida* 207, 210, emphasis added).[19] This passage violates reader expectations in many ways. She asserts, first of all, that she saw Christ and that it was *not* a dream, and, second, that she actually does not need the confessor to tell her whether her vision was valid because she has physical proof: the image of Christ miraculously perspired. Although she qualifies her interpretation—"I understood"—leaving space for her confessor to agree with or contradict her, she has, for all intents and purposes, already analyzed the significance of the vision herself.

The anxiety of authorship and alleged ineptitude in written discourse could also be used to the author's advantage as a means to suppress full confession of potentially damaging information or sensitive issues. On the pretext that she is only trying not to tire her addressee (and herself) by giving further details, she may omit entire sections of the life story, though this clearly goes against the exhaustive account recommended for a penitential confession. Toward the end of her lengthy account of her life, Francisca Josefa asserts: "I will write only one or two more things, because it would be an endless task to include all of them" (*Su vida* 144); a phrase reiterated by María Marcela "to declare everything would be an endless task" (118). Strategically evasive, the author often does not fully explain and at times willfully denies past incidents, declaring she cannot express herself in words. María de San José explains: "I could tell you more things about the mercies the Lord granted and grants me, but they are difficult to put into words and much less into writing" (III.4). "There are no words to explain the love of God for this poor wretch," laments María Manuela, "I have no words for the mercies that I am receiving from all the divine mysteries" (folio 11, *Vida* 188; see also folio 5, *Esquela* 237; folio 6, *Esquela* 239).[20] In a different context, Úrsula Suárez suppresses mention of a delicate situation with a confessor on his request: "I told him this and that . . . but I do not want to repeat anything here because I gave him my word I would not tell" (258); although if she were at liberty to recount all her sufferings, she notes, "it would fill a great volume" (263). María de San José is particularly insistent on this point. Although she complains that she writes only out of obedience, she continually states she could write much more: "I could write and say much more than what I have written if it were not for the difficulty [writing] causes me" (II.19); "If I were to tell what I suffered in this [episode] alone," she writes, "it would take up an entire book" (III.53); and she concludes the third (surviving) volume of her life, adding, "I could have written two [notebooks] beyond what I have written so far if I had the capacity to do so" (III.88).[21] María did indeed have more to write: at least eight volumes would follow (*Word* 199–207).

Although the rhetoric of humility and obedience could be and was used strategically by many women authors, for others, the anxiety of authorship and fear of Inquisitorial repercussions in which their own words could be used as evidence against them represented a real and present danger.[22] For some women, the anguish experienced in revealing their interior lives is palpable. Continually insisting that she writes "only for Holy obedience," Sebastiana Josefa de la Santísima Trinidad reiterates her difficulty in and repugnance toward writing in every letter she writes, pleading with her confessor to allow her to stop, begging him not only to burn her papers but to erase them from his memory (145, 209). The anxiety that writing produces in her is such that: "Sweet Jesus, how is it possible that I suffer such anguish, and for my greater torment, I am obligated by obedience to write, and I do so forcibly and with such despair that it would be better . . . to suffer the tortures of hell than to take up a pen, and moreso experiencing such fear and so many obstacles, that in setting myself to write, the paper and ink serve only to stain me, and it seems to me that such things are not good for me. But to obey you, Reverend Father, I will forget all doubts that come to mind" (49).[23] Sebastiana's writing is continually impeded by both God and the devil. As she is on her way to the chorus loft, where she normally writes, the candle falls out of her hands and onto her notebook, staining the pages; it falls a second time as she is writing and is extinguished (50); later, she falls asleep with the candle in her hand and the chair catches on fire (87). In other episodes, flies cover the paper as she tries to write, the devil throws the food from her hands so she will be late for her duties, and he disorients her on her way to the chorus loft (Valdés 70, 292–93). Although Sebastiana comments only that "these things . . . *do not* lead me to believe it is not pleasing to God that I come [to write]" (50, emphasis added),[24] the symbolic association between flies and the devil, understood by her readers, implies that there are demonic forces attempting to impede the word of God that Sebastiana transmits. If the devil did not want her to write, then her expression could not be diabolical (Ferguson 18; Velasco 81).[25]

Using a similar logic, Francisca Josefa obligingly offers to burn her papers but has no intention of doing so. Invoking the authority of her confessors and of God himself, she decides that to destroy her writing would be almost sacrilegious: "I had wanted to burn those papers . . . but on the other hand, since reading them encouraged and consoled me, I was hesitant. I gave them to you so that you would tell me what to do, and you told me that they were from God, and that I should be grateful for His gifts. . . . Our Lord opened the eyes of my soul and I realized that this was the same thing you, Reverend Father, had always told me, as had Father Juan de Tobar, Father Francisco de Herrera and Father Juan Martínez" (122).[26] María de San José insists: "Father of my soul, if these papers seem bad to you, take them and burn them, it is no great loss" (III.130)[27]; yet she complains on several occasions of the drudgery of rewriting parts of her life story that had been burned or lost (IV.4, IV.13–15, IV.88). María Coleta asks her spiritual father not only to destroy her papers but to avoid acknowledging them in his own correspondence: "when you write me, do not send me anything that would reveal that I write you, rather, let it be completely disguised so that nothing may be suspected, and so that no one knows I am writing, as soon as you read this, tear it up or burn it, I beg this of you for the love of God" (folio 167, carta 43).[28] María Coleta's fears turned out to be well founded: her confessor did not destroy her letters; he turned them in to the Inquisition.[29]

The Inquisition was an important factor in the production of autobiographical discourse. In fact, the autobiographical confessions produced for Inquisitorial trials may have influenced Teresa de Jesús, on whose life story most Spanish-American narratives are modeled (Weber *Teresa* 43; Gómez Moriana 72). The judicial confession regularly included genealogy, autobiography ("*discurso de su vida*"), and interrogation on particular issues of Christian doctrine. Notably, manuals on Inquisitorial procedure point to a key difference between religious and judicial confession: in penitential discourse, the subject is to be believed at all times, whereas the defendant in the judicial context is to be trusted only when speaking against him- or herself

(Slade 13–14). However, when the (writing) subject is a woman, the boundaries between public and private confession are complicated by divisions of gender. Because she was ostensibly unable to distinguish between good and evil without the guidance of her confessor, a woman's word was always suspect.[30] Defending the veracity of her narration, María Marcela concludes her life story with a formulaic declaration more typical of the courtroom than of the confessional. Certifying that all she has said is true, she adds: "if any of this seems suspect, I will swear before the tribunal of the confessional or outside it that all and every part of what I have recounted here, what I say and what I will say from this point on [is the truth]" (169).[31] Since her visionary experience could only be admissible if the confessor could interpret it as divinely inspired, the confessor/reader had not only the power of interpretation and spiritual salvation but the authority in this world to protect or to denounce his spiritual ward to the Inquisition. In fact, with the specter of the Inquisition, penitential confession in Spain and Spanish America often functioned, as Carole Slade observes, as "prelude" or "adjunct" to judicial confession (13). The regulation of women's thoughts through confession and written communication was thus also a way to isolate exceptional women and to maintain control over the sometimes unruly convent community. Since the confessor, and only the confessor, was qualified to interpret the nature of the penitent's sins and to grant absolution, he could either act as advocate or adversary. If accused of heresy, a woman would need the support of her confessor to contest charges against her; conversely, if he did not approve of what he read, her papers could be introduced as evidence to the Inquisition or "mercifully" destroyed. Inés de Ubiarte, a nun from Lima, was denounced by her own brother in 1623 when he turned her notebooks in to the Inquisition. Although the case was suspended, it was reopened in 1629 when another notebook, written in obedience to her confessor, was discovered. She was sentenced to prison for pacts with the devil but her sentence was later suspended (Medina *Historia del Tribunal de la Inquisición en Lima* 44–45; Glave 70).

* * *

Handbooks for confessors (*summae confessorum*), often written in vernacular, delineated rules and regulations for confessional practice, further systematizing the analysis of the will (Tambling 39); T.C. Price Zimmerman considers these handbooks the "matrix of early Renaissance autobiography" (126). Although early medieval manuals retained a legalistic tone, confessional works of such fifteenth-century thinkers as Cavalca, Passavanti, and Saint Bernard shifted emphasis "from the nature of the sin to the conscience of the sinner, their object being to encourage periodic and systematic examination by the layman of his acts and motives" (126). Kathleen Myers suggests that autobiographies of religious women may often constitute an alternative confession manual from the perspective of the confessing subject (introduction 36).[32] Although other mystics had discussed the importance of a competent confessor, it is the articulate defense of Teresa de Jesús in *El libro de la vida* that set the standard for religious women in Spanish America. While Teresa concedes that it is the priest's responsibility to interpret women's visions and decide whether they should be published or destroyed, confessors who judge her visions as demonic are ultimately discredited by the author, who sets up as a necessary condition that they be educated or at least well informed. Indeed, Teresa asserts that she fears an ignorant confessor more than the devil himself, since a confessor may do her irreparable harm by leading her astray, whereas God will always protect her from the devil (XXV.22, 319/166). Further defending the visionary authority of female mystics, she comments: "I know that there are persons ... to whom the Lord is granting these favors; and if those who are directing such persons have not themselves experienced them—more especially if they have no learning—they may think that, when enraptured, they ought to be as if dead. It is a shame that such suffering should be caused by confessors who do not understand this" (XX.21, 272/126–27).[33] Echoing the words of her Spanish precursor, Francisca Josefa Castillo specifies her qualifications for a good confessor, which implicitly limit the degree of her obedience: "I have always believed solely in what the (well-informed) confessor tells me" (69, parenthesis in original).[34] Similarly, María de San José interrupts an account of a divine revelation, to note: "on this I will be silent because only someone who has had such an experience can know what it is" (III.12).[35]

The confessant had the right, in principle, to resist confession to a priest suspected of moral or intellectual weakness; however, to change confessors required the permission of the current spiritual director, making this in practice a difficult move to make (Tentler 124–27).[36] María de San José, fully aware of the implications, inadvertently contradicts herself in her account of this delicate subject. The first time she mentions the episode she alleges that the confessor, Gonzalo Piñero, left her: "the hand of almighty God saw to it that without my dismissing the confessor, he took his leave from me in writing, never again to return to the confessional." This miraculous turn of events is further sanctioned by a vision of the Virgin Mary, who assures her it is "written from above" that she change confessors (III.73).[37] In a later volume, however, María reveals that the relation was discontinued on her initiative, and that, moreover, their parting was significantly less amicable than she had originally admitted: "When I proposed to him that I could speak to . . . Father Plácido, he was so offended and angry that, not content with what he had said to me in the confessional, he went to his cell and wrote me a letter, taking leave of me and never again returning to the confessional" (V.4).[38] Such separations could be quite traumatic, as is evidenced in a passage by María Coleta de San José in which she begs her addressee/confessor not to reveal her "infidelity" to her official confessor and is devastated by his reaction when he discovers the truth: "Even the most saintly of women could not have helped but be hurt. . . . He told me that he wished it was in his power to bring me another [confessor], and then I told him, Sir, but I never have told you I want another, and even if I did, I would not tell you. And so he told me, I do not understand you and you do not understand me, and so I do not want you to fill my head with crazy ideas . . . I am not well and neither are you" (carta 3, folio 120).[39]

Because she could not confront her confessor directly, a female confessant's contestory agency is often glimpsed only through silences and tensions in the text. Sebastiana Josefa de la Santísima Trinidad blames herself for difficulties with her current confessor, yet effects a silent challenge to the authority of an earlier confessor who condemns her visions as demonic. "It seems pointless to me to confess with you, Reverend Father," she tells her addressee, "who can neither understand me nor tolerate me, when I can not even stand myself" (27).[40] In the retrospective episode, in contrast, although she retains her subordinate discursive position, Sebastiana willingly suppresses confession: "This holy man . . . told me that I was deluded and that all my things seemed very bad to him. . . . There were no reasons I could provide that could change his low opinion of me. . . . With all he would tell me, I finally came to the point of losing my patience and what little sense I had left." Though the priest warns her she will lose her soul without him, Sebastiana refuses to be intimidated: "I refused to listen to him and left him very upset; although he called for me I did not return, but his words remained engraved upon my mind for a long time after" (67–69).[41]

Open hostility was not the only obstacle confronting female penitents. Úrsula Suárez and María Marcela take a more direct approach to defuse their obvious frustration with confessors who were not so much cruel as simply incompetent. "When I recounted [my sins] to him," Úrsula recalls, "he never said anything except 'all is well.' I said to myself, 'What is this! What am I supposed to understand by "all is well"? What does that have to do with what I am saying? Surely, this confessor must not be paying attention to what I am telling him'" (207).[42] So incredulous is Úrsula of this confessor's inattentiveness that she is tempted to peek under the cloth divider to make sure he is not actually the devil (207). Christ convinces her to return to the confessional, but the results are the same: "And when the Father arrived, I confessed all [my sins] and he said, 'All is well, well then, have patience!' I said to myself, 'What nonsense! But that's another matter entirely! I come to the Father in pain and all he can come up with is "All is well" and "patience"?'" (208).[43] Úrsula, who fifteen years later continues to be mystified by this confessor, ultimately ceases to speak to him (220). A disheartened María Marcela also recurs to silence in response to an inept confessor. Although educated, her confessor appears unable—or unwilling—to communicate meaningfully with his spiritual daughter, relying, as did Úrsula's director, on stock phrases that leave her dissatisfied and troubled. His only response to her confession, she recalls, "was to tell me to be patient and nothing more. This was the greatest cross I had to bear, because I think if I had had a confessor who had understood me, everything would have been more bearable." Finally, like Sebastiana, Úrsula, and María de San José, María Marcela stops going to the confessional: "I left the confessional with no intention of returning until I could find someone with whom I could unburden myself. Because with him, I tell you, it was impossible . . . not only was I bad for him but he was bad for me" (112–13).[44]

To not only disobey but to later criticize the competence of this powerful representative of the Church undoubtedly attenuated some of his authority by revealing him as human, and, indeed, sometimes even the intellectual inferior of the author. Such forthright commentary was, nonetheless, at root territory already explored: precursor texts by Teresa de Jesús, Juan de la Cruz, and other mystics had commented on the difficulties of expression with unenlightened confessors. There was, however, a much more immediate (and less contentious) goal involved: to complain of an earlier confessor's shortcomings could also enhance the qualities of the current addressee. In fact, the main point of María Marcela's story is that the arrival of her current addressee, after sixteen years of searching, marks the end of all her illnesses and persecutions (120).[45] His appearance in her life is, in fact, described as a miracle: Saint Michael and her guardian angel appear over the confessional and place her inside, finding the priest like an angel ("un serafín") himself. The reticence of the past gives way to an open and effortless confession (163).

Such hyperbolic description of a confessor/addressee was a common rhetorical device. Weber notes in relation to Teresa de Jesús's life story that the use of "coded flattery" and "private references" with her addressee was a means to "undermine his status as adversary and critic" and transform him into the ideal reader, receptive to the writing subject's self-evaluation and self-justification (*Teresa* 71). A particularly ingenious use of this strategic ingratiation is activated when the nun suggests she has the power of intervention to save her confessor's soul. María Marcela blatantly exploits this tactic when she writes that "Our Lord revealed the soul of the priest to me, burning beautifully and brilliantly white, showing me also how much this blessed priest gratified him (I do not name him so as not to embarrass him, since this [notebook] is destined for his hands), I was left full of joy" (157).[46] She further defers to her addressee by following this statement with the expected reiteration of obedience: "Our Lord . . . led me to understand that I should believe what the confessor tells me" (158).[47] In a similar vein, Úrsula Suárez pleases her Jesuit addressee in a dream in which her salvation is not through the doors of the church but through the house of the Society of Jesus, where she finds a Jesuit priest whom only later she discovers to be her current addressee (226–27); in another vision, she sees her confessor and a future governor, Francisco Ibañez Peralta, in heaven (218).

The inclusion of the confessor in the mystic realm could be used to validate visionary authority while respecting his interpretive privilege. In her description of the death of one of her early confessors, Manuel Barros, María de San José insinuates that her mediation with God allowed the priest his place in heaven, but grants Barros the last word as he tells her: "with the love and compassion with which I guided you in life I now do so from heaven" (III.89–93).[48] In her deathbed vision of a later confessor, Plácido de Olmedo, the priest promises to speak to God on her behalf, as well as for the bishop, María's addressee in this volume (V.11). Of her visionary encounter María Manuela de Santa Ana reports to her confessor: "realizing that I had received this favor thanks to your intervention, I gratefully removed my heart to ask God to intervene for you. . . Heaven is yours, my spirit was there yesterday and again assures me that it is so" (folio 7, *Esquelas* 239–40).[49] Another example of coded flattery, such incidents also reflect on the writing subjects, since the ability to intervene with God to save another person's soul implies that in the visionary realm they exercise powers that exceed those of their immediate addressee, the confessor. This power affiliates them with the saintly model of the Virgin Mary, as mediator between the divine and worldly realms, and further reiterates the human fallibility of those sent as spiritual guides.

* * *

Perhaps nowhere was this human fallibility made more evident than in cases of solicitation in the confessional. Although the authority of the confessor is that sanctioned by the structures of power, this very authority, along with the intimacy of communication between penitent and spiritual guide, could lead to serious misunderstandings and, occasionally, to transgressive behavior. Just as union with Christ was mapped onto a heterosexual relation in mystic discourse, the complicity between the confessor (himself affiliated with Christ) and female penitent was often shaded by worldly temptation. Lea points to the danger in relations between female penitents and their male confessors: "the manner in which a female devotee is absorbed by her confessor and endeavors to absorb him, looking for salvation to him and not to Christ, desiring to be always with him and jealous of his other penitents, and thinking that she can employ her property in no better way than in contributing to his comfort" (Lea II.442).[50] Cynical references to "property" aside, Lea's assessment bears consideration: solicitation was a problem throughout Spanish America, cutting across all religious orders (González Marmolejo 247). When a woman denounced a priest for any reason, she was required to sign a document stating she had no ulterior motives for making the accusation; nonetheless, that these charges were apparently taken seriously by Church hierarchy is indicated by the number of council measures and theological treatises dedicated to this problem.[51] In Spain, solicitation became an offense punishable by the Inquisition beginning in 1559, and it was included in the Edict of Denunciations which required anyone with knowledge of such an offense to denounce the parties in question. All confessors were required to have episcopal approval beginning in 1622, and in 1670, it was stipulated that each convent would have its own spiritual director, approved by the bishop. To further safeguard against possible abuses, it was declared that a confessor could serve in one convent only and for a three-year term, although he could reapply again after three years had passed. It was also specified that confessors in convents had to be at least forty years old. Moreover, if a female confessant believed the confession of a certain sin might "excite his lust" she was permitted to suppress it (Lea I.258, 349). However, as late as 1709 the Spanish Tribunal found it necessary to issue an edict forbidding priests from confessing in religious women's cells and in private chapels; and in 1850 the Council of Rouen directed itself to the problem of priests coercing the women they seduced into oaths of silence (Lea I.396, II.442). In Spanish America, continuing concern and inconsistent enforcement of such precautions was manifested in a series of edicts to control the means in which confession was performed. In 1606, Archbishop Bartolomé Lobo Guerrero of Santa Fe in Colombia specified that only elderly priests could confess nuns; in Mexico, an edict stipulating that women be confessed only in the confessional box was first passed in 1668 and reiterated on several occasions. In 1709, the Franciscan Manuel Vigil demanded that all confessors under his jurisdiction in Mexico be at least forty years old and educated. A 1783 decree specified that confessionals in convents could not have revolving doors (Lavrin "Vida conventual" 82; González Marmolejo 244–45). While the number of reported cases in South American viceroyalties gradually began to decline, in New Spain the problem refused to disappear: solicitation cases actually increased during the eighteenth century, particularly between 1712–13 and 1778.[52]

Although some argued that solicitation charges should only be pursued in cases of sexual relations, Spanish-American Inquisition records suggest that touching and provocative remarks could constitute an abuse worthy of investigation. Sentences were relatively light: a priest found guilty of solicitation would no longer be allowed to confess women; in serious cases he would be exiled from the community.[53] Charges would usually not be pursued if the woman involved did not cooperate; however, if the relations were proven to be consensual, the punishments were sometimes more severe (Lavrin "Vida conventual" 76–81).[54] In Manila, when a guilt-ridden María Zerafina de Nazareth denounced her confessor/lover for solicitation, he arrogantly replied: "I am a man, and although I confess the very thought of it frightens me . . . We have played enough, my dear, and now we must face the consequences" (folio 141).[55] Whether an abuse of authority or mutual seduction, solicitation was a painful reminder that the confessor was also human.

Among the myriad cases of solicitation documented in Spanish America, the incidence of *reported* abuses in the convent is relatively low.[56] Lavrin maintains there is no evidence that religious women were assumed to be at fault for seducing their spiritual fathers since solicitation of a nun, as the bride of Christ, would have been a grave offense to divine authority ("Vida conventual" 81).[57] There is, on the other hand, no reason not to believe some cases went unreported, particularly in the convent, where the denunciation of a priest could create tension among the sisters. María Marcela alludes to such a situation when she finds herself the object of convent gossip: "On one occasion they said that I had denounced a priest, and the accusations that were cast upon me were so slanderous that I dare not put them to paper" (109).[58] In reality, a woman was not obligated to denounce the offender if she had "reasonable fear of grave injury to life, reputation, or property, to herself or to her kindred to the fourth degree." Lea suggests that the practice was tolerated and perhaps even condoned by local authorities to avoid public scandal, and Lavrin cites at least one case in which another priest tried to convince a nun not to press charges. More troubling still, the confessor had the authority to absolve the woman he seduced, and, in the Franciscan and Dominican orders at least, the absolution would be valid (Lea I.383–90; Lavrin "Vida conventual" 81). Taught to believe salvation hinged on the mediation of the confessor, and trapped within the often delicate politics of the convent, nuns very likely were reluctant to betray their confessors. In fact, denouncing a confessor could have serious consequences for a religious woman. In 1576, when María de San José, abbess of the Reformed Carmelite convent in Seville, complained to authorities of the ignorance and abuses of the priest assigned to her monastery, *she* was punished, losing her position as abbess and condemned to solitary confinement in her cell, forbidden to see or speak with any of the sisters (Perry 72). And in 1610, María de San Rafael was sentenced by the Inquisition in Quito to six years of solitary confinement after accusing her confessor of solicitation, even though he admitted to the charge (Glave 67–68).

While actual violations may have been few, priests' presence within convent walls, as McKnight notes, was "never entirely above suspicion so long as nuns and priests remained women and men underneath their self-control" (95). Rhetoric such as that of the influential Jesuit manual of Giovanni Battista Scaramelli fueled such suspicions, warning that men and women could not be trusted in each other's presence; as P. J. Stockman explains in his 1921 revision, "Men and women when near each other are like fire and straw which burn together at the least contact, and if they touch, they will both most assuredly burn with the ardent fire of an impure love" (200). It is no wonder that relations between confessors and their female penitents sometimes became strained. In an especially tense passage, Sebastiana Josefa de la Santísima Trinidad expresses ambivalent feelings toward her confessor as if trying to discover whether she holds a favored position with him: "there is no more compassionate heart than yours, and being so merciful with me, how must you be with your other beloved souls? How well must they experience the sweetness of your love? It truly is the greatest treasure, which must be desired with all the forces of the Soul, and the pleasure you give us has troubled me many times, and we are thankful for the knowledge that you love us" (151).[59]

María Coleta de San José, charged by the Inquisition for illicit relations with her confessor, provides further insight into the competition to win a confessor's favor and the degree to which he could be conflated with Christ: "You have been my Father and my sanctuary, and consolation for my soul, and although I may be, not your daughter, because I no longer deserve this honor, even in your heart, but I content myself with being the servant of your daughters, my mistresses . . . Pray to God, for pity's sake, ask him, I say, that I may be His [yours] alone, and that I may know how to return this love, because I am very ungrateful with my God. Mother María complained to me that you no longer include her among your favored daughters. Mother F. and I have laughed at her nonsense, because she tells me that you are already hers, and that for her you must dismiss all the rest, that you must drive them out and that I alone should be the most beloved" (folio 117, carta 2).[60] In this labyrinthine passage, María Coleta plays with the ambiguous construction of second-person formal (the confessor) and third person (Christ) when she asks the confessor to pray that she be "toda suya" [His/yours alone]; "suya" being used in the sentences following to refer to the women's competition for the confessor's favor. She also reveals/conceals her own desire with an ambiguous lack of punctuation in the final sentences that veil the speaking voice by confusing it with the subject (Mother María) that desires exclusivity with the confessor.

Rather than invoking a direct appeal for his favor, Úrsula Suárez pursues a more playful strategy as she invites her reader to take vicarious pleasure in her flirtations with other men. In one particularly provocative episode, she blames herself in retrospect for misunderstanding when she tells her cellmates that a confessor "seems to want to be my devotee"; later realizing, apparently, that she was mistaken: "how distant was I from what the Father wanted: desiring my soul, I offered him my body" (184).[61] The narrative strategy Úrsula uses to recreate this scene is exceptionally astute: although she accuses herself in the past tense of misinterpreting the priest's intention, the original accusation is retained by presenting it as dialogue in the present. María Marcela takes a similar approach as she narrates a series of daring episodes from her youth with vivid, albeit sometimes dubious, detail. In María Marcela's narration, frequent allusions to possible transgressions are suggested but rarely elaborated. The most intriguing of these assertions is perhaps her relation to a childhood suitor. Noting that she had several admirers, she confesses that one stood out: "I loved only one, and it was he upon whom I set my sights, since from my earliest childhood I recognized his fondness for me and I also felt that way toward him"; but after this important revelation, she interrupts the thread of her narration to change to another subject: "But let us leave his story for now and later we will see what Our Lord did to him just because I loved him, and we will see what the Lord God began to do with me" (18).[62] Eventually María returns to her account but it remains deliberately ambiguous. Although she notes her embarrassment when the suitor continues to visit her, her uneasiness seems more due to his seeing her in plain clothes than to the presence of a man in the convent: "He started coming to the window to see me, which caused me great mortification, since before he had known me as haughty and vain, and to think he would see me now in simple clothes and the submissive manner of a novice made me blush." Later, humiliation is similarly misdirected when she mentions her embarrassment when, sent outside to deliver *atole* to the chaplain, she is surprised to find her admirer following her, and spills the liquid down the front of her dress. For good measure, the incident is repeated a few days later with a pitcher of water. However enticing, the story comes to an abrupt end when "I did not come to the window for some time, and with this, the man returned home and I was relieved of this burden" (52–53).[63]

María Marcela's mention of possible transgressions following her profession are expressed more ambiguously: an encounter with a man at the door of the convent is interpreted as a vision of the devil, but she does not elaborate further: "I will not say anything more here so as to not stain the paper with filth nor summon vile acts to my memory" (47). In another incident, when a nun with "too much affection" toward her defends her from the rest of the sisters, she is more cryptic still. Apparently, this defense only makes the other women in the convent more suspicious: "because she wanted to rectify things and take on my cause, she made everything worse and gave the other women more reason to accuse me of more serious offenses" (144). María never directly states what the suspicions of the other nuns are, nor does she clarify the nature of the other woman's "excessive fondness" for her. She excuses herself from further details, alleging, "to attempt to explain everything would be an endless task. I will say only that the suffering extended to everything and for every conceivable reason, in as many matters as can be imagined, and I swear that I do not find in my conscience to have given even the most incidental of motives for the nuns to persecute me as they did, nor did I ever bear them ill will" (118).[64]

It could be that María Marcela is not so much trying to escape punishment from the confessor as to avoid further scandals in the convent. At any rate, by shifting attention from the (unspecified) accusations leveled against her to the carriers of these charges, María Marcela positions herself as the persecuted victim, thus reframing the questionable incident into what will later be identified (in chapter 3) as a hagiographic model. At the same time, by re-creating these incidents she is engaging in a visual confirmation of her identity that suggests some attempt on her part to stimulate voyeuristic pleasure in her male reader. As Margo Glantz observes, there was more than a trace of voyeurism implicit in the curiosity of priests to know the most intimate details of a woman's life, as evidenced by Manuel de Santa Cruz's impatient demand for more (and more) material from María de San José, with a particular interest in her life prior to profession: "Make her hurry to tell the rest of what happened to her in twenty years of secular life, because it is not possible that she does not have more, and if she mentions that she had temptations, or other interior labors, and spiritual comforts from God, make sure that she remembers to write them down" (Santander y Torres "Al Lector"; Muriel *Cultura femenina* 376; Glantz *Sor Juana Inés de la Cruz* 57).[65] Whether expressed directly, as in her overpowering awareness of her body as revealed to her suitor (its contours further revealed when she spills *atole* and water on herself), or indirectly, through the male fantasies of demonic seduction (a scene too "vile" to stain the paper) and convent lesbianism, the line between edification and titillation is thin indeed.[66] It may even be that these narratives of seduction are played out for the benefit of the confessor, whose complicity in the game is assured by the interplay of narrative strategies that protect both performers behind the masks of earlier addressees.

Whether or not confessor and penitent ever acted out their fantasies is irrelevant; most of them probably did not. Rather, this eroticized tension is played out within *and as* a struggle for discursive power. In other words, the woman's narrative is not so much a desire for her confessor as the wish to be the object of his desire and perhaps also of his respect. Indeed, it could be asserted that for all the repressed tensions between male confessors and female penitents, what really is at root here is the seduction of power and knowledge. As Jane Gallop has observed in another context: "The father's refusal to seduce the daughter, to be seduced by her . . . gains him another kind of seduction (this one more one-sided, more like violation), a veiled seduction in the form of the law" (70). By revealing the humanity of the confessor, through implied transgressions and shortcomings of others as well as his own guilty pleasure in reading such narratives of desire, the writing subject may undermine his omnipotence while perhaps gaining some pleasure of her own. Her control of the narration is a power play in itself: she can manipulate the viewpoint of the text, revealing only as much as she wishes to disclose, or drawing the reader into the narration through partially exposed indiscretions and deliberately ambiguous pronominal references in which an eroticized second person/Christ is transferred onto the confessor/reader. As was noted previously, although discursive authority resides in the confessor, this control may be subverted by multiple "points of resistance" within the power network (Foucault *History of Sexuality* 61–62, 94–96). The problem is that presenting herself as body, as a spectacle for her reader's enjoyment, only further underscores his control, for the pleasure of voyeurism, as will be elaborated in chapter 3, is ultimately linked to domination and disparagement and is sometimes even shaded with sadism.

Susan Bernstein notes that it is a standard assertion that "people are susceptible to suggestion; people need to please an authority, to believe an expert, to submit to a master" (4). Regardless of the degree of subordination in such narratives, the gratification of writing to please the confessor could also have played a part in alleviating women's anxiety of authorship. In other words, the author also derives some pleasure or at least reassurance in a form of communication that promises her reconciliation with her self and reintegration into those social norms she has internalized (Tentler 12–13). Confession was also, potentially, a creative channel, because it was one of the few instances in which women were asked—and indeed, were obligated—to express themselves. Furthermore, this submission, related to her position as the "weaker vessel," was also an assertion of a special place in Christ's heart, since, redeemed by the grace of God, she would hold a privileged space in the next world.

* * *

As historian Jodi Bilinkoff observes, relations between male confessors and female penitents were "more complex, more nuanced, and more reciprocal than conventional wisdom might have us believe. . . . Far from occupying positions of unqualified control, male confessors were strongly attracted to the idea of directing spiritually advanced women and, in turn, became deeply influenced by them, identified with them, and even became dependent upon them" (83–84). This dependency was rooted perhaps in their own insecurities and guilt, as the transgressive narration of the penitent acts as a medium for "analogous ambiguous identifications and desires" of the confessor (Kahane 20). As Foster notes, the confessor is "infected with the doubt and loss evoked by the narrative of confession. . . . He traffics in the sins of others, which must at some level recall to him his own sins, his own estrangement from God's coherent being" (3). When María Manuela de Santa Ana wrote a letter to her confessor, Pedro Loayza, in which she described a vision of the two of them with Christ, he responded: "I am a wretched sinner. I must attribute whatever other favors of the Savior she transmits to the Lord's mercy and the prayers of this woman, his handmaiden" (*Esquelas*, folio 7, 240).[67] The understanding between María Manuela and her confessor demonstrates how reassuring guidance could alleviate the fears and tensions suffered in isolation. The priest often returned María's letters with his commentary written on the texts themselves to ensure they would not fall into the wrong hands.⁶⁸ Carefully interpreting each letter, Loayza provides textualized authority from the Bible or the works of the saints to support María's visions, reassuring her of their orthodoxy and encouraging her to write (*Esquela* s/n, 290, 298).

As this relationship shows, confession is also a communicative act: it represents a reciprocal attempt to understand the terms and the limits by which people are defined, both as they listen to the confessions of others and they recount their own transgressions. It is this demand for understanding that the other narrative will repeat as an integral part of their production and effect (Foster 7). As long as she is writing her inner life, her confession, for another/others, the author is not alone. Alluding to the communicative impulse in confession, Stephen Spender asserts that "one of the things that the most abysmal confessions prove is the incapacity of even the most outcast creature to be alone. Indeed, the essence of the confession is that the one who feels outcast pleads with humanity to relate his isolation to its wholeness. He pleads to be forgiven, condoned, even condemned, so long as he is brought back into the wholeness of people and things" (120). On the other hand, just as the penitent could refuse to speak to a hostile confessor, the confessor could exercise the prerogative to refuse to listen, no matter how insistently his spiritual daughter tried to make her perspective heard. Francisca Josefa Castillo recalls a particularly traumatic incident with an early confessor, Francisco de Herrera: "They told the father some things about me that made him very angry: he said some cruel things to me, abandoning me in the confessional without hearing me, and then stopped confessing me altogether. . . . I see now that the best path would have been to humbly beg his forgiveness, but what I did was to express remorse and *try to give him my reasons,* and after being *reprimanded four or five times,* I gave up and took my leave" (35, emphasis added).⁶⁹

Although the "things" that so infuriate the priest are never fully revealed, Francisca obliquely insinuates that her confessor was at fault when she comments shortly after that he was prohibited from confessing in convents, a common punishment for priests accused of solicitation (37). This revelation is followed immediately by a discussion of the Inquisition (37–38).⁷⁰ When Herrera attempts to visit Francisca a year later, he is refused entry (37). Although clearly she seeks to absolve herself of responsibility for the altercation, her motives in implying a parallel between her confessor's eviction from the convent and the Inquisition are less obvious. It was, after all, Herrera who had ordered Francisca to write her mystic *Afectos* at the age of nineteen, offering words of support and suggestions for revision to refine her style (32), and according to her account, they continued to correspond for many years after until his death, although such epistolary relationships had provoked "all too human" rumors within the convent (37, 113, 122). Michel de Certeau writes of the "will to hear" as a necessary precondition for the establishment of dialogic spaces in the visionary encounter (*Heterologies* 91). As Francisca's repeated attempts to communicate with her confessor demonstrate, the same expectation underlies the confessional exchange. Foster refers to a shared expectation of understanding, an understanding that "is deferred as the conclusion fails to arrive: the writer will keep trying to tell the story if the reader will keep trying to understand" (3–4). Confessors who fail to respect this pact, who do not listen or who respond with hostility, are resisted. Moreover, since God condones the inner life of the subject, the message to current and future addressees is clear: confessors who refuse to listen should be resisted and indeed declaimed as impediments to the divine word.

While they may not have expressed their feelings openly, intelligent women intrigued their confessors and stimulated them intellectually. Bilinkoff relates the admiration of one of Teresa de Jesús's confessors, Baltasar Álvarez, who commented to another priest that Teresa "flew so high" that he had to read enormous quantities of devotional books just to keep up with her. However, this same confessor, like so many others, sadistically "experimented" with his daughters, testing their obedience through insults, mortifications, and the arbitrary granting and denial of the Eucharist (91, 95). María de San José provides a detailed account of a similarly complex and sometimes difficult relationship with Plácido Olmedo, one of her later confessors and the addressee for most of her surviving work. The roles of confessor and penitent converge as the father shares his thoughts with his spiritual daughter: "he came to speak openly and frankly of matters of his soul with me . . . He started coming to the confessional just to talk to me and tell me of his great troubles and difficulties" (V.2). Nonetheless, and although she contends that Olmedo was the first confessor with whom she was able to fully express herself (V.4–5), María recalls her frustration with not being able to share her problems on a regular basis (V.3).[71] She is particularly troubled by the distance he imposed between them: "I was very hurt by the way he treated me. . . . He would speak to me as if he were speaking to someone else and not me: when he would tell me to do something he would say: 'Madre María, do this, do not do that' . . . and so I asked him, 'Father, who is this Madre María?' and he responded, 'The Madre María with whom I am speaking.'. . . . In the seven years that he was my spiritual father I never heard a single word from him that would lead me to believe I was his daughter of confession" (V.7). María was also disappointed that Olmedo rarely commented on her notebooks, and when he did, it was to clarify a specific point rather than offer an interpretation. On his deathbed, however, he returns her papers organized and bound. Many of María de San José's earlier writings had either been burned or lost, and she is deeply moved by the generosity of her confessor: "I found the notebooks bound by his saintly hands, conveying to me the great effort he had taken to put them in order because of those that had been lost. Of all the confessors I have had, there has been none other as caring and kind as the venerable Father Plácido Olmedo, who collected my papers and put them in order" (V.16–17).[72] María later has a vision of Olmedo on his deathbed in which he explains to her that his mistreatment was not due to lack of affection but to set her on the path to salvation (V.11).

The inconsistencies (or, perhaps, conflicting agendas) in María's narration (that, for example, Olmedo was the only confessor with whom she could speak freely, and yet he rarely let her speak) may be explained in part by the fact that María is writing this version of her relation with the priest for Ángel Maldonado, powerful bishop of Oaxaca and a close friend of Olmedo. On the other hand, there often appears to be an attraction on the part of the authors toward those confessors who were most demanding, whose trust was not easily gained, and whose verbal abuse would ostensibly save their souls from more serious torments in the afterlife. These demanding confessors command respect and loyalty in female penitents because their motivation is to help bring them closer to God. This is illustrated by the ambivalent relationship of Francisca Josefa Castillo with Juan Manuel Romero, a Jesuit missionary whose aversion for women was so pronounced that he made it a practice not to confess them. Winning over his indifference and cruelty and gaining his favor becomes a challenge for Francisca. The first time she sees him inspires a mystical-erotic vision that justifies her daring: "while with Our Lord, I saw myself with the denotation or semblance of a little garden, with the door very narrow and closed, although somewhat mistreated. . . . The garden had abundant water, but with no current nor direction, it was stagnant. . . . This blessed father was inside, making way for the water and clearing the vegetation with great fervor and free of obstacles, and he was working under the supervision of God, who was presiding there and giving orders like the lord and master of that poor little piece of land" (121).[73] The use of bodily and sexual metaphors for the awakening of the soul is not especially transgressive in itself. Specifically, Francisca may have remembered the image from the Song of Songs ("A garden locked is my sister, my bride, / a garden locked, a fountain sealed"

[4.12]), a text she often evokes in her *Afectos espirituales.* Garden and fountain imagery was also associated with the Virgin Mary. What makes Francisca's version particularly suggestive is the active role posited for the confessor rather than Christ in this passage, only marginally veiled by the divine intervention of God overseeing as ultimate Lord and master. In courtly literature, the orchard was a common space for lovers to meet and secrets to be exchanged, symbolic of, as Danielle Régnier-Bohler suggests, an obsession with boundaries—both physical and social—and their ambivalence (322). By playing with these boundaries and imagining herself in the center of the vision as, quite literally, the virgin land to be cultivated, Francisca nonetheless strategically deflects her desire through the use of biblical text. Her desire is further displaced when, following this vision, she mysteriously finds herself confessing to Romero: "without knowing how, I found myself confessing with that blessed father, so much so that people later told me that it made one stop to think what could have moved him to come to me against his resolve not to attend to nuns" (122).[74]

Once Francisca Josefa has convinced Romero to confess her, however, conventional boundaries and power relations are sustained. Luce Irigaray has alluded to the complicity of the female subject in the structure of patriarchal exchange systems as part of the disempowered daughter's desperate need for the love and recognition of the symbolic father (106). In her anxiousness to please Romero (and, by extension, her current addressee), Francisca willingly submits to his humiliation and erratic demands. Forced to choose between abandonment and abuse, she would rather be submitted to Romero's tests of will than face his indifference:

> My confessor humiliated me as much as he could. . . . He treated me badly, whenever possible, verbally, and his responses were terribly harsh. Sometimes, and this was customary, he would become so extremely and genuinely angry with me, scolding me for things I had thought to be good, that I was left trembling and fearful, and then later he would tell me to proceed, that all was well. Sometimes he threw me out of the confessional with such rage and disdain that it seemed as if I had given him some serious cause; in particular, on some occasions he wrote 'that he had realized that I and all my things deserved only to be burned, and that he had decided to leave me because my path led to ruin' and other very cruel things . . . but later he would return and again would scold and reprimand me for not knowing how to bear that humiliation and cross. . . and in this way, his severity was what gave me the most strength to go on (123–24).[75]

Francisca embraces her confessor's sadistic treatment precisely because of the suffering it entails. This pain becomes the principal focus of the story because it is the only action she is allowed to perform, her only way to please and her only access to power in the narrative. As Francisca Josefa explains: "He used to tell me later that although he felt inclined to help me bear my crosses, he could not, on the other hand, help but treat me that way ... but that he only desired what was best for me and that my soul would be cleansed and purified for God. It seems to me that I would have thrown myself into a burning oven to obtain such joy" (134).[76] Francisca Josefa maintains the jealousy of the other sisters led to the dismissal of Romero as her confessor (126); nonetheless, he later defends her against a priest who threatens to denounce her to the Inquisition (170) and is called to her side when she is near death (173).

Romero tells Francisca that "what he wanted from me was that my name would go unheard in the world and that I would suffer greatly" (134)[77]; she is willing to risk complete annihilation of her identity to continue to be recognized by the confessor. In return, by pleasing him through her self-mortification, she binds him to her through his own sense of guilt. Ironically, as Gallop suggests, precisely because this seduction cannot be consummated, power relations remain intact (75). Fearful of her desire and perhaps unable to admit his own, the authority figure translates and sublimates these tensions into the "lasting seduction" of the law. When translated to the text, this struggle between law and desire inevitably reflects on questions of discursive authority.

Although also maintaining hierarchical gender divisions, the narration of Gerónima del Espíritu Santo, who had a particularly affectionate relationship with her confessor, portrays a gentler form of submission. She imagines herself a lamb (64), a little dog (72), and a small child (64, 80), helpless and dependent on the support of her spiritual director: "I saw the Lord walking on a very rough road, full of obstacles. He was leading me by the hand, and to my right went my guardian angel and my confessor, helping clear the way. And when there were places where I might stumble, the Lord ordered my confessor to lift me in his arms and help me over, and so he did, to the Lord's great happiness and satisfaction" (64).[78] The role of the confessor as a benevolent patriarch is further explored in another richly symbolic vision in which Gerónima imagines herself as a small child just learning to walk; her confessor, like a patient father, holds her up, since each time he tries to release her she teeters as if about to fall.[79] Although in this passage dependence on the confessor is absolute—"if it were not for his help, I could not have walked" (80)—it would seem that Gerónima's affection and respect for her spiritual father, Juan de Olmos, was mutual, as he details at length his grief at the death of his spiritual daughter: "the pain of her absence pierced my heart" (33).

The darker side of this dependence on the spiritual director is suggested in the narration of Sebastiana Josefa de la Santísima Trinidad. In a compulsive search for new transgressions to confess, Sebastiana expresses a piteous fear of abandonment. In one passage she confesses: "I am overcome with fears, with such painful anguish . . . that I want only my Father, yet with the fear of the thought that he loathes me . . . and no longer wants to confess me. . . . What I suffer within is great . . . and it is all your fault, Reverend Father, you could stab me and it would hurt less" (29); on another occasion she increases her self-mortification in an attempt to keep her confessor from leaving her (110). Similarly, María Coleta, who describes herself as "your little daughter who wishes to obey you" (carta 4, folio 121), declares: "I perform the examination of conscience continually, my dear little Father: my desire is to give you an account of every breath I take" (carta 2, folio 117).[80] While it was not uncommon for confessors to be older than their spiritual daughters, the women envisioning themselves here as helpless children were actually mature and perhaps even well beyond middle age at the time of writing. Whether portraying the confessor as benevolent father or harsh disciplinarian, by situating themselves in the position of child these authors underscore the level of dependence and subordination to the confessor.

At the same time, occasionally a careful reading of what is narratively inscribed as dependence actually reveals inner strength. In a moment of desperation María Manuela de Santa Ana writes: "I beg of you, do not fail to write me . . . so I may continue . . . Pray to God for me. I can go on no longer" (folio 14, *Esquela* 250). In a letter one day following, however, she reports that the problem was solved on her own initiative: "My Father, at your feet I beg your forgiveness for bothering you yesterday. . . . With the help of God I began my spiritual exercises and in an instant God's mercies poured upon me" (folio 15, *Esquela* 251). María Manuela clearly indicates here that, with the help of God, she had resolved the crisis alone, yet she subsequently gives credit to her confessor: "My father, I was greatly consoled yesterday by what you wrote me. . . . I was so relieved that I set myself to praying and could . . . do all my exercises" (folio 15, *Esquela* 251).[81] Although, like Gerónima del Espíritu Santo and Francisca Josefa, she regularly qualifies her statements, noting that it seems to her ("me parece"), María Manuela does nonetheless often interpret her visions without the benefit of her confessor: "Three days before the fall, the interior chapel of my soul was revealed to me as half fallen. And it seems to me that the Lord God was demonstrating that not all would be destroyed, only half, as we had envisioned it" (folio 3, *Vida* 167).[82] Invoking her visionary authority, María both asks the questions and supplies associations, making the intervention of her confessor unnecessary. Indeed, in the visionary realm María Manuela posits equal discursive authority with her spiritual guide. In one revelation in particular, she summons her confessor to assist her as she releases Christ from the cross. In the manner in which she describes the scene, she has assumed the active role of initiating the untying of the ropes, while the priest kneels passively; they then proceed to work together to unbind him: "Last night the desire to untie Our Savior during the procession of the Passion awoke in me. I immediately begged Him to bring you along in spirit and he conceded me this [request] so you could help me untie Him. I saw you very clearly with a supernatural vision, kneeling with great love, you on one side and I on the other untying Our Savior" (folio 7, *Esquela* 240).[83] The vision underscores the close relation between María Manuela and her confessor, and, perhaps, her desire to be united with him in the next world, where they will be equals. At the same time, the image of "tying"/"untying," as Elia Armancanqui-Tipacti notes, is explicitly related to the absolution of sin by the confessor in Matthew 16.19: "I will give you the keys of the kingdom of heaven, and whatever you bind on earth shall be bound in heaven, and whatever you loose on earth shall be loosed in heaven" (135).[84] What makes María Manuela's revelation especially subversive is that it should be the confessor, and not the confessant, who holds the keys to the kingdom. This inversion of authority is further reinforced when Saint Peter himself, with Christ at his side, gives her communion and she pleads that the soul of her confessor might enter heaven (folio 9, *Esquela* 243).

Direct experience of Christ gives the subject a discursive advantage over even her confessor. After she speaks with her spiritual guide about a vision of purgatory, Christ himself intervenes to reassure María de San José: "I began to fear and doubt that this could have been a trick of the devil or my own imagination.... 'Have no fear, my daughter, it is not a delusion of the enemy, and so that you may see how much I love and cherish you, I will show you the soul of your father in all its glory'" (*Word* 81).[85] As Myers points out, the fact that this interchange took place in the confessional and that indeed, because of it María was unable to respond to her confessor, insinuates that her direct relation with Christ makes the priest's participation unnecessary (introduction 33). In another episode, sensing the presence of Christ on her bed one day as she is sewing, María de San José asserts, "I had no doubt that it was not a delusion of the devil," immediately qualifying her boldness, clarifying that she did not *see* him but *felt* him, further admitting "although it is always with fear that I explain such things to myself." What Christ tells her in this vision, however, is designed to reinforce the confessor's authority by obeying his command to write: "it is time you told your confessor of the wonders I have worked in you . . . I do not want my greatness to remain in silence" (II.14). Although she gives credit here to the confessor, her discursive authority is affirmed on many levels. Encountering Christ in the humble surroundings of her cell as she completes her daily routine, María not only speaks directly to Christ but is able to distinguish between good and evil without benefit of a priest, and Christ himself demands that she articulate her visions, thereby legitimizing the act of writing. In another notebook she inserts a similarly independent defense into a formulaic expression of obedience: "My Father and Lord, to obey you I will continue with what I have begun although with repugnance and difficulty. . . . Although, on the other hand, *I have no doubt that what I say is as I say it and so it is that I say it*" (III.59, emphasis added).[86] In this passage, although she again defers to the confessor by professing she writes only out of obedience, it is her own will and conscience that reassure her of the validity of her assertions.

Although the acceptance of a nonverbal visionary realm did not ultimately offer resistance to the ruling order, it is possible to recognize, as Bernstein suggests, "elements of testimony or bearing witness to inequities that define the transgression and the transgressor and that compel and mediate confession itself" (2). If the structural demands placed on how one confesses make telling the truth impossible and maybe even dangerous, the truth may be less important than the strategies used to structure and present this truth, and the means in which the confessional model is respected and challenged. Because the priest, and not the writing subject, was authorized to determine the "truth," the author must position herself in a subordinate position in which hierarchies of authority are reinforced. At the same time, the assertion of a visionary authority in which a direct relation to Christ is attributed to the writing subject and not the confessor suggests a subtext that questions the nature of this authority and, moreover, uncovers the mechanisms of power in which the discourse is situated. Bernstein refers to the "latency" of confessional discourse, of provisional, partial, and occluded "margins and moments of testimony . . . embedded within confession, particularly confessions of those who are disempowered, those who are culturally prohibited from speaking a different 'truth'" (39). Meaning is conveyed by implicit or explicit contrast, by a complex system of internal differentiation that is not always readily apparent on the surface. On the margins and between the lines, the *vida* has the potential to effect a critical renegotiation of self-representation as process and product.

2

Immaculate Conceptions
Madre Castillo Wrestles with the Truth

> Nosotros no somos ángeles, sino tenemos cuerpo; querernos hacer ángeles estando en la tierra . . . es desatino.
> Santa Teresa de Jesús

Sor Francisca Josefa de la Concepción (Francisca Josefa de Castillo Toledo Guevara Niño y Rojas, 1671–1742) was literally a product and reflection of her birthplace outside Tunja, New Granada (Colombia). Although at one time a major center of power, by the mid-seventeenth century Tunja was an isolated and arid city in decline (Achury ix). Since the convent was often an option for the elite class to maintain racial purity when the prohibitive expense of a dowry made suitable marriages difficult, the mining crisis of seventeenth-century New Granada (Colmenares 244) led to a most unusual situation. Although the city had barely 3,500 inhabitants, it had no less than three parish churches and six monasteries and convents, each with a large population of men and women religious, giving the town a particularly desolate character. As Darío Achury Valenzuela notes, hyperbolically: "Water is increasingly scarce and firewood limited, the land yields no crops, and men and women do not reproduce, because nearly all have taken refuge in the convents, to quench there the fires of the flesh" (xiii–xiv).[1] Francisca's father, a Spanish functionary, opposed her entrance into the convent; nevertheless her mother and one of her two sisters joined her there as widows; all six of her brother's daughters took their vows at the convent of Santa Clara and two of his three sons became Jesuits (Domínguez 219).[2]

Although her family was apparently affluent, Francisca Josefa never attended school and was instructed by her mother in their home; when her mother became ill she taught herself to read and write, spending many hours a day reading both spiritual and secular texts (*Su vida* 7).[3] During her life Francisca had numerous confessors—Achury counts twelve and perhaps thirteen mentioned by name (lxii) although she did not write for all of them. She corresponded with several former confessors, most notably with Francisco de Herrera, with whom she communicated from 1695, when he left Tunja, to his death (37, 113) and Juan de Tobar, with whom she confessed from 1697 to 1702 and continued to correspond for at least eight years thereafter (69).[4] Herrera was the first confessor who had her write down her thoughts in an organized fashion (29); he likely motivated the first *Afectos* when Francisca was barely nineteen years old (Achury cxxxi, ccv). Though at times harsh with his spiritual daughter (35; 39–40), Herrera provided the young Francisca with literary models and suggestions for revision to refine her style (*Afectos* 32). The next confessor with whom she would have a frequent exchange of letters was Diego de Tapia. References to Tapia appear in chapters XLIX to LV (188, 192, 200, 205, 208, 213) and she directs herself explicitly to him as "vuestra paternidad" in chapters XXVI and XL (139, 153–55). Significantly, Tapia had consulted with Herrera regarding Francisca's case and he mentions his colleague in a letter to his spiritual daughter (*Afectos* 537). Engaged as her confessor for only five years, Tapia nevertheless exercises an important influence on Francisca. Although she finds his insistence on regular reports burdensome, she suffers when he is absent (166, 187, 200, *Afectos* 544). It should be noted that by now Francisca was a mature woman: her affiliation with the priest began when she was about forty-seven or forty-eight years old.

Although Francisca occasionally mentions her age and certain events that can be historically verified, the text is primarily based on the liturgical calendar, even though, given the number of administrative positions she held, she was more than well acquainted with secular chronology. Since in the first chapter of the text her mother has already died, the earliest possible date during which she could have initiated this version is 1701, when she was thirty years old. In chapter XXIII she mentions, in past tense, that she was thirty-two years old (79); in chapter XXIX, also in past tense, that she was thirty-eight (116), and in chapter 41, that she was forty-four (160). While there is no question that the *Afectos espirituales,* which span the years 1690 to at least 1728 (Domínguez 217), were written for a series of confessors, it is not clear when or for which confessor Francisca began the definitive version of her life. The "phantoms of earlier addressees" mentioned by Weber further cloud the author-reader pact (*Teresa* 66–67).

Francisca Josefa mentions a key historical referent in the second chapter of her autobiography that suggests that the existent version of the text was likely written for Diego de Tapia. She recounts seeing her addressee, "vuestra paternidad," when she was twelve or thirteen years old and when he was still a novice priest (8). Though a native of Medellín, a seventeen-year-old Diego de Tapia studied as a novice priest at the Colegio de Tunja in 1684, when Francisca would have been thirteen years old (Pacheco 162; Restrepo 396). This hypothesis is reinforced by the fact that Tapia is the confessor mentioned most in direct address by Francisca and the last confessor named in the text.[5] Chapter XXXVI brings her addressee up to date as she notes the arrival of "vuestra paternidad" (139); and she apparently takes as completed the retrospective vision of her life a few pages later when she concludes: "In this way, I have spent most of my life. I will now write only a few more things, because it would be a never-ending task to recount all of them, which at any rate have almost always been the same" (144).[6] This statement strongly suggests that the main body of the text, including thirty-seven chapters on her life and four additional entries, was written for Tapia. This would explain the uniformity in style, noted by Achury (cxxxii), the differentiation between "vuestra paternidad" and "mi confesor" in earlier chapters (see, for example, chapter XIV: 45), and the fact that Tapia's departure leaves her life story truncated, though she would live eighteen years more. However, a clear break in the narration may be discerned between the end of chapter XLI and the beginning of chapter XLII. The chapter breaks in the original manuscript have been maintained in the published versions of the work and the chapters rarely have formulaic openings and conclusions. It seems likely, then, that they were designed as parts of a work, not as individual documents. Thus when Francisca concludes chapter XLI by reiterating: "And so I ask of you, my Father, that with the favor of the Lord, having overcome so much and gone through so many tribulations writing this to give you an account of my life, to look well upon it and the steps my soul has taken, so it is not lost; as I again put it in your hands" (160),[7] it may be deduced that with this chapter the manuscript was closed. The entries that follow are more like an appendix than part of her coherent life story, jumping from recent events to episodes from the distant past, with a greater integration of expressions of devotion and descriptions of her mystical visions, often transcribed from her *Afectos*. This is reinforced by the way she wrote the following chapter, beginning with an introductory formula of obedience and speaking of Diego de Tapia in the third person and in the past tense: "Trusting the promises and words of the Lord who said: that she who obeys his ministers, obeys the Divine Lord God, and seeing how you, Reverend Father, have ordered this of me, as has Father Diego de Tapia (to whom I revealed all the trials and tribulations of my soul), who has written me that I should obey Your Reverence in this" (161).[8] Domínguez implies that Diego de Moya, Francisca's last confessor and rector of the Colegio in

Tunja, had attended to her for an extended period (221); suggesting that perhaps it is to him that she directs her final chapters. On the other hand, the addressee could have been someone more highly situated in the Church hierarchy, since he is the only person to whom Francisca refers, repeatedly, as "vuestra reverencia" (164, 165, 166, 214) and is, moreover, perhaps someone who has had authority over her for some time, since she states that she had asked him many times for permission to burn her papers.

* * *

It appears fairly likely, as Achury suggests, that Francisca must have had access to baroque poetry (cxx); however, his logic that her difficult style proves that she "wrote only for herself" (cxxi) and that it never even "passed through her mind" that her work would be read after her death (cxxv) is less sound. Although clearly her primary audience is her confessors and Church authorities, and her antagonistic relation with her companions in the convent could have led her to hide her writings from her sisters (122), it seems unlikely that she could not have foreseen a future audience. Achury unwittingly reveals an important contradiction in Francisca's work when first he contends that she wrote only out of obedience and then, that she did not write for her confessors (cxxi). Francisca confirms that her confessors insisted on a regular submission of papers to evaluate: "I have written [these papers] in response to the many and repeated demands of my confessors, who have seen and examined them" (*Afectos* 207); she further states that she found this request difficult to fulfill.[9] Nevertheless, her autobiography seems to have been initiated during a period in which her confessor was not directly involved. It could well be, as Achury suggests, that she began to enjoy the act of writing for its own sake (cxxii) or as a means of catharsis for her daily tribulations (77). That Francisca had creative instincts that superseded the duty to her confessors is suggested by her *Afectos espirituales,* which she scribbles on any paper available without stopping to worry about grammar and spelling, sometimes, she claims hyperbolically, using her tears to make the ink last longer (58). Moreover, her request to burn her writing occurs more frequently in regard to her mystic *Afectos* than to her life story (122, 162; *Afectos* 8, 42, 67, 90).[10] As we have seen, the formulaic repetition of obedience (77, 86, 187) is common to nearly all such narratives and can be taken as at best an ambivalent reaction to her task (29, 34, 44, 63, 122, 160, 187). Another possibility, supported by the lack of overstrikes and corrections on the work, is that Francisca copied the material after it was revised by her confessor with the intention of preserving it, either for future canonization or as a model for other nuns. Francisca herself had been inspired by precursor texts; moreover, she spent many years of her life in the convent as an abbess and as mistress of novices, a role model and mother figure for her wards. Referring to possible future readings of her writings she expresses the hope that "if some day they could come to be known to some soul, it could move her to love such a benevolent God" (*Afectos* 227); in another passage she straddles the divide between humility toward her confessor and artistic pride invoking divine intervention: "With these things and others written in those papers, the infinite mercy of God consoled and lifted my afflictions and kept me from burning what I had written, as many times I had proposed and asked of Your Reverence" (164).[11]

Francisca Josefa protects herself by claiming that God has given her knowledge and inspiration. She also claimed, as had Teresa de Jesús and Catherine of Siena, that her knowledge of Latin was a case of divine intervention (23, 26, 30, 157, 197; *Afectos* 28, 34, 98), and she cites only the permitted *Oficio Divino* (16, 23, 26, 30, 37, 157, 197).[12] Her usually uncited glosses of the Bible, both in her *Afectos espirituales* and in *Su vida*, derive principally from Psalms.[13] Achury speculates that the sometimes awkward versions of biblical text and frequent Latinisms indicate Francisca was translating from Latin (clvi–clviii). Another possibility is that she was citing from memory phrases she had heard in sermons. Nonetheless, Francisca's citations of biblical texts from a variety of books strongly suggest that she had access to texts besides the *Oficio Divino;* perhaps, as Achury contends, to the *Brevario Romano* (clv), and possibly the Bible itself. Whether or not the confessors who read and approved Francisca's work believed it was divinely inspired, that she was allowed to appropriate biblical passages (and was, indeed, encouraged to do so, as evidenced by the gift of Luis de la Puente's work) suggests that Francisca enjoyed a particularly advantageous position of protection through her confessors.

In 1813, the Convent of Santa Clara turned over what remained of Francisca's papers to her great-grand nephew, Antonio María de Castillo y Alarcón, who bound them into four notebooks, titled the chapters, and commissioned three copies. *Su vida* was published in Philadelphia in 1817; the *Afectos espirituales* were published in Bogotá in 1843 (Achury cxcv–cxcvii). Why a biography was never written about Francisca is somewhat of a mystery. Neither Moya nor the high Church authorities of the time demonstrated much interest in writing her biography, as requested by her family, although when the papers were finally presented for approval prior to publication (*Afectos* 548–50), the censors detected nothing that could be considered heretical (224–26, 235–39). Another nun from Tunja, Francisca del Niño Jesús (1665–1708), was the subject of a *vida* published in Spain in

1723. Kathryn McKnight suggests the lack of interest for Francisca Josefa's life story has something to do with her relation to authority, which could have made her an unlikely candidate for canonization (125). Nonetheless, as one of the few women whose autobiographical writings were published before this century, Sor Francisca Josefa de la Concepción, or "Madre Castillo" as she is commonly known, has the distinction of being the only woman studied here to appear in mainstream literary anthologies and textbooks.

*   *   *

Francisca Josefa recreates her childhood closely following the hagiographic model in general and Teresa de Jesús in particular. A relationship to the divine is established from earliest childhood: "My mother used to tell the story that before I could walk and barely able to form words, I told her with great fear and joy that an image of the Baby Jesus . . . was calling out to me" (4).[14] Following this miraculous event, her family began to call her "the Holy Child" and dressed her in a nun's habit as a gesture of gratitude to Rosa of Lima for saving Francisca from a life-threatening illness (4–6). Francisca further recounts that she was set apart from other children at a very young age and began a regimen of penance before she was eight. Although she claims not to understand the meaning of marriage, her aversion to it is such that a playful exchange with a boy at the age of six or seven leads her to contemplate suicide, and she is saved from death only by an act of divine intervention (5).

Significantly, her religious inclination is inspired by a reading of Teresa de Jesús: "My mother would read me the books of Teresa de Jesús, and her *Fundaciones*, and this gave me such a great desire to be like those nuns that I tried to do some penances and pray some devotions" (5).[15] At fourteen, after her confirmation, her commitment to ascetic practices intensifies: "I was taken with a resolve and longing to imitate the saints. . . . I abandoned my fine clothes and dressed in a plain skirt. I went about burdened with hairshirts and iron chains until the flesh grew over them. I slept dressed or on boards" (11).[16] Although Francisca's parents are alarmed at the degree of her self-mortification, her father sets up an altar so she may worship at home. Nonetheless, fearful of the gossip and distractions in the convent, Francisca has no interest in professing. After all, two of the most revered women in the New World had not been cloistered nuns: both Rosa of Lima (canonized in 1671) and Mariana of Quito dedicated themselves to religious contemplation in their homes. When, under pressure from her confessor, she does finally decide to enter, her father's reaction, typical of hagiographic narrative, is to discourage his daughter from entering: "Speaking of this, my father would begin to cry, even though he was a very serious man. If I was at the table, he would have the food taken away. It seemed in those last days that I was in his house, that he came to love me more, or demonstrated more that which he had for me. He would wait outside the door of my room for a long time until I finished my devotional exercises and opened it. Then he would enter, greeting me with tender words. . . . Sometimes he said that if I were not in the house, he would not enter it, because I was his only consolation"(16).[17]

The turning point in Francisca's life occurs the day she meets her confessor: "God . . . through you, Reverend Father, saw to it that I would enter one day by chance into your confessional, to reconcile my soul, and I will never forget the first words you said to me, that were: 'Come now, be brave, and together we will find the strength to serve God.' Those words made such an impression on my heart that from that moment on I put myself at your disposal and put my soul in your hands to direct it toward God, unable and unwilling to stray from your guidance" (15).[18] When Francisca's father dies shortly after her entrance into the convent, she interprets this as God's will to position the confessor in his place (21, 29).

* * *

In the seventeenth and eighteenth centuries, the evangelization of the Orinoco region had resulted in the violent deaths of several Jesuit priests, chronicled in Juan Rivero's *Historia de las misiones de los llanos de Casanare y los ríos Orinoco y Meta* (1736) and Pedro de Mercado's four-volume *Historia de la Provincia del Nuevo Reino y Quito de la Compañía de Jesús*, composed between 1682 and 1685 and possibly circulated among members of the society, although its publication was delayed by censors in Spain until 1741 (Pacheco 311, 314–15).[19] There were five principal Jesuit missionary expeditions in the region of New Granada, four during Francisca's lifetime: in 1662, 1681, 1684, 1690, and 1694. The uprising in Marañón, which resulted in the torture and death of two Jesuits, had occurred in 1666 (Mercado IV.145–374). Even if by the time she professed such activities had declined, certainly they were contemporary enough to form part of the popular lore during Francisca's lifetime. More important, many of her confessors were directly affiliated with these missions and their publication. Rivero's chronicle, which includes earlier *relaciones* and other archival materials, was commissioned in 1728 by Diego de Tapia (Rivero xiii); among the documents it includes is the 1692 account of Manuel Pérez to another one of Francisca's confessors, Juan Martínez Rubio (282); and

Francisca's active campaign to win the favor of Juan Manuel Romero is undoubtedly related to his renown as a missionary priest (421, 432).

Although she describes her term as abbess as a period of martyrdom, fitting her life story into the paradigm of sainthood is not an easy task for Francisca.[20] Her attempts to portray herself as a model of obedience and humility are continually undermined by her own narration as she activates the hagiographic model of persecution in which those around her accuse her of excessive pride and refusal to follow the rules. She complains repeatedly of the tremendous hardships suffered at the convent: that she eats flowers for lack of food (25); that she must work in the infirmary to purchase a private cell (52); that she is publicly humiliated when the convent vicar berates her family's "poverty" (72).[21] Yet she brings two servants with her (25), and is accused on more than one occasion by other nuns of secretively eating convent rations and of hiding jewels in her cell (90, 143, 214). Similarly, mirroring Teresa de Jesús's commitment to conventual reform, Francisca alleges that she had began instituting reforms prior to the official demands (29–33), yet she recounts that she is accused of resistance to change by the other members of the community (103).[22] Significantly, Francisca continually reiterates her desire to profess in the more ascetic Discalced Carmelite convent in Tunja, but does not take advantage of the opportunity when her brother and brother-in-law set in motion the necessary documents to do so, despite what she describes as a particularly unhappy period in Santa Clara. Although she describes herself as "very inclined" to make the change, she somehow is able to intercept the documents and burn them (96). Since her family name was more closely associated with Santa Clara, the intervention of her powerful relatives would seem to have alleviated any anxiety she might have had about "disloyalty" to the Clarissan order, and fear of offending her confessors/addressees is also unlikely, since they were Jesuits and not Franciscans. She may have feared entrance into the more vigilantly cloistered Carmelite order would prejudice her access to her confessors. Perhaps the more difficult lifestyle, without servants and slaves, was not as desirable as she claimed. Conceivably, although her surviving male relatives were in favor of moving her, she believed her family honor would be compromised if she were to leave Santa Clara. At any rate, her expressed desire to escape from worldly concerns is contradicted by her actions.

Self-representation, as Roy Pascal affirms, is not so much the truth as a "wrestling with the truth" (75). And it is this wrestling with the truth that is frequently exploited by Francisca in a simultaneous attempt to admit sin and to be absolved from responsibility. She portrays herself as innocently drawn into corrupt activities: she obediently wears fine clothes "with the pretext to please" and not so innocently continues to correspond with an "important person" who wishes to become her devotee: "the enemy ... saw to it that [this person] would write me many times, requesting what they call *devociones* from me, of which there were many at that time. I acted badly, since after receiving the first letter, I received the second and the third knowing what they contained, although I always responded that I did not understand why he was writing me" (20).[23] Inexplicably, she claims, her rejection of the suitor provokes the anger of the other women in the convent, who, along with their wards and servants, spit on her and call her names (21). This narrative of persecution persists throughout Francisca's text. Significantly, the episodes she chooses to emphasize—both as gossip about her and the rumors she spreads—usually center on inappropriate relations with men. In one case she is accused of stealing suitors from other women: "The stories and insults they said to me were endless, in particular, some things that offended my honor, such as that I was seducing their suitors and propositioning them, etc." (25); in another, of inventing pretexts to admit men into the convent: "They called the convent vicar and told him things so shameless that I do not know how I can repeat them here. Among them: that I ate the convent's rations of food, that I got away with whatever I wanted, ... [and] that I feigned illness to have the convent open at all hours and the priests inside" (90). In another incident that underlines the tense environment of the convent, Francisca is accosted by a nun seeking her "amistad particular" [special friendship], a euphemism for lesbian relations (xlix, Lavrin "Vida femenina" 48). "I found myself made into the scandal of the convent. They said and did intolerable things against me. If I read a book in the chorus loft about special friendships and the damage they do, they said I intended to steal their girlfriends to have them come to me" (53). This friendship, or her rejection of it, apparently, compromises her position with Francisco de Herrera; "This woman had gotten friendly with my confessor ... and this caused me great difficulties and distress" (54, 57). Soon afterward, she has a vision of the priest severely reprimanding her as he witnesses her interaction with the other woman, and it is only then that she is freed from the relationship (58). However, by giving the confessor credit for her salvation, she ironically admits some level of involvement in the situation.[24]

As this incident suggests, the contradictory demands of obedience and self-defense are often difficult to reconcile. Even without the intervention of the confessor, the logic of Francisca's discourse is at times suspect: for example, when one of her nieces turns against her and later goes blind and dies, the narrative defies chronology, connecting the two incidents as if the sudden death had been an act of divine retribution (97). There are, in fact, at least three separate occasions in which someone who has treated Francisca badly becomes mortally ill and begs her forgiveness before dying (96, 104, 189). Symbolic flames are said to emerge from another nun as she accuses Francisca unjustly and dies soon afterward "of the rage she had against me" (109), and in another case, incredulity masks a deceptively offhand remark in the margins about one of her former persecutors that "it was a strange thing to see her body decompose" (202), that is, that she did not die a virgin or, at the very least, could not be considered a candidate for sainthood.[25] Another curious inconsistency in Francisca's text is how she held important posts in the convent and indeed was elected abbess on no less than three occasions (1715, 1719, 1738) if, as she claims, she suffered continual persecution at the hands of other nuns.

In her descriptions of the cruelty of her companions in the convent, Francisca ingratiates herself to her confessor by declaring her innocence in all such altercations. Although she employs the expected formulas of her inherent sinful nature: "my vileness, my vain conceit and contemptible character" (73)[26], she rarely directly admits to any specific example of wrongdoing and continually seeks to misdirect her reader's attention from her transgressions. Francisca simultaneously confesses her guilt and absolves herself from the same by portraying herself as an innocent victim, allegedly unable to understand why she is being martyred. In one particularly dramatic episode, "Our Lord arranged that when I was *escucha* [grille attendant], an older nun in the convent attacked me so furiously (*without me knowing why*), that shouting and boxing my ears she loudly ranted 'crazy dog, crazy, sanctimonious dog, you are going to be the eternal damnation of us all, Eucharistic fanatic, I will bar you from confession and communion: Why do you dishonor me so?'" (71, emphasis added).[27] It may be inferred that in this incident, Francisca has listened to an exchange between this nun and a visitor and reported her for "dishonorable" behavior; yet she claims to see no connection between her role and the nun's angry reproach.

In another episode, without elaborating the truth or falsehood of an accusation that she used her niece, a novice under her care, as a servant, she discredits her accuser by claiming to see the devil dressed as a priest entering her cell (89). Whether interpreted as the devil himself or a sly intimidation of illicit activity, Francisca further deflects attention from her possible guilt by claiming a servant tried to suffocate her (89).[28] The tension and gossip among women in the cloister is frequently evoked, although Francisca usually sidesteps the details; at no time does she directly admit that she also engages in gossip or that any of the claims against her might be rooted in fact. Only the devil, she says, could have been responsible "for some of the things said [about me], such as: that I incited conflict between so-and-so and you-know-who; that of another I had said this or that, disputes in which I, through God's mercy, was not involved" (108–9).[29] Such a statement seems suspicious since she had already admitted that she did gossip about and effectively betray other nuns as part of her duties as *escucha* and, albeit less directly, through her accusation of a man or devil in a woman's private cell. Later in the same passage she specifies an accusation that does not seem to correspond to the original claims, but to which she confesses: "they told me I had moved the bed of a mulatta servant which I had found almost on top of mine in the dormitory, and they had told a certain nun that it was her servant's bed that I had removed, etc." (109).[30] Francisca begins her statement in the same way she has before, framing it as a false accusation. However, by stating that the bed "was almost on top" of her own and that, moreover, it was the bed of a servant, she admits her role in the altercation. Nonetheless, there is no logical relation in the narration between this infraction and the supposed attempt of a servant to suffocate her, even if it was the same woman whose bed she had moved. By confessing to what her superiors would undoubtedly consider a lesser charge, that of offending a mulatta servant, she takes attention away from the more serious and never elaborated claims of her mistreatment of her niece and denunciation of the woman who had accused her of this abuse. Moreover, she makes her accusers look petty. The theatrically villainous response of the abbess further defuses any doubts the reader/confessor might have about her innocence: "the Mother Superior responded 'tie her up with strong cords until she croaks.' On other occasions she would say, 'I've been sharpening a knife to send you to stab yourself with, and I will send you rope so you will hang yourself'" (90).[31] In addition, she reinforces her argument with a skillful counterposition of the persecution of her fellow nuns with the solace she finds with her confessor: "My only solace was when I was in the confessional, and so I counted the days until your return" (21).[32] The absence of and longing for her confessor is evoked with images from mystic literature: "as in a desert and dark night" (21); "in a dark night as he who loses his guide on the harsh path upon which he walks blindly" (34).[33] Explicitly situating the confessor in the place of Christ (for it is of course Christ to whom mystics such as Juan de la Cruz refer with the image of the dark night of the soul) works as an effective form of securing her alliance with her spiritual guides, essential for her protection within and outside the convent.

No sooner has this conflict been resolved than Francisca discovers a black tumor in her mouth (110); although doctors pronounce the tumor as incurable and widespread, it spontaneously bursts with a river of blood on the evening of Pentecost, also the day of Mary Magdalene of Pazzi (117). McKnight suggests a correspondence between the tumor and Francisca's unspoken sense of guilt as an unwitting participant in convent gossip, which she evokes in the *Cuaderno de Enciso* as a social disease. Significantly, in the meditation copied into the *Cuaderno,* the innocent victims of gossip are the most worthy (190–91). It is perhaps also relevant to note that, according to medical doctrine of the time, menstruation was a purgative process that could occur in any part of the female body, including the mouth (Laqueur 105), further associating transgressive speech with gender. More important, as McKnight points out, the resolution of the illness on the day dedicated to one of her preferred saintly models is no coincidence (158–59). Many pages of the life of Mary Magdalene of Pazzi are dedicated to a series of mysterious illnesses that physicians could not explain, including an explosion of blood from her mouth (72). Mary Magdalene's (and by extension, Francisca's) illness is associated with the suffering of Christ: "she understood from her Jesus, that her sickness proceeded not from natural causes, but was otherwise permitted by the will of God for her greater glory and probation" (Puccini 110). Ironically, in the lines copied from the saint's life in her devotional book, Francisca underlines those that have to do with *murmuraciones* [gossip or rumors]: "They never saw her angry or upset nor say an injurious word or murmur" (*Devocionario* 94, ctd. McKnight 159; Puccini 26).[34] By affiliating herself with this saint and suggesting her influence in the miraculous recovery, Francisca contradicts what might otherwise be interpreted as a sign that the accusations against her as a gossip were legitimate. She is, in fact, taken to the chapter of faults, where accusations against her are presented for two hours (104), and subsequently finds an *auto* against her signed by the entire convent for teaching novices to read and write (a charge she denies, saying the only thing she had done was teach one novice to sign her name) (107).

On the basis of the letters that have been found, McKnight speculates that Francisca's correspondence with former confessors who had been promoted to higher positions in the archdiocese was much more than a spiritual exercise: cultivating private relationships with her former confessors was, perhaps, a means to consolidate and ensure her own position and power (116). Thus, the isolation that Francisca experiences from other women in the community—and her contrived silence about their motives—may have less to do with petty jealousies than to concrete political conflicts. Indeed, Francisca's rise to positions of authority was unusually rapid.

Shortly after taking her vows, she was appointed convent secretary, eventually working her way up as mistress to the novices and finally abbess; conceivably her diligent attempts to gain the favor of her superiors during her period as *escucha* played some part in the older nun's anger over the young Francisca's impudence. In the 1715 election, which Francisca lost by a few votes (158), she claims that the winning candidate had attempted to discredit her with outside authorities; however, convent records show this same abbess reappointed her former rival as mistress of novices (McKnight 117). If there are indeed two moments in the text, then we can situate the production of *Su vida* during a period in which Francisca was building a power base within the convent. If this is the case, her claims of persecution and martyrdom may be simultaneously read as confirmation of her special status in the divine realm—that is, that God has selected her to suffer in this life so she may be with him in the next—and ingratiation to her confessors as a means to ensure her political position in the convent.

In fact, although Francisca alleges ignorance of administrative duties in *Su vida*: "I was completely ignorant, I did not even know how to speak in the style of secular people" (181),[35] McKnight's study of records of her first two terms as abbess show that she alone performed sixty-six of the seventy-one economic decisions—including sales of land and approvals of dowries—recorded in the Archivo Regional de Boyacá, without the approval of the governing council (119). Whether or not these records indicate an extremely centralized locus of power during Francisca's terms as abbess, they do corroborate her involvement with worldly concerns and contradict her self-representation as weak and ignorant. Indeed, as McKnight points out, these documents represent only a fraction of the legal and economic transactions in which Francisca would have been involved. Tenant receipts were not retained, but legal documents in which Francisca sought retribution for tenant violations or collection of debts have been uncovered that sharply counter her claim that she did not know how to express herself in secular matters (118–21). On the other hand, since the "secular language" to which she refers was standardized and her legal documents drawn up by scribes or convent secretaries, even if she was at that time uninitiated in this type of discourse, it would have had little impact on her ability to run the convent. As was customary, she also had apparently hired a male administrator, or *mayordomo*, to help manage the convent's income (184); notarial archives indicate that Francisca's nephew, Francisco Joseph Cayzedo y Aguilar, was contracted to fill the position in 1719, a move that further reinforced her power and influence in the convent (McKnight 121).

The final chapters, in which Francisca's addressee has changed, are those which cover her first term as abbess (1718–21): she has yet to consolidate a strong majority in the convent (the election, again, was close) but she has achieved a more solid ground toward this end.[36] McKnight speculates that her work guiding the novitiate—a post she held at least five times—as well as her family's influence in the convent, are likely responsible for the nearly unanimous vote in her second and third terms and that, moreover, cryptic references to certain "projects" in her exchanges with Diego Tapia and, especially, Felipe Arguíndegui, suggest "the way in which she developed private relationships with specific confessors in order to work out her own political concerns and those of her convent" (117). Specifically, faced with the concrete problems of ensuring the economic survival of the convent, Francisca enlists the help of her former confessors by portraying herself as a victim of internal conflicts. *Su vida* does not cover the final period of Francisca's life, but McKnight demonstrates convincingly that the mystic *Afectos* written during this period, and particularly those she revised in the so-called *Cuaderno de Enciso*, indicate a stronger authorial voice; in this document, direct address to the confessor disappears almost entirely (195).

Because their authors were faced with multiple and sometimes conflicting reader expectations, autobiographical writings by these marginalized subjects become, as Sidonie Smith suggests, a narrative artifice within which alternative or deferred identities continually subvert any pretensions of truthfulness (5). Written precisely in a moment in which she was consolidating her power in the convent, the notion of "truth" produced by Francisca's text ultimately is situated not so much in the correspondence between word and past, but in the interstice between the disparate discursive conventions she manipulates. In the end, as Francisca's life story demonstrates, the recreation of the past becomes secondary to what the female writing subject's rhetorical strategies reveal about her present experience of self in relation to her reader/confessor and the dominant society he represents.

3

Cloisters of the Soul

Spiritual Autobiography and the Hagiographic Tradition

> En los claustros del alma la herida / yace callada, mas consume hambrienta.
>
> Francisco de Quevedo

In Early Christian religious thought, saints and martyrs were regarded as mediators who could intercede on behalf of the living. Although the veneration of saints was criticized by proponents of the Reformation, the Council of Trent reaffirmed the practice as a significant expression of Catholic doctrine and popular worship.[1] With the proliferation of the printed word, people who had previously received nearly all their instruction from the priest on the pulpit and in the confessional could now meditate through books, and sainthood and hagiographic discourse were, as Weinstein and Bell affirm, a "powerful medium for teaching religious values" (4). While theological treatises were destined only for an elite minority, hagiographies and, in particular, the short daily readings of the *Flos sanctorum* appealed to a wider audience with their distinctive combination of edifying example and heroic narrative. Popular demand for stories of saints led to the production of hundreds of hagiographies: in the holdings of a single personal library in Seville, José Sánchez Lora counts 697 hagiographies, 320 of which were published between 1610 and 1629 (360–61, 375, 401). In Spanish America, the lives of the saints were widely distributed: devotional readings of the saints formed part of family readings and structured daily monastic life. Muriel found forty-four examples in a single Mexican convent (Muriel *Cultura femenina* 20; "Lo que leían las mujeres" 169). Individual religious expression was further consecrated by the canonization of such figures as Teresa de Jesús and Ignacio de Loyola. Promoted as models for the examination of conscience, these empowering figures were nonetheless also associated with political influence and the act of writing. In the library examined by Sánchez Lora there were eight hagiographies of Teresa de Jesús alone (377, 400).[2]

Foster refers to the "economy of discursive exchange" in which the writing subject realizes that to articulate her understanding she must use languages and models of others. It is precisely through this "object of exchange" that the author may appropriate this model as a source of power (14–16). In baroque Spain and Spanish America, hagiographic literature and women's life stories are intimately intertwined, with autobiography borrowing patterns, rhetorical strategies, and even passages from earlier works. Kate Greenspan proposes the term "autohagiography" as a way to better understand the model within which the *vida* is framed (157). As in hagiographic discourse, modern or secular notions of "life" and "time" are not relevant in the *vida*; the subject's life is intended to be more exemplary than real.[3] It is, nonetheless, precisely this lack of individuality that endows the *vida* with meaning. As Greenspan notes, *vidas*, like hagiographies, "convey what their authors perceive to be a universal spiritual rather than a personal truth. They make little distinction between natural and supernatural events, tending, in fact, to favor the latter . . . traditional hagiography and women's autohagiography both *reconstruct the lives of their subjects to conform to the expectations of what constitutes holiness*" (159, emphasis added). In one way or another, this "autohagiographic" model frames nearly every biography and most autobiographies in the Spanish-American baroque. By reshaping the details of a life into the hagiographic paradigm, authors could "legitimize their moral authority, providing edifying examples of virtue to secular readers that . . . served as a guide and inspiration for others" (Lavrin "Vida femenina" 28). Moreover, since the saint was the one figure who could equal or, in some cases, supersede the confessor's powers of mediation with God, self-representation within the hagiographic paradigm permitted the author to assert a more equal relation of power to her immediate addressee.

The appropriation of another's word, accepted and to some degree expected in many literary genres, was willfully deployed in Counter-Reformation texts to protect the author from accusations of heresy (Bakhtin *Dialogic* 69; Moraña 233). At the same time, the inclusion of hagiographic narrative further challenges boundaries of discursive authority through a complicated network of mutual contaminations that underscore the role of the author as reader. The imitation of other texts in baroque spiritual narrative suggests a profound respect for the power of the written word, and both Ignacio de Loyola and Teresa de Jesús had made their roles as readers an essential part of the conversion experience (*Autobiography* 23, *Libro de la vida* III.7, 137/19).⁴ Following these canonical models, secular books are frequently denounced as an incitement to evil, while lives of the saints are specifically cited as an inspiration. María Ana de la Encarnación, advised to stop reading *libros de romance* to recover her health (2), receives a hand-copied version of the *vida* of Teresa de Jesús and, perceiving in it her own road to salvation, decides to enter a Carmelite convent (8–9).⁵ Francisca Josefa Castillo describes a long illness that results from reading comedies, "the plague of souls," for pleasure (7); her religious activity, in contrast, is inspired by reading Teresa de Jesús (5).⁶ As a child, María Magdalena (1572–1663) read the lives of the saints in the *Flos Sanctorum,* and was "delighted to read of the torments they endured, and I wanted to suffer for the love of God as they had . . . I applied cilices and fasted as much as I could" (3).⁷ For her part, María Anna Águeda de San Ignacio (1695–1756) recalls being "very much inclined to reading, studying as many lives of the saints as I could find." She resolves to imitate them, taking particular affection for Rosa of Lima (Bellido 16). María de San José's first exposure to the lives of the saints is through nightly family readings; she miraculously learns to read while holding the hagiography of Anthony of Padua (*Word* 88, 124). As a small child Micaela Josepha de la Purificación (1681–1752) dresses as a Carmelite and pretends to be a nun in the order of Teresa de Jesús; reading Teresa's life story, she decides to become a nun (Miqueorena 9). Francisca de San Joseph, frustrated with a confessor who did not understand her and refused to listen, reads Teresa de Jesús and Catherine of Siena to reaffirm the validity of her visionary experiences (Quiroga 293–95). Although Úrsula Suárez confesses to reading lives of the saints for pleasure when she was a girl (149), she cites the biographies of two Spanish nuns, María de la Antigua and Marina Escobar, as models essential to her conversion (208, 230). As Sebastiana Josefa concludes: "In my view everything one may consider moral comes from prayer and the reading of good books" (70).⁸

Bynum affirms that female hagiographic narratives differ from those of male saints in that crisis and decisive change are more likely in men than in women: both men and women saw female saints as models of suffering and inner spirituality, male saints as models of action (24–25).⁹ Although in reality the most venerated male saints during the baroque period were also associated with ascetic activity (most notably, Francis of Assisi and the often-cited Pedro de Alcántara), life stories of female saints and of women imitating this model continued to differ from their male counterparts by emphasizing a progressive movement toward sanctity revealed at an early age rather than a single conversion experience (some authors, such as María de San José, appropriate both strategies). Predestination was a means to prove that the woman's visionary powers were divinely inspired, even though they had been granted to a weaker vessel.

Although it was often the biographer who organized the chapters to illustrate the righteousness of his subject, this discourse of virtues is also exploited by women themselves.[10] The most frequently cited manifestations of saintly calling are a precocious knowledge of God and early dedication to penitence. Rosa of Lima had already begun penances at three and by age four was having her indigenous servant spit on her, strike her, and step on her "to imitate Christ" (Ribadeneyra I.539). Francisca de San Joseph's first word as an infant was "Jesús" (12); she began fasting and disciplines when she was five and was rewarded by her mother with a hairshirt and chains when she was seven (Quiroga 24–25). Francisca Josefa Castillo recalls her mother telling her that, barely old enough to speak, she told her parents that an image of the infant Jesus was calling her; dressed as Rosa of Lima, she began a regimen of penance before she was eight (4). Antonia de la Madre de Dios dedicated herself to a life of solitude at age three and began disciplining herself at five (Sánchez de Castro 20, 27), and it was also at age five that Guatemalan Anna Guerra de Jesús began a regimen of eating a single tortilla and drinking five sips of water a day (Siria 7). Describing a calling or an election from early childhood set the stage for a progressive manifestation of destiny. Significantly, the role of the confessor was subliminally displaced in this process since moral discernment—the "age of discretion" or "reason"—was associated with the child's first confession (Lea I.402). While early Renaissance authorities and many hagiographies specify seven as the age for the first confession, by the seventeenth and eighteenth centuries sainthood was measured by a progressively hyperbolic earlier calling.[11] María Anna Águeda de San Ignacio's biographer reports that "the age of reason awoke in her" when she was only two years old: she discovered that "she was nothing" (Bellido 16). María Marcela contends that "reason . . . awoke in me at a very young age . . . I was three years old" (8), even though she did not realize her potential until much later, and Gerónima de la Asunción, a Clarissan nun in the Philippines, reportedly had her calling at age four when she read the life story of Claire of Assisi, the founder of the order in which she would later profess (Letona 4). María Magdalena does not specify an age but asserts that "from my tender infancy and since I reached the age of reason and knew how to use it, I had great desires to love God" (2)[12], while Venezuelan Bárbara Josepha de San Francisco, her biographer assures us, "había mamado la virtud con la leche" [had acquired virtue with her mother's milk] (Torres 18).

Whether or not the reading public was expected to believe these narratives was incidental: the saint was a heroic figure and therefore extraordinary; as such s/he could not have an ordinary background (Certeau *Writing* 277; Sánchez Lora 414). Indeed, because the saint's life was understood as itself an imitation of Christ, the repetition of certain patterns was an accepted and expected discursive device; as Thomas Heffernan notes: "the sacred model reclaims past models and in turn is authenticated by them as these past lives are reintroduced into the present" (20; see also Certeau *Writing* 276). In hagiography, individuality counts much less than character. Modeled after the hagiography, the repetition of recognizable passages from other texts in the *vida* serves a similar function. In many cases, in fact, a long chain of mutual influences and textual contamination may be traced. For example, María de San José, as Myers demonstrates, integrates almost verbatim entire passages and rhetorical formulae from the founder of her order, Mariana de San Joseph, into her life story (*Word* 23–31). Mariana had herself borrowed from Teresa de Jesús, who in turn had used Augustine and Catherine of Siena. Francisca Josefa Castillo and Sebastiana Josefa de la Santísima Trinidad reproduce episodes from the life story of Mary Magdalene of Pazzi, who duplicates passages from Catherine of Siena. Further tracing this complex bricolage of hagiographic discourse, Catherine of Siena's life story had been influenced by Mary of Egypt, herself associated and sometimes conflated with Mary Magdalene.

Narrations of childhood seem to be where authors are most likely to borrow ideas, words, and entire phrases from precursor texts. To mold one's own formative years into the frame of a familiar childhood narration was a way to establish trust with the reader and to confirm from the beginning one's saintly calling. Thus Teresa de Jesús describes her parents as "virtuous and God-fearing" (I.1, 119/10), while Francisca Josefa Castillo writes that hers are "Christian and God-fearing" (3); and María de San José specifies that she was "the granddaughter and daughter of very Christian parents" (*Word* 85).[13] Teresa affirms: "My father was fond of reading good books" (I.1, 119/10), while María de San José asserts: "both [my parents] were fond of virtue and good books" (87); and Francisca cleverly modifies the axiom to include Teresa herself: "My mother read the books of Saint Teresa de Jesús and her *Fundaciones*" (5).[14] Teresa's declaration: "My father was a man of great charity to the poor, was good to the sick and also to his servants" (I.1, 120/10) is repeated by María Marcela: "My parents . . . were very kind to the poor" and Úrsula Suárez: "my parents . . . were extremely good, very charitable and philanthropic" (116). Francisca embellishes her version of her father's benevolence to include charity to animals: "With his eyes full of tears . . . he gave alms to the poor . . . and even with sick animals he was very kind" (3, 13).[15] Of her father Teresa recalls: "He was strictly truthful: nobody ever heard him swear or speak evil" (I.1, 120/10); qualities that resonate in the narrations of Francisca: "from my father never was heard a dishonest word, nor was ever seen an action that was not [honest]" (3); and María de San José: "I knew in him a continual silence, he never spoke badly of anyone but well of all" (*Word* 88).[16] Teresa's childhood desire to die like the saints (I.4, 121/11) and live in isolation like Mary of Egypt (I.5, 121/11) is repeated in Francisca (5–6), María de San José (139), and Úrsula (124, 127). All are favorites of their fathers (Teresa I.3, 121/10; Castillo 6; Suárez 93; María Marcela 19);[17] and often blame others for straying from their principles; in Teresa's case, her "cousins" (II.2, 125/13) and servants (II.5, 126/14); in Francisca's, "some very close relatives" (9); in María de San José, "an orphan girl" who lived nearby (91); and in Úrsula Suárez, mixed-blood wet nurses (91) and men in general (185–87).

María Marcela, admittedly "of sharp wit," "lively and sociable" as an adolescent, skillfully although none too subtly recreates her secular life to demonstrate an early inclination to the convent. Although she describes several adventures in which she escaped from the house with her friends, she repeatedly insists on her natural propensity for the cloistered life: "I was only allowed to go to decent places because . . . my father was very strict and extremely opposed to my leaving the house" (8).[18] María also reports an innate predilection for charity—"I was by nature very pious and charitable"—a quality revealed in four strategically graded examples of her kindness (an old woman, a paralytic, a leper, and a prisoner).[19] Moreover, although self-described as "bright" and "attractive," she is careful to mention that *those around her* considered her chaste: "neither evil talk nor frivolous words were to be spoken in front of me. . . . They used to say that I commanded respect" (12).[20] María Marcela had apparently finished her life story and perhaps shown it to her confessor when she remembers to add further examples of her observance of the seven virtues (faith, hope, charity, prudence, temperance, justice, and fortitude).

Authors further set themselves apart as candidates for sainthood by their prophetic powers. The use of historically verifiable facts was one way to counteract suspicions surrounding mystical experience; and prophecy had long been an accepted gift in the narrations of female saints. Indeed, Heffernan notes that women were thought to have greater access to prophecy than men (187). María Manuela de Santa Ana contends that she had visions of an earthquake two years before it occurred; her heroism (and the exactitude of her vision) is asserted as she demands that the stairs to the choir loft be reinforced "at any price," saving many women's lives when the earthquake hits (folio 3, *Vida* 167; folio 7, *Vida* 175). Somewhat less credible is her claim to have foreseen the expulsion of the Jesuits, suspect because she did not mention it to anyone at the time (folio 7, *Vida* 176). This kind of unverifiable prophecy is a convenient and common narrative device: in many *vidas*, there are revelations in which the death of an individual is supposedly foreseen by the nun; and she may intervene at this time or following the death to save the person's soul. Because such visions are affiliated with historical facts that may be corroborated, narrative authority is strengthened. Francisca Josefa Castillo cleverly protects herself by transferring a potentially arrogant vision, in which Jesus says he is Francisca's alone, to the mouth of another nun who has, conveniently, died (59). Prophecy could also be used to assert predestination. Úrsula Suarez finds her convent cell exactly as imagined in a dream (140); María de San José has visions of the convent in Puebla where she later professes (*Word* 144, II.4) and of the convent in Oaxaca she will help found (III.52).

As appropriate for saintly heroines, biographers regularly described their subjects as beautiful, since outer beauty reflected inner serenity.[21] Juan de Olmos describes his spiritual daughter, Gerónima del Espíritu Santo: "Our Lord endowed our Gerónima with striking natural features. For she had a tall and very well-proportioned body, her face was very handsome, her eyes beautiful and bright. Proportional to this [beauty], her mind was clear, subtle, delicate and sharp" (37).[22] On the other hand, admission of beauty was also a way to reinforce a confession of the childhood sin of vanity, a common topic in women's life stories. María de San José recalls: "I started to enjoy . . . fixing myself up to look nice . . . especially my hair, which was very pretty" (93). Úrsula Suárez confesses: "I had been very partial to silks and showy adornments since I was a child" (94).[23] Teresa de Jesús admits: "I began to deck myself out and try to attract others by my appearance, taking great trouble with my hands and hair, using perfumes and all the vanities I could get—and there were a good many of them, for I was very fastidious," specifying, nonetheless, that "*There was nothing wrong with my intentions,* for I should never have wanted anyone to offend God because of me" (II.2, 124/13, emphasis added).[24] Francisca Josefa also affixes a disclaimer to her confession of childhood vanity: "seeking to amuse myself, and taking more care in my fine clothes and in my appearance, so that I no longer did anything besides take care of my hair, *although not with any specific intention,* but only with that vanity and egotism, that it seemed as if the world was not big enough for me" (8, emphasis added).[25]

María Marcela, in contrast, admits that she does seek to attract attention: "I was full of vanity, with pride, with the *desire to be seen*" (8, emphasis added).[26] With declared suitors alone numbering more than ten (18), María boasts: "*I caught everyone's eye* and was ... celebrated by all" (10, emphasis added). Similarly, and in apparent contradiction to her biographer's narration of her childhood propensity to solitude, Sebastiana Josefa de la Santísima Trinidad asserts "I thought myself *queen of all attentions*, beautiful, with all the adornments of nature and wealth of the land, *recognized and celebrated by all*" (49, emphasis added).[27] Although the description of physical attractiveness is included ostensibly to illustrate the sin of vanity and pride that the writing subject was subsequently able to overcome, it is interesting to note that both for Sebastiana and María Marcela, their pleasure derives from the gaze of others who confirm their beauty.[28] This external (male) gaze is further evidenced in biographical accounts. Valdés describes Sebastiana's exceptional beauty from the perspective of those around her. The day she took her vows, he reports, "her rare beauty and loveliness ... *captivated the attention of all who were able to see her*" (136, emphasis added); he also specifically cites the testimony of Father Diego Maldonado, who, giving her communion, is reportedly overwhelmed by her beauty: "He saw in her face such loveliness, such clarity, such a stunning beauty, that he nearly burst out shouting. Captivated by impulse ... in his heart he gave thanks to the Divine Lord God who cultivates these chaste and honest beauties so He may rest among beautiful lilies" (191).[29] That the only appreciable difference between the two accounts is the hyperbolic prose of the biographer reveals to what extent the female writing subject has assimilated the male gaze into her own version of self. The visual confirmation of identity through the narrative of beauty caught the attention of the reader not only through the direct appeal of an attractive heroine, but also indirectly on a moral level, since the beauty of the subject also could be used to reinforce the sacrifice of her self-denial. Sebastiana's beauty is willfully destroyed when, shortly after entering the convent, her confessor submits her to a rigorous program of mortification and abstinence. As Valdés reports: "In just a few days, her appearance was altered; having entered robust, she became gaunt, pale and exhausted. Her zealous confessor continued to encourage her fervently and in keeping with his desires, the daughter obeyed God and his minister" (32).[30] Such sacrifices were indispensable to the hagiographic model.

Voluntary destruction of external beauty was just one example women could cite as proof of their religious vocation and submission to divine will. The most commonly evoked scenario was that of family opposition and separation anxiety upon entrance into the convent. Francisca Josefa notes that many saints had entered the convent against their parents' wishes and she wanted to imitate them: "When my family heard of my entrance [into the convent] their sorrow and tears were incredible.... Continuously weeping at the door of my room, my father spent three days refusing to drink even a sip of water. My mother began to have seizures, and so on" (16, 20).[31] Her first impression of the convent, she says, is that "It seemed as if I was in hell, or in an Inquisitorial prison" (20).[32] In Úrsula Suárez's case, because her father has been disabled by an apparent stroke, it is her mother who opposes her entrance into the convent, violently threatening, "'if you so much as mention being a nun, I will kill you.... I will suffocate you between two pillows or strangle you on the bedpost!'" (118).[33] Despite the melodramatic fury of this reaction and a clear dislike for her mother, Úrsula recasts the incident within the model of Christ's persecution, describing her response to this opposition as "a lance that pierced my soul and tore my heart with pain" (138). Similarly, María Marcela evokes her family's continued opposition as "daggers ... plunged into my heart" (56).[34]

A pierced heart often represents contrition, repentance and, in this case, "devotion under conditions of extreme trial"; the lance is of course associated with the torment of Christ (Ferguson 49, 177). When María Marcela has her godfather speak with her father to convince him to let her enter the convent, her father objects virulently to the idea of allowing his favorite daughter to become a nun: he cannot eat or sleep and refuses even to look at María. He is plagued with doubt and confusion until a visit to the convent changes his mind. Although he consents, resentment from the family continues, and no one notices when María leaves the house a year later (37–39). Upon entering, she compares the convent to heaven: "Entering the doors of the cloister seemed as if I was entering the gates of heaven ... lowering myself and kneeling on the ground I asked to go to the chorus loft on my knees; this moved the Mothers and they did not permit me to do so" (56).[35] Soon after, however, she begins to have second thoughts. Her description of the horror of isolation is evoked dramatically:

> The mistress [of novices] ... asked me many times if I was content; I told her I was, because although sorely tried, I concealed it and said nothing so that no one would know I could not sleep because my nun's habit made my bed so hot, that the food left me empty and disgusted and so I ate nothing, that the hours in the chorus loft seemed an eternity to me; I battled with myself, saying "What is happening to me? What happened to those desires, those longings to enter, overcoming all obstacles that were not enough to make me renounce my

goal, neither the opposition of my father, nor the adulation and pleas of my sisters, nor the entreaties of my admirers? What is this? If I leave, what will they say about me? . . ." I looked inside myself and said . . . "I have already entered and will not leave . . . I am destined to suffer alone and in silence" and so I did. (58)[36]

María de San José has an almost identical experience when, after years of fighting the opposition of her brother and older sisters that she enter the religious life, she finds separation from them unbearable. Taking leave of her family, she feels overcome by a strange sensation "as if they had come and pulled my heart out by the roots of the love I had always had for my family . . . I began to sob and felt . . . as if each part and every limb of my body was resisting the separation of my heart from the affection I had always had for my loved ones" (II.1–2).[37] In retrospect, however, María thanks God for making this sacrifice possible: "That day that I was ready to enter the convent . . . I did not find nor did I have anything else to offer the Lord God except this affection I had for my loved ones. . . . Since that day I have lived and live as if I had not been born nor even descended from human beings" (II.2).[38] It was common to renounce the family name for a new religious identity; María further reinforces her separation from her earthly family by also changing her first name from Juana to María (*Word* 90).

* * *

Claims of austere conditions aside, religious women's narratives regularly indicate the presence of slaves and servants to attend them, and records clearly suggest that most nuns in Spanish America were well fed, well dressed, and hardly isolated. In their life stories they insistently return to their suffering and persecution within the convent because pain and obedience were the single most important defining principles for the humanity of Christ in the Hispanic baroque as well as an essential component of power relations with the reader/confessor. "Take pleasure in being reprimanded," advises Luis de Granada, "and do not defend yourself with pride, but, in imitation of your Lord, desire only to suffer more in silence" (*Memorial de la vida cristiana* IV:7, 282); and in *Arte para servir a Dios*, Alonso de Madrid declares: "Let us, then, jump for joy a thousand times when we are mistreated with insults and injustices" (132; ctd. Weber 46).[39] In the widely read *Imitation of Christ*, Thomas à Kempis (1379–1471) further underscores that the progress toward salvation is not possible until "you look upon yourself as inferior to all others" (57).[40] As Asunción Lavrin confirms: "Abstention, mortification, renunciation and humiliation are all key words in the religious vocabulary of the colonial period. They point to a total loss of personal will and the obliteration of the self in Christ and God" ("Unlike Sor Juana" 78). For cloistered women in Spanish America, persecution symbolically reenacted the martyrdom of Christ and the divine mandate to "love your enemies and pray for those who persecute you" (Matthew 5.44); Teresa de Jesús also associates persecution with the figure of Mary Magdalene, imagining the taunts of the community after her conversion (*Las moradas* 7.4.13, 209/192–93).[41] In the *vida*, the tormentors are not the severe and abusive confessors but other nuns unable or unwilling to recognize the virtues of the writing subject.[42] Notably, the attacks continually return to a stereotypical vision of women as hysterical and manipulative. Thus, Sebastiana Josefa reports being attacked as "self-righteous," "deluded," and "hypocritical" by a certain person "who had taken great effort to fashion her [Sebastiana] a crown of thorns and make her a saint as her expense" (Valdés 32, 77–79).[43] Isabel de la Encarnación (1594–1633), a nun from Mexico, was regarded as "possessed, delusional, deceitful and degenerate" (Salmerón 25–26); and Úrsula Suárez as "deceitful, scheming, contriving" (256). Francisca Josefa Castillo, who expressly manifests her desire to imitate the saints, is accused by her sisters of being "possessed" and that all her experiences "originated in [her own] hypocrisy and arrogance" (30).[44] María Marcela complains that the other nuns call her "sanctimonious, crafty, conceited, hypocritical" (107). They give her "ridiculous nicknames" and denounce her to the mother superior. When she refuses to listen to the accusations, she is punished by not being allowed to take communion (108). She describes her torture both in physical terms and in terms of her humiliation, as the nuns "tighten the rope" around her, treating her "like an Indian [servant]"; "with all of this my life was unbearable" (110).[45]

Whether or not these episodes—or at least the writing subjects' innocence in them—were exaggerated, the persecution motif could have had a therapeutic effect, as daily personal conflicts with other women were recast into the martyrdom of Christ and the saints. More important, this rhetorical strategy could also serve as a means to explicitly situate the writing subject, for her confessor and for future readers, as the most beloved bride of Christ by emphasizing the cultural fiction of the isolated and solitary saint (Donahue 238).[46] When other sisters are mentioned, they are an anonymous mass of persecutors; and even individualized, other women are rarely, if ever, named, although most priests are referred to by their full names. This image of the singularity of the subject also has ideological implications when exploited by a biographer or confessor since, as Tambling points out, "Power maintains itself on the basis of separating and confining each person separately, each in their confessional" (85). Viñuales reports that in some colonial convents walls came to divide not only confessor and confessant but separated each nun from the other (210). Not coincidentally, this architectural modification was recorded in large convents in Peru and was in part designed to contain uprisings such as those of Quito and Santiago. With the high number of documented cases in which nuns banded together to challenge Church authorities, isolation of particularly intelligent women from their peers was a way to prevent collective action. Ironically, by criticizing other nuns as an unholy pack of tormentors, the author herself is an accomplice to the undermining of female power.

Clearly implicit in this discussion is the specific historical context of documents written in colonial Spanish America and why biographers emphasized the lives of women more attuned to bodily mortification than political authority in the convent. Although ascetic practice was extolled in the New Testament (see, for example, Matthew 6.16–18, 10.38, 19.12, 19.21; John 12.25; Mark 2.18–20, 10.28), it was not until the early fifteenth century that the doctrine of the "imitation of Christ" developed (Cross and Livingstone 113). By the seventeenth century, Jesuit "ascetic directories" such as that of Giovanni Battista Scaramelli dedicated entire chapters to technical descriptions of instruments of torture and exemplary cases of penance, which nuns could use as a base to improvise in their continuing search for creative forms of pain. Although women learned from other women's examples, the textual model of ascetic perfection for Spanish-American nuns was Pedro de Alcántara (1499–1562), whom Teresa de Jesús had met and profoundly admired. Mentioned in nearly every Hispanic religious woman's text as a paradigm of virtue, Pedro, according to Teresa, customarily ate once every three days and often went eight days with no food. As a young man he reportedly never raised his eyes and never looked at women, and even as a well-known holy man, he spoke little (XXVII:16–18, 332–33/176–77). According to Teresa, he wore a metal cilice continuously for twenty years (XXX:2, 355/194). Teresa's reiterated remarks of "as everyone knows" and "as is well-known" when referring to Pedro strongly suggest that even during periods in which his works were banned, the oral legend surrounding this figure persisted, thanks in some part to Teresa's narration.

Although self-torture rarely occupies center stage in surviving autobiographical narrations, exaggerated acts of self-mortification abound in hagiographies and imitation of these deeds is extolled in biographical treatments of saintly women.[47] It was this side of sanctity rather than abstract spiritual values that most appealed to the "passion for the outlandish" of the baroque reading public (Maravall *Cultura del barroco* 461/229). Even women who achieved positions of importance in the Church were often textually defined by their bodies. Although Catherine of Siena (1347–1380) was actively involved in important Church issues of her time, the biography in Pedro de Ribadeneyra's *Flos sanctorum* emphasizes instead her extreme humility and asceticism: "She had nothing left her but skin and bones and [had] become a perfect picture of death. The marks and prints the devil gave her appeared in her body" (667/283).[48] How a woman who supposedly spoke only to her confessor and never left her cell could influence two popes is only one of the questionable assertions expounded by this popularly distributed version. Similarly, the life story of Teresa de Jesús related in Ribadeneyra and in the processes of beatification and canonization emphasizes, to a far greater extent than in her own writings, her fasts, illnesses, and physical disciplines (*Procesos* xlii; Ribadeneyra 280/800).

The grotesque fascination of the reader for graphic descriptions of mutilated bodies further reveals the sadistic implications of the commodification of the female body as narrations glory in the most gruesome details of ascetic practice. After the death of Mexican nun Ana de los Ángeles, chains and an iron cross were found fully incorporated into her flesh. Her biographer celebrates the discovery, considering these instruments of torture an "adornment that enriched her life" (Vetancourt 71).[49] In *Parayso occidental,* Sigüenza y Góngora recounts how doctors had to use scissors and knives to cut off the trusses, wires, and chains imbedded in Marina de la Cruz's body while she was still alive, tearing out chunks of her flesh in the process (103).[50]

Mary Magdalene of Pazzi was "so greedy of suffering," her biographer reports, that "she neither thought, nor exercised herself upon any other thing than mortifications and acts of humility, finding ever new inventions how to suffer" (Puccini 118–19, 140).[51] And indeed, some women seemed obsessed with the creation of new ways of suffering, either in imitation of the amazing feats they read about in hagiographies, or by designing their own variations. Isabel de la Encarnación applied hot coals to her body, wore a crown of thorns and a rope around her neck, and spent hours kissing the ground and the feet of other women in the convent. She stopped eating and even drinking water until her stomach developed ulcers (Gómez de la Parra 534–36). Peruvian Luisa Benites ate dirt and, imitating the Spanish holy woman Juana de la Cruz (and Saint Jerome), hit herself in the chest with a rock until she bled (Blanco 371). While the prevalence of such narrations in published biographies undoubtedly appealed to the baroque fascination with the grotesque, these accounts also served an important social function. José Antonio Maravall suggests that the bloody spectacles mounted by the Church in Spain (and repeated in Spanish America) were a way for rulers and their collaborators to terrify people into accepting their places in the social order (*Cultura del barroco* 163/336–37).[52] More specifically, because the women who received public recognition were often also those who most flamboyantly abused their bodies, this became the model according to which they were told they must measure their worth. Through this methodical manipulation of the body the ideological apparatus was inscribed on individual subjectivity. With women's energies engaged in self-monitoring and self-destruction, control over their bodies—and their minds—was ensured at all times.

* * *

Ironically, as Jean Franco suggests, the denial of the body may have actually encouraged an awareness of physicality and an erotic vocabulary (7). María Marcela notes that prior to entrance in the convent she had no conception of "impure movements" and "evil thoughts"; it is not until she becomes a nun that she experiences "rebellions" of the flesh and struggles with her conscience (196–97). As Foucault points out, the sublimation of sexuality transformed the moment of transgression from physical act to the "all the insinuations of the flesh: thoughts, desires, voluptuous imaginings, delectations, combined movements of the body and the soul" (*History of Sexuality* 19–20).[53] Because mental temptation extended to dreams and visions, it was sometimes reframed as combat with the devil (Lavrin "Vida femenina" 40; "Espiritualidad" 168–69). Medieval theologians had defined female possession by the devil (and heresy) in terms of sexual intercourse, and this association remained typical of Counter-Reformation texts (Slade 10; Blanco 372). In chapter 1 a complicity was suggested between the writing subject and reader in the production of fantasies that could be mutually pleasurable. But by far the most graphic examples of female violation that appear in the *vida* are found in the explicitly sexual narrations of struggles with the devil. Most descriptions of demonic possession use similar terms as the accounts of mystic union with Christ. In both, authors allude to painful blows; in both, the body is fragmented and destroyed. Nonetheless, in contrast with the sublime pain of mystic union with Christ, the devil in the *vida* does not seduce but assaults, and such assaults are violations of the body and of the will. In her many struggles with the devil, Sebastiana Josefa de la Santísima Trinidad reports shortness of breath or suffocation, fainting, and, especially, the reiterated detail that the devil hit her in the stomach or that a hand reached inside her to pull out her entrails

(121). Sebastiana envisions him as: "Huge, nude, and very rough . . . he pressed down upon my body with such force that I was crushed" (16). It was, her biographer comments, as if "all the bones of her body had crumbled into little pieces" (Valdés 287); a description that is similar to that of the hagiography of Rosa of Lima, in which the devil appears as a giant who "clenched her in his arms with so much force that all the bones of her body seemed to have been disjointed and broken to pieces" (Ribadeneyra II.160).[54] María de Jesús Ágreda also feels the devil on top of her, "with a heavy and unbearable weight, as if he were making her suffer as he crushed her" (Ximénez Samaniego ixxxiv–ixxxv).[55] Francisca Josefa Castillo's visions of the devil are particularly explicit. In one episode she feels the devil mount her when she is in bed and experiences "many temptations"; when he returns another night he tells her his name is "Crecerá-bulto" [bulge-rising]; again she is tempted and is left "exhausted." One night he appears beside her bed, threatening to "penetrate her body" (147, 150–51, 205).

Although it is conceivable that some repressed erotic desire was unleashed by the authors in such descriptions, the contrast between the ecstatic physical pleasure (and pain) of union with Christ and these frightening nightmares of violation and penetration seems to put into doubt that many women derived pleasure from recreating such experiences in writing. Moreover, racial and class biases of the criollo hierarchy are evident in many of these visions. Francisca's describes the devil as a "dark Indian," a mulatto, and a black man (150, 151, 205). María de San José also envisions the devil as a "dark nude Indian," a nude mulatto, and a black man (*Word* 95, 133, 135, II.8–11, V.12–13), and Úrsula Suárez mistakes the devil for a black slave brought in from the hacienda (109). One of the reasons women were kept under surveillance was precisely to avoid contact with the nonwhite majority; yet black and indigenous slaves and servants attended them at home and in the convent. Demonized, sexualized, and transformed into an antagonistic force by the discourse of conquest, women's fear is translated into the unknown.[57] Although struggles with the devil were understood allegorically as representations of obstacles women would have to overcome in their quest for spiritual perfection (Eich 71), the logical question as to how women came upon such explicitly sexual visions to describe this struggle and why they shared them with their confessors could perhaps suggest that women were encouraged to recreate such episodes in writing. In some cases, authors may even have believed they were meeting their readers' expectations, since by far the most graphic depictions of demonic possession are usually detailed in *male* narratives.[58] One case in which a contrast may be noted is that of Sebastiana Josefa de la Santísima Trinidad.

In Sebastiana's original notebooks, the blows of the devil focus on her stomach and intestines, a detail perhaps related to real pains she suffered as a consequence of her severe program of self-starvation. Although her male biographer does repeat this detail, he also embellishes the image of the devil to create a more sexually charged presence. Appearing in human form, the demonic figure in this narration "moves her imagination" with "horrible suggestions" and "furious flames of sensual fire" (Valdés 286).[59] This version is mild in comparison to some of the more extreme cases such as that of Luisa Benites, whose confessor, Francisco del Risco, reported that 6,666 demons (by his count) appeared nightly to terrorize the young nun with sexual temptation in the form of a "fierce black man" or a huge phallic serpent: "they immobilized her so that she could neither move nor escape (although the child wanted to and tried) and performed the act with her"; sometimes, he reported, she felt the male member inside her all day (ctd. Blanco 371–72).[60]

* * *

Whether a union with Christ or a struggle with the devil, in baroque culture the affirmation through the senses was the clearest indication of existence, be it through pleasure or, usually, pain. Nonetheless, rather than emphasize self-inflicted pain, the preferred form of suffering for many women was that made visible *through God's will,* usually in the form of a serious and prolonged illness, even if such conditions occurred as a result of overly rigorous disciplines. Although the representation of health and illness is common to the hagiographic narration of an ascetic or moral type in both men and women, it is particularly exploited in the lives of female saints (Certeau *Writing* 280; Weinstein and Bell 234).[61] Some mention of painful illness is almost obligatory in the *vida,* and women who suffered lifelong debilitating illnesses were especially revered, because illness was regarded as a divine gift (Valdés 29). In the *vida,* illness is nearly always expressed by conspicuous, public, and sometimes even theatrical inscriptions on the body: seizures, paralysis, anorexia, vomiting, or unexplained bleeding. Teresa de Jesús reports that she vomited every morning for twenty years, and that at night she would often induce vomiting with feathers "or in some other way"; she also mentions heart problems and paralysis as chronic conditions (*Libro de la vida* VII:11, 162–63/42). Like Teresa, who suffered extended periods of insensibility and even a coma as a young woman, Francisca Josefa Castillo suffered a strange trance that she says lasted for fourteen years: "I stuck pins in my mouth and did not feel them, I tried to pull my hair out, but my hand remained submerged in that lethargy. I put knots of rope beneath my knees when I knelt and felt nothing. I put verbena and other bitter herbs in my mouth and rubbed tobacco in my eyes, and none of this cured me. As we prayed the Divine Office, I made the novices twist and press my fingers but to no avail, although they did so with all their might, as I had ordered" (70).[62] Her doctors, suspecting this condition might have to do with "weakness," submit her to several different eating regimens; she is also advised to appeal to the saints, but nothing relieves her, as she reports with a rare touch of humor: "They ordered me to perform . . . many devotions to the saints and apply holy water, etc., and although I was soaked with holy water and laden with crosses I remained as I have said" (76).[63]

As Elaine Scarry points out, in the Scriptures disobedience or doubt is often described as a "withholding of the body" and, particularly, of a hardened heart, which God must shatter and repossess (202–4). Gerónima del Espíritu Santo describes her illness as a choice she made to free her body from worldly temptations and open her heart to God. Praying to Saint Francis Xavier to help her withdraw from worldly distractions, she hears a voice "speaking to my soul that told me that a chronic illness would be the only way for me to remove myself. I cannot deny that this proposition relieved my heart because it seemed to be the only way for me to achieve what I desired, which was to save myself from all dangerous temptation; and so I accepted it, surrendering my will and embracing it with great joy" (Nava 60).[64] Soon afterwards, Gerónima begins to regret her decision and begs the saint to find another way to effect her salvation. But it is too late: within a month she is assaulted by an illness reportedly so terrible that no doctor is able to diagnose its origin.

Gerónima's biographer adds the dramatic detail that she was first afflicted with the illness that ended her life at the symbolic age of thirty-three (38). Although Gerónima herself states it was later, the perceived connection between illness and the agony of Christ is a common motif in women's life narratives. For María Magdalena, bedridden for thirty-three years after a crude operation, the only solace in her suffering is that she is replicating the pain of Christ (11–12).[65] Associating physical pain over which she had no control with the suffering of Christ endowed it with meaning. As Scarry notes, "hurt . . . becomes the vehicle of verification. . . . the incontestable reality of the sensory world becomes the incontestable reality of a world invisible and unable to be touched" (202). Women's symptoms were often specifically affiliated with Christ's torment and crucifixion. María Marcela suffers a dislocated shoulder which, improperly treated, regularly slips out of place, and headaches, especially on Fridays (113–14), a condition also suffered by Teresa de Jesús and associated with Christ's crown of thorns in the hagiographies of Catherine of Siena and Mary Magdalene of Pazzi. María Coleta also suffers chronic headaches that impede her from carrying out her daily routine; she needs to get up earlier than the rest of the community because the noise of the other women causes her physical pain (folio 110, carta 1); and Gerónima del Espíritu Santo reports suffering headaches so painful that she feels as if her eyes are being torn out (43). Another symptom directly related to Christ is pain in the ribcage, as suffered by Sebastiana Josefa de la Santísima Trinidad (Valdés 265).

Isabel de la Encarnación, the subject of no less than three biographies, was venerated in her lifetime as a saint by the local community. Yet her only claim to fame was that she suffered violent epileptic seizures and a series of other illnesses that left her blind, paralyzed, and bedridden for the last sixteen years of her short life. In fact, it is unlikely that many women were able to exceed the staggering list of ailments reported by Isabel's biographers. She suffered "pain in her side, pain urinating, pain in her lungs, ribs, heart, ears, stomach, jaw, teeth and molars, with inflammation of the liver and spleen, which she suffered along with pain in her back, feet, and hands, without a single part of her body not enduring its own torturer and singular torment, suffering often in the forehead, eyes, head, with interminable chills and fevers, and copious sweats from the injurious humors that infected the convent."[66] In addition to these afflictions, Isabel bled from the nose and mouth and could not swallow without vomiting. She spent most of her adult life bedridden with "sharp and intolerable pains" except, as one biographer recounts, on those occasions when the devil would levitate her and throw her against the walls of her cell. In addition, she regularly suffered seizures in which her eyes and tongue rolled back into her head and convulsions sometimes so uncontrollable that the other nuns had to drag her down the stairs to receive communion (Agustín de la Madre de Dios 316, 326, 328, 339).[67]

Brought on by extreme fasting, Isabel de la Encarnación's illness is interpreted by those around her as an active and saintly enterprise.[68] Notably, in Agustín de la Madre de Dios's version of Isabel's life story, her condition was supposedly brought on when, after six days of denying herself water, she was refused permission by the mother superior to drink (315). Rather than challenge her superior—since in the Discalced Carmelite Order, even a sip of water required authorization—Isabel takes the opportunity to destroy her body (315–16). Thus, although the exaggerated detail of horror was a typical baroque trope, the use of such grotesque bodily excesses as an indication of sanctity could be read as a powerful social message since the mortification of the senses corresponded to a program of self-control and exemplary obedience encouraged in many reformed orders (Agustín de la Madre de Dios 48–50). Isabel was also revered because through her suffering she effected a literal enactment of Christ's taking away the sins of the world, itself repeated during communion (John 1.29). It is this conception that transforms the graphic description of an ill woman into the paradigm of a saint valiantly struggling in retribution for the sins of others. Taking on the sins of others is visibly marked on her body as she expels repulsive excretions from every orifice. As one of her biographers recalls: "the pestilent humor infected her entire body, causing pus and excretions of putrid odor and dark green color from her mouth and other parts" (Agustín de la Madre de Dios 316). Another biographer recounts: "She suffered an intolerable stench that the other women could barely abide, and the rancid odor so penetrated the bed frames that they had to be burned, and the mattress was destroyed outside because it smelled so bad" (Godínez, ctd. Loreto 548).[69]

Narrations designed to repulse the sensibilities of the reader are common to hagiographic literature. However, in some life stories more attention is placed on ingestion of the fetid fluids of others; in such narrations, the subject's body is not so horrifically implicated and the notion of taking on the sins of the world is underscored. Catherine of Siena drank the pus from the cancerous sores of one of her patients; Angela of Foligno drank the water in which she had bathed a leper's rotting flesh; Catherine of Genoa swallowed the leprous flesh whole. Rosa of Lima drank a dish of rotting blood, and María Anna Águeda de San Ignacio varied her consumption to include "all kinds of foreign refuse" from her patients; she also sucked the blood from her wounds (King 123; Bynum 144–45; Mazzoni 183–84; Sánchez Lora 418; Peña 2; Bellido 38). When a leprous scab lodges in Angela of Foligno's throat, she ecstatically declares that it tastes "as sweet as communion" (Mazzoni 183). Catherine of Siena experiences pus as the most "sweet and savory" sustenance she has consumed in her life; that night Christ rewards her by allowing her to drink the blood from his side (Ribadeneyra 668/283).

Reading these life stories, one might wonder how convents populated by weak and ill women could continue to function. Were women chosen for biographical treatments exceptional in their penitential fervor? Did autobiographies and biographies exaggerate bodily abuses for rhetorical effect? This is impossible to determine with certitude; however, logic suggests that although many women chose to abuse their bodies for the pleasure of recognition, the exaggerated narrative description of women's penitential activities ultimately presents a distorted view of women's religiosity. In reality, as will be discussed in detail in the next chapter, in viceregal Spanish America anything that would call attention to a woman's presence was discouraged, and evidence suggests that for most women, unexplained illness was not attributed to divine intervention but viewed as demonic or simply unhealthy practice. While self-annihilation and psychosomatic illness presented little threat to the dominant order, undoubtedly the political ramifications of an entire convent population engaged in such activities were too dangerously subversive to be fully endorsed. Indeed, proof of good health was required for entrance into many convents, as the documentation for the entrance of María Francisca González Carrillo attests. Witnesses were required to vouch for the professant's health, both mental and physical: "In witness whereof . . . he has no knowledge that she has vices; suffers defects; deformities in the body; incurable, contagious, or debilitating disease; seizures or heart defects that render her unconscious, nor that she has ever been insane, hysterical, possessed by spirits or the devil, nor excommunicated" (*Declaración* 521).[70] When María Marcela develops a mysterious illness after six months in the convent, the other sisters want her removed and it is only through the intervention of the mother superior that she is allowed to remain (68–69). María de San José was refused entrance into the Convento de Santa Clara in Puebla because her fasts and disciplines had made her appear ill (*Word* 155–56, 169), and when she has difficulties walking as a novice, the abbess tells her she cannot proceed with her vows until they find out what is wrong with her. When doctors try to heal her by burning her feet, her condition worsens. She finds herself afflicted with sores and blisters throughout her body that they treat by burning and letting blood; she is bled eighteen times. This "cure" continues for two or three months during which time María is expected to continue her duties in the community (II.12, 15–16). María Magdalena is not so fortunate: when a case of rheumatic fever is accompanied by uncontrollable physical twitches, she is confined to her cell, whipped repeatedly, and exorcised before a barbaric operation paralyzes her completely (9–11).

As Mary Ann Doane suggests, given femininity's historical association with the pathological, disease and women are both marginalized elements that continually "threaten to infiltrate and contaminate that which is more central, health or masculinity" (152). Women not attracted to a life of pain were obligated nonetheless to somehow fit their life stories into this paradigm, because that is what the reader expected. Although she also dedicates several pages to the virtue of discipline, gaps and inconsistencies in María de San José's life story reveal that her commitment to penitence is less clear in retrospect. Before entering the convent, she says, she ate only herbs and tortillas, and three days a week, half a tortilla and water; she recalls that her hands were black with bruises and that lice entered the wounds from her hairshirts, leaving puddles of pus where she slept (*Word* 113–16). Confused by the comforts offered in the convent (chocolate and other sweets, beds with blankets), she nevertheless sleeps in the bed, she says, out of obedience and eats when God appears to her and says: "María, eat, in this life one cannot go on without eating and what the community gives you is to be eaten, no matter what it is, and I am not displeased by eating" (II.5–7, 31).[71] A similar ambivalence is reported when one day, tempted to eat at an inappropriate hour, she transgresses both the virtue of abstinence and the rules of the convent. Although she falls to her knees and begs forgiveness "*as if I had committed a very grave offense,*" her apology is tempered, again, by God's tolerance for such minor infractions: "Our Lord God revealed to me clearly how much it displeased him that one would fail to follow that ordered in the rules and regulations [of the order] *even in very small things. . . .* Asking Our Lord to show me how to be a saint, he led me to understand that I should not be distressed, because it was an exercise to which he had submitted me, because it pleased him so to see the tears and pain with which I wept for a mistake or imperfection, *however minor,* as a very serious offense. I was consoled" (II.17, emphasis added).[72]

* * *

When Úrsula Suárez is sentenced by Church authorities for instigating an uprising in the convent, the most painful part of her severe sentence is not the nine days of whipping but the forty of solitary confinement, during which she is to be denied communion (262). And no wonder: with the Eucharist, physical and spiritual nourishment were united. In contrast to the repulsive nature of worldly nourishment, the Eucharist was considered "spiritual nourishment" for the soul; in the Jesuit order, members of the spiritual community who failed to confess were not allowed to partake of food for the body until they had first nourished their souls. María Manuela de Santa Ana's greatest trials were chronic stomach pains alleviated only by taking communion. She reports taking the host as many as five times a day, since the act of eating anything besides the Eucharist was intolerable to her soul, she explains, precisely because of the pleasure it gave her body: "Eating caused me immense suffering, because the more flavorful the food, greater was the resistance and bitterness for my soul" (folio 1, *Vida* 162).[73] Eucharistic devotion in a ritualized sense was not gender specific. Nonetheless subsisting solely on the Eucharist seems to be a practice to which women were more vulnerable. It also has a different connotation for the female communicant because of her disparate relation to the body of Christ (Curran 67, 95–96). Bilinkoff suggests that the emphasis on women's "hunger" for communion might have been emphasized in biographies by confessors because of their own power to grant or take away this privilege (88). This observation can be extended to autobiographical writings designed to meet the expectations of the confessor/reader, since it is another way to defer authority to the priest. At the same time, as Bynum observes, there is little doubt that the Eucharist had a very real symbolic connotation for women: "To religious women food . . . was flesh, and flesh was suffering fertility. In renouncing ordinary food and directing their being toward the food that is Christ, women moved to God not merely by abandoning their flawed physicality but also by becoming the suffering and feeding humanity of the body on the cross, the food on the altar" (5). It is through the Eucharist that María Manuela is able to be with Christ in the visionary realm, a miracle that she recreates each time she takes communion: "An interior chapel was constructed for me, where the Lord God was placed within its structure, and around him all his adornments from the stages of the procession of the Holy Passion. And so it has remained to this day. And it is renewed and the Lord again placed within it every time I receive the consecrated host" (folio 2, *Vida* 163–64).[74] Gerónima del Espíritu Santo writes that when swallowing the Eucharist she feels as if Christ has entered her heart (76): in one vision Christ opens his heart, and inside she finds her heart and a dove eating grains of wheat, which he tells her is her soul, sustained by the host (124).

When women spoke of abstinence and Eucharistic ecstasy, Bynum notes, "they called it imitatio Christi. 'Imitation' meant union—fusion—with that ultimate body which is the body of Christ. . . . The eucharist was an especially appropriate vehicle for the effort to become Christ because the Eucharist is Christ. The doctrine of transubstantiation was crucial. One became Christ's crucified body in eating Christ's crucified body" (246, 256–57). Because of this identification with Christ, pain, whether self-inflicted or brought on by illness, inscribed one's own monotonous routine into a heroic narration. Moreover, by recontextualizing mundane life experiences such as illness, isolation, and depression into an imitation of Christ, these ordeals were transformed by the serenity of a future resurrection. As Gerónima notes: "I understood that the Holy Apostle had negotiated this suffering for me, commuting through it the terrible punishments that awaited me for my grievous faults" (Nava 61).[75] By accepting (or initiating) her own pain, she pays for her sins while on earth rather than after death. In this way, she asserts a measure of control, as Gilmore suggests, rather than being a prisoner to a suffering body "passivity turns to passion as her wounded body is conflated with Christ's" (144).[76] Because she was defined by her body, a woman's corporeal pain was also inextricably linked to an expression of identity before the eyes of her confessor/reader. In this way, a woman's pleasure was not as much through suffering in itself but through the satisfaction felt when her pain was recognized by her confessor, God, and conceivably also her female peers. On the one hand it could be said that such narratives manipulate the power structure to the detriment of other women, since acceptance of the paradigm of the suffering saint only served to perpetuate a model of female behavior that ultimately was ineffectual. On the other hand, given the limited options for female expression in Counter-Reformation Spain and Spanish America, the silent but nonetheless subversive protest of self-torture and self-denial effected a transformation in which, as Susan Bordo suggests, conditions that are "constraining, enslaving, and even murderous, come to be experienced as liberating, transforming, and life-giving" (93). Rather than a passive subject with no agency or volition, the model of sainthood actively abuses her body, asserting discursive power through seduction and spectacle, endowing it with meaning through the imitation of Christ, a ritual Gilmore appropriately terms "embodied sympathy" (134). In this way religious extravagance becomes a means of self-affirmation.

Framing life experience in the language and imagery of work that had been recognized and accepted allowed the writing subject to assert her own discursive authority just as female authors before her had done. As Jean Franco affirms, the hagiographic model provided a story in which a woman could imagine herself as heroine (xiv): by fashioning a textual self to conform with the paradigm of the solitary saint, the author was not only encouraged but obligated to engage in self-centered discourse. Extreme asceticism and literalism of women's spirituality must not, then, be evaluated only as an annihilative impulse but, rather, as Bynum notes, as an effort to gain power and impart meaning (208). The body, and especially the virginal, cloistered body, becomes a private and inviolable space, the only space truly her own, where the female writing subject could transform monotonous and sometimes even painful experiences into the heroic and empowering narrative of the saint.

4

Geography of the Sacred

Sebastiana Josefa de la Santísima Trinidad and the Hagiographic Representation of the Body

> Para el alma no hay encierro / ni prisiones que la impidan, / porque sólo la aprisionan / las que se forma ella misma.
>
> Sor Juana Inés de la Cruz

As evidence of the humility of Sor Sebastiana Josefa de la Santísima Trinidad (Sebastiana Josefa Maya Marín Samaniego, 1709–1757), her biographer cites "sixty documents" that demonstrate the extent of her virtue: "The sixty documents I offer are the letters she wrote to her confessors, because each one is proof of her humility" (306–7).[1] And indeed, the "letters" of Sebastiana Josefa, written over eleven years' time, are exceptionally and sometimes torturously burdened with the rhetoric of humility and obedience. The only organizing principle in these documents, often written in haste and late at night so other nuns would not see her, seems to be the author's unrelenting obsession with her shortcomings, temptations, and bodily torment. From her own account and that of her biographers, Sebastiana Josefa's life seems notably devoid of experiences in this world: she never held a single office, never administered any account, was not involved in the foundation or expansion of her order. Nonetheless, and perhaps precisely for this reason, her life of penitence was held up and praised to her sisters at her funeral as an edifying example of the *perfecta religiosa*, "the clearest mirror in which religious souls could see the most heroic virtues epitomized" (Saldaña 2–3), and the biography by Joseph Eugenio Valdés is similarly conceived as an example for other religious women, through direct address and the inclusion of spiritual exercises (22, 207–9).[2] Although the lives of women who openly challenged the system reveal an essential gap between official rhetoric and everyday practice, a close reading of Sebastiana Josefa de la Santísima Trinidad's life story offers an equally important vision of the extent to which women internalized embodied rhetoric into their discourse, simultaneously conforming to and challenging the hagiographical image of the penitent saint.

* * *

Sebastiana Josefa Maya Marín was born in Mexico City in 1709. Little is known of her childhood beyond that pieced together (and occasionally invented) by her biographer, except that her family was unable to provide her with a dowry, without which her options were extremely limited. Determined to follow her religious calling, she first chose to enter the Colegio de San Miguel de Belén, an institution affiliated with one of the most austere orders in New Spain.[3] Because women there had to do their own work, there was little time for anything more than the most rudimentary education. Although Sebastiana's family was not wealthy—hidalgos were the lowest rank of nobility—she had little in common with the uneducated working-class women with whom she lived. Because she lacked financial backing, however, no convent would admit her as a black-veiled nun. Finally she was allowed to enter the Convent of Corpus Christi, which required no dowry, but there her tribulations continued, since this convent had been founded to educate descendants of indigenous nobility. Sebastiana had been used by Pedro Navarrete, the Franciscan general commissary of Spain, and the criolla abbess as a political pawn. Navarrete opposed self-rule for indigenous women and had admitted three criolla novitiates to "strengthen" the community (Gallagher 155). Shortly thereafter, he was taken to court and Sebastiana, along with the other two criollas, was expelled. Nonetheless, after some time in the home of a wealthy benefactress, she was able to enter the Franciscan convent of San Juan de la Penitencia in 1744 with 1,000 pesos, on the condition that she pay the remaining 2,000 pesos at the time of her profession. When the time came for her to take her vows, her parents were unable to pay the balance. Finally, with funds pooled from several sources, the dowry was paid off and Sebastiana was allowed to profess. Valdés is careful to note that during this long and frustrating process Sebastiana never lost hope (one of the cardinal virtues), framing these difficulties instead within the narration of persecution: "this prolonged delay served as a very heavy cross for her to bear" (162).[4] The impasse was extended indeed: Sebastiana took her vows in 1746 at the relatively late age of thirty-seven.

Sebastiana Josefa would live only ten more years as a professed nun. Before she died, she detailed her spiritual life in a series of notebooks she had written at the request of her confessor. These notebooks, or "letters," were copied by hand, distributed among other women religious, and later used by her biographers as the basis for her life story. Sebastiana's confessor, Miguel Lozano, died one year after she did, so the task of writing her biography (1765) fell to Valdés. In addition to Sebastiana's letters, which form the main body of the text, Valdés supplements his version of her life with testimonies of those who knew her. Significantly, although male clerics who were only marginally acquainted with Sebastiana are cited by name, her sisters in the convent remain an anonymous mass of eyewitnesses until the final chapters when more specific evidence is presented as an argument for her sanctity. While it is true that the original notebooks set out to be neither a model for other women nor an assertion for sainthood, it is important to note that Sebastiana, like many authors, evokes her sisters in the convent only as persecutors and never as friends, even though her biographer mentions at least one woman who was a close companion. Thus, although Valdés does edit and reorganize Sebastiana's narration, her letters already are intended to conform to the hagiographic model of singularity. Valdés speculates that Sebastiana deliberately muddled chronological referents in response to her anxiety of authorship (311). More tenable, perhaps, is Muriel's suggestion that the lack of chronological order and absence of details from her life stem from Sebastiana's rejection of temporal existence in favor of eternity. Thus, although the author mentions details from her life, they are only used as a means to illustrate her relation to God (Muriel *Cultura femenina* 425). Readers expected edifying examples of virtue in the *vida,* which closely follows hagiographic conventions. The didactic intention of Valdés's text is especially hyperbolic when the Franciscan virtue of poverty is described: "And so the Venerable Sebastiana was able to become more poor than she was before, having been extremely poor before, and becoming the living portrait of poverty. What she wore was poor, what she ate, poor, what she spoke, poor, and poor in what she thought until she achieved the finest heights of apostolic poverty" (182).[5]

Nonetheless, and although Valdés dedicates a chapter to each of the vows and cardinal virtues his subject incarnates—obedience (165–74), poverty (174–85), chastity (185–93), faith (193–200), hope (209–19), and charity (219–27)—it is clearly Sebastiana's dedication to penitence that has made her exceptional, as is suggested by the titles of both her funeral sermon, *La penitente paloma, o gemebunda Maya* ([Penitent dove, or moaning Maya] 1758) and Valdés's biography: *Vida admirable y penitente de la V.M. Sor Sebastiana Josepha de la SS. Trinidad* ([The amazing and penitent life of the venerable mother Sor Sebastiana Josefa de la Santísima Trinidad] 1765). According to her biographer, Sebastiana began abstinence from the moment she was born, never crying for her mother's milk and weaning herself alone; her spiritual vocation was reportedly first observed when at the age of three months she wept inconsolably before the image of Christ (7–9). She never shed tears for worldly matters, even after falling down the stairs and cracking her skull (7–11). As a child, Sebastiana had neither an interest in playing with other children nor with pretty clothes, contenting herself "with only that necessary to decently cover her body" (10).[6] Modest even as an infant, she reportedly spurned the caresses of her father; she never gave her hand to men and rarely to other women and often refused medical care for fear and shame that the male doctor would see her body (185–86, 189).[7] As a child, she never left the corner of her room, never spoke more than necessary, and then in a "low and submissive" voice, and never raised her eyes from the ground. She engaged herself with needlework, read devotional books, and pursued "other similarly honest and religious activities" (19, 268).[8] As Valdés concludes: "these were the first steps of Doña Sebastiana down the blessed path of virtue" (19).[9] Although Valdés is reconstructing a saintly childhood narrative for his subject—Sebastiana gives few details of her secular life—he is faithful to a narration in which the textual image of sanctity is expressed through the body. In an appropriate allegory, Valdés notes that Sebastiana's propensity for the cloister was such that she demanded that the windows of the house be nailed shut; when her parents refused her request, she closed the "windows of her body" with "doors to her senses, padlocks on her lips and shackles on her feet" (18).[10] According to her biographer, Sebastiana had no difficulty separating from her family; in fact, she wished to take a vow to renounce her parents, but her confessor would not permit it (263–64). As Valdés, in a typical flight of flowery prose, declares: "like a pearl in its shell, like a dove in its nest, like a rose in its own garden, so happy was she in the Recogimiento of Belén that in a few short days after entering, her relatives' visits became an annoyance, and even those of her parents offended her natural inclination" (27).[11]

* * *

Although practiced by both men and women, the torture of the body had a special connotation for women, whose identity was based on their corporeality. In acts of self-abjection, the body becomes the privileged space of encounter in which the flesh and the law are reconciled (Kristeva 127–28). Restricted to a limited space in which every movement was monitored, the penitent sought to achieve perfection not by denying her flesh but by making her body overpresent. To be one with Christ in the eternal order required the mastery of the body to "direct the attention of the retreatant from externals to inner experience, thus preparing the individual for openness to divine inspiration" (Curran 6). Again, women express themselves as gendered subjects: they are imitating the hagiographic models of women who spoke with their bodies as a means to access power and prestige as well as to provide a meaning for themselves, as they become one with God. The subjugation of the body, then, is, as Mary Giles affirms, "but the necessary and preliminary elucidation of a historical state of affairs: it constitutes the point of departure for the task of offering a body to the spirit, of incarnating discourse, giving truth a space in which to make itself manifest" (80). Catherine of Siena makes this distinction clear: "Perfection does not consist in mortifying and killing the body, but in *killing perverse self-will.* . . . It is necessary for us to build the foundation out of killing and drowning perverse self-will, and with this will submitted to the will of God, we will devote, sweet, hungry, infinite desire to the honor of God and the salvation of souls" (Petroff 265).[12]

Marginalized from discursive authority, female autobiographers counter by defining their textual selves through the suffering body of Christ. Even within this context, Sebastiana elevated penance to a torturous art: she flagellated herself daily with thorned scourges, nettles, nails, iron chains, and wooden rods, applied until she lost consciousness. She wore nettles and thistles in her underwear, clothes of maguey, hairshirts, and iron cilices, although her confessor had her remove them periodically since the points opened wounds in her skin. Among her other adornments was an iron cross covered with barbs, worn on her chest until her confessor insisted she move it to her back; a gag over her mouth, and a rope around her neck from which she hung a heavy stone. She put steel spikes and rocks in the soles of her shoes and always kept bitter herbs in her mouth. Sebastiana slept no more than two hours a night, on the floor, and barely covered; she often put her head on the corner of a platform to remain awake all night (Valdés 181, 331).

The ideological implications of this kind of "praiseworthy" behavior are particularly evident in an episode in which Sebastiana is ordered by her confessor to continue her penances even while ill. Unexpectedly, Valdés reports, she finds that in disciplining her body she recovers her health, to which he smugly comments that such pain is a "fine medication to cure many illnesses" and that in fact the medical profession would benefit greatly from learning this maxim from the "pulpits of Penitence" (336–37).[13] To illustrate this precept, the episodes of Sebastiana's bloody bodily mortifications are described in detail by her biographer. On one occasion, he recounts, "she performed such a cruel, bloody and rigorous discipline, that blood gushed out everywhere, staining with its warm crimson not only the snowy jasmines of her body but the bricks of the room to which she had withdrawn" (119–20). In one episode Sebastiana removes the pools of blood from her cell with a bowl and hides it beneath the floorboards, while in another she reportedly spills so much blood that she has to pour it out the window of the nun's choir with buckets, leaving horrific stains on the walls (334–35).[14] Nonetheless, the most richly symbolic bodily practice exploited by Sebastiana was the subjugation of her tongue. As her contemporary Domingo de Quiroga observed: "The tongue . . . is a world unto itself of evil" (28);[15] the control of the mouth and especially of the tongue was particularly emphasized by baroque authors (Loreto 549). An entire chapter of Scaramelli's *Ascetic Directory* was dedicated to the tongue as an obstacle to spiritual perfection. Scaramelli maintains that by regulating the tongue, one could control all other parts of the body and subdue all sensual appetites (Stockman 234). Sebastiana crawled on her knees, making crosses on each tile of the courtyard with her tongue and then crosses with the blood of her tongue, soon staining the patio with bloody crosses as the raw skin of her tongue began to bleed; according to her biographer she would then add to her pain by pouring vinegar over the raw flesh, a ritual he heralds as: "Adding pain to pain and torment to torment. Oh blessed tongue, what reward must you have received for such a raw penitence. Oh joyful Penitence, what glory must you have received, as we so faithfully believe!" (44–46, 332–34).[16] Extravagantly theatrical, Sebastiana's bleeding tongue is a powerful reminder of her inability to express herself in any other way.

The tongue, as Sebastiana's readers knew well, had many functions beside that of speech. It was upon the tongue that she received the body of Christ in communion, and it was this spiritual nourishment that contrasted with the physical nourishment of everyday meals. Food—or the denial of it—is a theme that resonates both in the original letters and in Valdés's recontextualization. As early as the sixth century, food was associated with carnal pleasures, and women, ostensibly less able to control their sexual appetites, were encouraged to fast to repress lust (Bynum 45, 79, 214; Stockman 215). Sebastiana explicitly associates the temptations of the flesh with meat when she envisions a condemned soul eating a huge slab of raw meat; she stopped eating meat after her first communion ("after tasting the delights of the spirit") and when forced to eat it she would immediately vomit (Valdés 154, 300–301, 317).[17] According to her biographer, Sebastiana ate only once a day and then only food that was spoiled, purging herself regularly, although this sometimes left her too weak to leave bed.

Usually she limited her intake to two or three sips of *atole,* or, in imitation of Claire of Assisi, her patron saint, she would wait until the other nuns had eaten and would satisfy herself with table scraps, garbage from the kitchen, or in one case a piece of fish she allowed to become fetid in her cell (317–19, 321–22, 326–27). Emulating Catherine of Siena, Sebastiana ate the ointments and compresses used on her patients "as if they were a delicacy" (326).[18] When most thirsty, she would put a glass of water to her lips and then renounce it; even on her deathbed she had another sister bring her some chocolate, only to insist she drink it in front of her (382). She survives, spiritually and physically, on the Eucharist, which, by her own account, she takes daily (39).

Nonetheless, Sebastiana mentions the temptation of eating as her greatest trial. On one occasion she indulges in something sweet and is severely reprimanded by her confessor. Her own guilt leads her to intensify her efforts at fasting until she loses consciousness from lack of food (185). The next time Sebastiana's hunger compels her to give in to temptation she criticizes herself harshly: "sometimes I lose consciousness and, exhausted, my head feels as if it is going to burst, and I am so despondent that I do not have the strength to do good, and my body is powerless, and with this weakness the appetite to eat forces me against my will to surrender and eat something I had not tasted for a long time, and that was sweets. Seeing myself so perverse distresses me so that I am disgraced and ashamed before God and all others, as a loathsome thing" (295).[19] Yet it is not the act of eating itself that Sebastiana condemns, but rather her inability to control her appetite: "It happened . . . that for dinner I ate a little piece of bread and a little bit of corn and this was enough to dishearten me because of my lack of mortification. . . . When will I be free of my appetites? It might seem that this was not something to get so upset about . . . what was wrong was that I did not have any need [to eat] and I had not intended to have dinner" (295).[20] Sebastiana's admission of guilt is a misconstrued act of contrition because the shame caused by her supposed sin (lack of self-control) lies in the way this transgression has offended her confessor (who had previously reprimanded her for this temptation) and by extension, God and "all others"; a distorted aggrandizement of the confessor that is nonetheless expected in the unequal power structure in which she exists. Her rebellious and alien appetite marks her conflict and complicity within a hierarchy of power in which she is no longer able to distinguish her desires from those of her confessor.[21]

Rosalva Loreto López suggests that sensorial impulses were inextricably linked to symbolic practice and, as such, formed part of the road to perfection, continually threatened by demonic temptation (543). To control the consumption of food is, moreover, the last defense of the powerless, it is "one element of human existence that each controls for himself or herself. . . . It requires no clerical intervention and indeed avoids it. If one is powerless in all other regards, one still has power in this: not to eat, but to love" (King 125). This literal hunger forms the physical counterpart, moreover, to the discourse of longing textually expressed in mystic narratives and baroque art. As Susan Bordo confirms, through the denial of the body the woman discovers "what it feels like to crave and want and need and yet, through the exercise of her own will, to triumph over that need. In the process, a new realm of meanings is discovered, a range of values and possibilities that Western culture has traditionally coded as 'male' and rarely made available to women: an ethic and aesthetic of self-mastery and self-transcendence, expertise, and power over others through the example of superior will and control" (100).

The use of masculine attributes to describe saintly women has a long history in hagiographic and devotional literature: Catherine of Siena urged her followers to "labor manfully" (Petroff 269), and Thomas à Kempis described love for God as "long-suffering, and manly" (94); it also appears in the writings of Augustine and Claire of Assisi.[22] In the hearings for the beatification of Teresa de Jesús, she was praised as "a virile woman" for her "manly" soul and "manly" courage (*Proceso* xiii, xxii, xlii). The Peruvian nun, Gerónima de la Madre de Dios, described as a "spiritual Amazon," was lauded by her biographers for her "manly reason" (Calancha 1.937; Torres 2.787). Juan de Olmos commends the intelligence of Gerónima del Espíritu Santo, noting that "she did not have a womanly mind. . . . she was so benevolent and strong that, I can attest, she could compete with the greatest manly fortitude" (37–38).[23] And both María de San José and Sebastiana Josefa are lauded for their "fearless" and "manly" hearts (Valdés 15, *Word* 4). As Darcy Donahue notes in relation to biographies of holy women, describing the subject as "heroic" or "manly" was "a way of asserting her superiority over the rest of her sex. In doing so they separate the subject from normal or 'inferior' women" (232). This superiority is manifested most clearly in the "male" ideals of control and self-mastery; and the space upon which it was inevitably played was the space in which woman was most vulnerable: her body.

* * *

Contemporary theories of hysteria as pathology or protest (105) are relevant to an understanding of why women, much more than men, actively sought to weaken and destroy their bodies. Indeed, if woman is defined by her body, the act of making that body, or at least its feminine marks and dangerous sexuality, disappear may seem to be the ultimate act of humiliation, the ultimate erasure of self.[24] At the same time, however, when all other aspects of one's life are rigidly controlled, as Bordo notes, "an unwillingness to limit oneself, even in the pursuit of femininity, breaks the rules" (102). This was especially true in Counter-Reformation Spain and Spanish America, where women's speaking voices were silenced even from prayer and openly demonstrative mystic raptures discouraged. In the *costumbrero* written with a female pseudonym by the misogynous Archbishop Francisco Aguiar y Seijas, individuality is strictly forbidden: "In singularity we are doomed. In dress, in modesty, in style and in all actions there must be uniformity, from the mother superior down to the last novice" (folio 58, ctd. in Bravo Arriaga 167)[25]; even singularity in eating habits was discouraged by some writers (Calancha 1.939).

The narrative insistence on bloody descriptions of women's self-mortification, while undoubtedly an effective tactic to satiate readers' perverse fascination with such spectacles, makes it difficult to determine to what extent these public displays were actually tolerated. After all, Sebastiana was merely electing to employ the model of exaggerated sanctity of the redeemed sinner, Mary Magdalene, rather than the dignified grace of Mary. As such, her behavior was not aberrant enough to merit disapproval, but neither was it unconditionally held up by Church hierarchy as a model to imitate, particularly if it bore the slightest trace of volition. Thus, although Valdés marvels at Sebastiana's often very public displays of abstinence and discipline as "Heroic action!" (321) and "amazing example!" (322), he undermines her authority as he tries to simultaneously fit her into the hagiographic model and the social order. In Valdés's recontextualization, Sebastiana's mystic raptures are extolled precisely for their *conformity* and, most important, for their *lack of corporeality:* "In none of them will there be discovered an inclination to the extraordinary comfort of the body and carnal pleasure but, rather, great *honesty* in every way. One will not find pernicious intranquility but rather, *gentle interior peace.* Nor will be discovered in them *impudence or indocility* but devoted obedience and submission to the prudent judgment of her confessors. . . . There will not be recorded any affectation, any desire to seem like a saint or virtuous woman, because she considered herself the most unworthy creature in the world" (131, emphasis in original).[26]

Physicality takes on a different cultural and psychological connotation for women, whose inferiority in general and exclusion from theological learning in particular were often expressed as weakness of the flesh. When men use the act of self-mortification as a corrective for the sin of pride, they are renouncing their cultural dominance; when a woman uses the same set of symbols, she is reaffirming a lowly status already assigned her. For a woman to control her body was a way to command respect in a male-dominated world. Ironically, however, by attempting to dominate their bodies, women like Sebastiana were actually *out of control*. Indeed, the extreme penances Sebastiana pursued clearly violate the almost universal call for moderation. Ribadeneyra himself points to Catherine of Siena's "heroic" mortifications as "more amazing than imitable" (667);[27] and Ignacio de Loyola insisted that the discipline of the flesh be accomplished with the authority of the confessor and only as the first step in a process. Moreover, he specified that self-mortification was intended only to cause the sensation of pain and not bodily harm: "What seems the most suitable and safest thing in doing penance is for the pain to be felt in the flesh, without penetration to the bones, thus causing pain but not illness" (*Ejercicios espirituales* 124/62).[28] For his part, Thomas à Kempis asserted that "bodily discipline ... must be undertaken with discretion" and that public displays were inappropriate, "for such personal things are better performed in private" (28). Catherine of Siena advised discretion in self-mortification and, should the body become ill, that "not only ought fasting be put aside, but meat should be eaten, and if once a day isn't enough, let it be eaten four times a day.... discretion proposes that penance be done *as a means and not as a principal desire*" (Petroff 268). Teresa de Jesús also counseled against fasting and excessive disciplines for women. Women are weak enough spiritually, she comments, to waste their time weakening their bodies; and when visions are invoked by such a state, she adds slyly, it is not "arrobamiento" [rapture] but "abobamiento" [foolishness] (*Las moradas* 4:3.574/92–93).[29] Discretion was also advocated by Church authorities in Spanish America. Antonio Núñez de Miranda recommended moderation in penance for his readers, commenting that their motivation should not be "extraordinary eccentricity but the intense love of God and solid desire to please Him" (*Plática doctrinal* 8–9).[30]

Despite running counter to all conventional and medical wisdom, Sebastiana's penitential exercises form one of the key themes of her biography, and the most torturous acts are celebrated by Valdés as exemplary behavior. Recounting an episode in which her confessor commands her to remove the iron cilices with steel points and she puts on an animal hairshirt that aggravates and infects the wounds, Valdés exclaims: "But what brilliant designs are invented by the gift of divine love!" (334).[31] For Valdés,

Sebastiana's behavior is admirable (and for that reason exceptional) because she conforms to the model of the penitent and suffering saint. At the same time, Sebastiana's refusal to alleviate her suffering may also be interpreted as a form of muted rebellion within the guise of obedience: she obeys her confessor by removing the iron cilices but defies his obvious intention by putting on another hairshirt that actually causes her more pain. Similarly, she obediently denies herself nourishment until her starving body converts her into a spectacle, compulsively digging food out of the garbage after the other nuns have left the table. Rather than suppressing the will, torture and deprivation allow Sebastiana to assert her determination over the wishes of her confessor and advice of her doctors.

Robert Stoller contends that self-inflicted pain is a "technique of control" because by torturing herself, the subject masters her own script and is no longer a victim; she may decide for herself "when to suffer pain rather than have it strike without warning" (125). Thus, self-destructive behavior that at first seems passive may in reality, as Michelle Massé notes, "display a startling amount of initiative" (42). By creating ever new forms of bodily torture, moreover, the passive object will be recognized and perhaps even revered by her confessor for her suffering, achieving "her own form of agency and object relations via pain: her passivity may control others; her conspicuous and silent suffering can shout an accusation at her tormentors" (47–48). Although conforming to the ascetic ideal of femininity, Sebastiana's spectacular public tortures transgress the boundaries of the enclosed space of her body, inscribing a corporeal discourse that denotes excess. Her flamboyant penances, leaving highly visible marks of blood on her body and even throughout her limited space (notably, in at least two episodes, the blood spills *outside* her enclosure) "speak" louder than any words.[32]

Sebastiana stubbornly continues her program of self-mortification, fully aware of the toll it has taken on her body. When a doctor treating her for her frequent stomach pains from lack of food advises moderation, instead of following his orders, Sebastiana takes matters into her own hands by increasing the disciplines to her body (10, 158). The loss of blood from these tortures, along with continual fasting, often leads to fainting that concerns both her confessor and her doctor, who, she reports with some satisfaction, is horrified by her self-imposed condition (66,77). By her own account it seems clear that Sebastiana starved herself to death, although her biographer is careful to note that it was God's will and not her own, since an illness was the immediate cause of her demise (375, 379). Arguing for Sebastiana's sainthood, Valdés affirms that her heart continued beating hours after her passing, similar to what had occurred with Saint Paula, whose heart had remained warm after her body was cold (386). Although he decorously defers to the authority of the Church by refusing to confirm whether or not Sebastiana's beating heart qualifies as a miracle, the biography clearly sets her up as a candidate for sainthood long before this concluding passage. Indeed, the rigorous asceticism of Sebastiana, evoked by Ignacio Saldaña as a "penitent dove," is specifically associated with Paula, who had relentlessly disciplined her body and identified herself with the dove.[33]

To torture the body is to renounce the temporal order of the physical world for the infinite order of the divine; it is a form of self-expression that transports the subject into a different realm of reality. If women's only power is the power of refusal, it could be argued that Sebastiana's radical appropriation of corporeal rhetoric can also be read as the frustrated and furious "power hunger of the powerless" (Gilbert and Gubar 285). Sebastiana gained immortality through her extravagant suffering, yet ultimately, by inscribing her pain within the representational system of her confessor/addressee, a system that eroticized, objectified, and sometimes even demonized the female body, she ironically relegated herself to silence and isolation.

5

The Hiding Places of My Power

Visionary Authority and Mystic Space

> Faith is the substance of things hoped for, the evidence of things not seen.
> Hebrews 11.1

The material world is shaped by and interacts with our social perceptions of it. Divisions of space and social formations are intimately associated not as cause and effect but in terms of a simultaneous interdependence: space defines the people in it and people define space. As Shirley Ardener notes, space reflects social organization, but once space has been bound and shaped it exerts its own influence (11–13). The limitation and classification of space within the convent contributed to the reproduction of the power relations on which it was modeled. Every space in the colonial cloister had a representative function that mirrored conceptions of the divine order, themselves a symbolic extension of societal divisions of age, gender, social class, and religious rank. Adjacent to the main chapel, and hidden behind woodwork, grating, and sometimes a heavy black curtain that allowed them to see out without being observed, religious women were simultaneously at the threshold and on the margins of the church building just as they were in the Church.[1] Daily routine, which centered on the cycle of the liturgical year, further consecrated the systematic use of space: although prayers and acts of contrition could vary, at any given hour of any given day the nun would be in the same place at the same time. Religious women were divided according to their positions: black-veiled professed women worshiped in the upper choir loft, the *coro alto;* with novices, servants, and lay religious women in the simpler lower choir.[2] The crypt in which they were buried lay directly below the choirs, and below that, the ossuary.[3] Once professed, the body of the cloistered religious woman never again left the convent, even after her death.

Symbolic and real power relations were further demarcated through the manipulation of the body, textually codified in confession manuals and the rules and constitutions of each religious order. Confession manuals instruct the penitent to kneel in deference at the feet of the confessor; many confession manuals also advise that she clasp her hands together (Lea II.187). The *reglas y constituciones* of each religious order, supplemented by the *costumbreros*, further ensured uniformity through the detailed description of daily activities, spatial organization, and even physical positions: women were instructed to kneel, lower their heads, and kiss the ground (Bravo Arriaga 167). This use of physical gestures to dramatize devotional acts was indebted to the spiritual exercises of Ignacio de Loyola (1491–1556). In his *Ejercicios espirituales,* Loyola instructs his readers to assume certain symbolic postures during contemplative activity: to kneel, to prostrate oneself on the ground, to lie face upward, eyes raised toward heaven, or humbly lowered in the presence of another; a hand on the chest indicated pain for having sinned or failed in some way, as did tears, a wordless and visceral response to Christ's sacrifice and glory (94, 122–23).[4] Margo Glantz suggests that we may speak of a "corporeal rhetoric" in baroque culture, a system of theatricalized signs through which sanctity itself is systematized ("El cuerpo monacal y sus vestiduras" 172–73). It is through this methodical manipulation of the body that the ideological apparatus is inscribed on individual subjectivity.[5]

In the baroque era a sense of theatricality permeated not only art but life in general. The architectural positioning of the colonial church itself, with its main altar and pulpit at the front, focuses the attention of the viewer as if in a theater: didactic and emotive paintings and sculptures form the backdrop. On an individual level, as Emilio Orozco Díaz suggests, theatricality may be considered an essential human feature, not unlike the self-fashioning effected in autobiography: on the one hand to present an idealized self and, on the other, to "express something different from what we appear to be or to set free our basic impulses" (117). As Sharon Magnarelli has pointed out, confession is in itself an inherently theatrical gesture (200), an affected rhetorical strategy. The narrator dramatizes a series of transgressions in an attempt to reformulate her (sinful) past self and create a new identity that conforms to the expectations of her audience (the confessor) and, by extension, to all the values he upholds as a representative of institutionalized religiosity. If she "played her part" convincingly, she could expect to be rewarded not only with forgiveness and recognition, but also, perhaps, with a power base she could use to her benefit. Thus it should not be surprising that autobiography intersects so notably with hagiography: by recreating their textual selves around model figures, religious women sought to cast themselves, literally, in the role of the saint.

* * *

Nowhere was this theatricalized system of signs more apparent than in the glorification of the "rhetoric of tears."[6] Jerome had written: "prayers placate God, but tears compel Him"; and penitent saints were regularly portrayed with tears (Knipping 314), an involuntary manifestation of *imitatio Christi* (Lochrie 117). Tears indicated empathy for the passion of Christ, and for his sacrifice for the sins of man; it is to a weeping Mary Magdalene, according to John, that the resurrected Christ first reveals himself, making her the first apostle (John 20.11–18).[7] Weeping was also an essential feature of the redeemed sinner (often conflated with Mary Magdalene), who uses her tears to clean the feet of Christ and is saved by her faith (Luke 7.38, 50).[8] Ignacio de Loyola, who was said to weep continually, codifies "the gift of tears" into a complex series of referents that vary according to the time they occur and their intensity (*Spiritual Journal* 12–13). Catherine of Siena distinguishes five kinds of tears that correspond to the five affective states or stages of the soul, each representing a progressive movement toward God (*Passion for the Truth* 129–32).[9]

Úrsula Suárez alludes to the penitential dimension of tears as she begins her life story "drowned in the sea of my tears" (90), specifying later that the torrent she sheds is a gift from God to cleanse her soul (194). It is, on the other hand, to cleanse the transgressions of others that a weeping Gerónima del Espíritu Santo uses her tears: "And [Christ] said: 'sins without tears will never be cleared.' And he remained there as if waiting for me to mourn those whose sins were not cleansed so that I would weep for them and erase them with my tears" (174–75).[10] Longing to share Christ's suffering, María de San José's eyes "were fountains of tears, continually, day and night, and at all hours . . . to this day my eyes are a torrent of tears."[11] This hyperbolic description of tears is further reinforced when she recalls: "At the time I had . . . a cloth almost six feet long to wipe the tears I cried and some days I let them flow to the ground. And today I do the same, because I drench three cloths and still do not have enough and so I let the tears flow without wiping them" (*Word* 130). In another episode, like the remorseful David who nightly "floods" his bed with tears (Psalms 6:6–7), María's bed is inundated by "a pool of water from the tears I cried" (*Word* 192).[12] Francisca Josefa affiliates her tears as an infant with a knowledge of human sin, although she cleverly qualifies her statement by attributing it not to her memory but to that of other witnesses: "They used to say that even when I could barely walk, I hid myself to cry . . . as if I knew the evils in which I would fall, offending our Lord" (4).[13] Although Francisca's observation that the sleeves of her habit are perpetually wet (46) from her weeping may be an exageration, she also uses common images from the rhetoric of tears to communicate her genuine sense of loss during a conflict with her confessor: "to write you, Reverend Father . . . I began to cry in the inkwell to moisten it with the tears I cried . . . I wanted to moisten it with my tears and write with them, and could do so easily because I was crying so much" (57–58).[14]

Through tears, eyes were used to express a spiritual devotion that went beyond words. Indeed, for the baroque sensibility, the eyes are, as Maravall observes, "the most direct and effective means that we can make use of in questions of affections. They are linked to feelings, as feelings are linked to them. To move the psyche, which we have seen to be what the baroque strove for, the most effective means are visual" (*La cultura del barroco* 504–5/253). The power of vision, an organizing principle of epistemology since the Greeks, may be traced back in devotional discourse to Christ's teachings ("The eye is the lamp of the body" Matthew 6.22), and is particularly notable in the Gospel of John (see 1:32–34, 38). As Miguel Ángel Ferrando notes in his analysis of the importance of vision in John, "The fundamental verb here is 'to see' . . . this is not speculation illustrated with examples. It is the testimony of a man who has seen with his eyes and touched with his hands another man, a man as real as himself" (98).[15]

To the denial of outer vision, the devout were encouraged to cultivate an imaginative inner stage. This method of spiritual orientation was advocated in *Meditations on the Life of Christ,* attributed to Bonaventure (1221–1274),[16] and Pedro de Alcántara also emphasized the visual nature of meditation in his *Tratado*.[17] The most influential text of the Counter Reformation, however, was undoubtedly Ignacio de Loyola's *Ejercicios espirituales*. Like that of the *Meditations,* Loyola's method is based on a visualization of devotional images expressed in tangibly corporeal terms. In each scene Loyola presents, he asks his readers not only to vividly picture themselves within the setting but to endow this pictorial vision with the corporeal stimuli of all other senses: with sound, scent, taste, and touch. This exercise is to be followed by general confession. The first step in spiritual contemplation, Loyola asserts, is to situate the imagination in a *physical space:* "The first prelude is a mental image of the place. It should be noted at this point that when the meditation or contemplation is on a visible object, for example, contemplating Christ our Lord during His life on earth, the image will consist of *seeing with the mind's eye the physical place where the object that we wish to contemplate is present*" (*Ejercicios* 103/54, emphasis added).[18]

Thus, although spiritual vision is interiorized, Loyola's form of mental prayer is *an experience* and not an intellectual abstraction; as such, it was a means of meditation accessible to women.[19] Teresa de Jesús repeatedly refers to the centrality of physical images to her spiritual life (VII.2, 157/38, IX.1–3, 177–78/57–59, XXII.8, 287/140). When she anguishes over the loss of her favorite devotional books following the Inquisitorial prohibitions, Christ reassures her: "'Be not distressed, for I will give thee a living book'... His Majesty Himself has been to me the Book in which I have seen what is true" (*Libro de la vida* XXVI:5, 323/168).[20] And to those who declare that envisioning Christ impedes higher spiritual contemplation, Teresa defends her vision of Christ's humanity: "It seems to me that if they had then had faith as they had after the Holy Spirit came, to believe that He was God and Man, it would have been no hindrance to them" and confesses that she wishes she could have the image of Christ before her eyes at all times because he is not engraved in her soul as much as she would wish (XXII.1–4, 284–85/136–38).[21]

Visual allegory points to a direct perception of spiritual reality. While book learning was a privilege limited to a small elite, art could communicate to even the most unlettered segments of the population. The power of images was promoted from earliest childhood. Sacred images—of the saints, and particularly of the infant Jesus—were recommended as a means to guide children toward God from an early age, suggesting that identification with an *image* is the first step toward spiritual ascent (Freedberg 4–5). As a textual strategy, iconographic references represented a common visual language shared by the author, her confessor, and the wider reading public. As Surtz notes in his discussion of women's visionary experience in late-medieval and early-modern Spain, "To the extent that an extraordinary spiritual experience is often translated into a series of visual or verbal images, such revelations were conditioned by verbal and iconic texts with which the nuns were familiar" (12). Just as hagiographic narratives were essential to the (re)construction of a saintly life, the use of conventional imagery was an effective way to convince the reader of the validity of her visionary experience (18). If a mystic experience conformed to the revelations previously experienced by the saints, then it was less likely to be viewed as heresy.

* * *

Loyola's exercises, and those that followed his model of mental prayer, transform meditation into an imaginative act, a powerfully visual force, and this fit perfectly into the baroque notion of art as a means to provoke an emotional and spiritual reaction (Maravall *La cultura del barroco* 501, 506–7/251, 254–55). Although the *Ejercicios espirituales* did not explicitly advocate the use of artwork to stimulate the imagination, the Ignatian method of visual contemplation inspired illustrated devotional works and allegorical emblem books from the seventeenth century on. Lorenzo Ortiz titled his emblem book *Ver, oír, oler, gustar, tocar: Empresas que enseñan y persuaden su buen uso en lo político y lo moral* [See, hear, smell, taste, touch: Emblems that teach and induce their good use in political and moral matters, 1687], and the eighteenth-century version of Loyola's text was abundantly illustrated (Orozco Díaz 144; Freedberg 180–83; Barthes 56).[22] Jesuits were, in fact, obligated to emphasize the Ignatian visual and corporeal approach to prayer, and one of Teresa de Jesús's confessors, Baltasar Álvarez, was reprimanded by his order for advocating silent worship (Sánchez Lora 210–11). Jesuits such as Juan Bautista Escarlo in his *Retórica Cristiana* (1674) go so far as to advocate the use of visual texts in sermons to facilitate the understanding of a given doctrine or spiritual effect (Maravall *La cultura del barroco* 502/252).[23]

Manuel Ramos Medina alludes to the "visual triumph" that the Catholic Church effected against Protestantism ("Esplendor" 498): it was through the eyes that artists sought to involve the viewer, and through art that the Church captured the imagination of the devout. Indeed, a 1562 edict of the Council of Trent advocated the use of "visible signs" of religion to help the faithful contemplate hidden mysteries (*Doctrina sobre el muy santo sacrificio de la misa,* 22a sesión, ctd. Chazal 23). Baroque spirituality, with its emphasis on the individual experience of God, converted the act of devotion into a work of art. No longer limited to the repetition of ritual formulae, a renewed notion of will and of an active calling to love God formed the nucleus of spiritual treatises throughout the Spanish world. This dangerous individuality was what eventually led to the suppression of many devotional works in the sixteenth and seventeenth centuries. Art, on the other hand, continued to encourage this approach to spirituality through the participation of the observer in both a didactic and sensuous way. The visual imagery for these mental pilgrimages was reinforced by the pictorial cycles in the churches and by privately commissioned panel paintings. Religious themes predominated, and paintings adorned churches, convents, and private homes.

The yearning aspirant quality of baroque affective art reflected and encouraged a vision of devotion codified in the position of the body. Polychrome sculptures strived for an intense palpability of the flesh, while intimate portraits of saints embraced by Christ were produced and reproduced throughout the Spanish world.[24] The center of these visual representations was Christ's embodiment. As Sarah Stanbury observes of Medieval England, which holds equally true in the Hispanic baroque, "it is difficult to overemphasize the importance of the image of Christ's body as a figure in daily devotion: as a visual presence in all forms of representation" (265). Underlining Christ's suffering, images from the Passion of Christ were favored and were integral to the development of the cult to the wounds of Christ that later developed into the image of the sacred heart, even though this image, ironically, was promoted to counteract the vision of the crucified Christ (Bargellini 45–46). The body in pain was further implicated by the profusion of images of penitent saints, a motif that was more pronounced in the New World than in Spain itself (Ruiz Gomar "La penitencia" 184).[25] Graphic images of penitent and bloody female saints adorned even the walls of young girls' *colegios* (*Arte y mística del barroco*, figures 49, 54). Margarita Peña suggests that this image of the suffering saint is one reason self-mortification reaches its highest expression in conventual art and literature of the baroque period (1).

In his influential 1633 manual, *Diálogos de la pintura* [*Dialogues on Painting*], Vicenzo Carducci instructs artists to represent saints "kneeling, hands together or raised to the heavens, or across the chest, head uplifted, eyes raised, tearful or joyful, or the head lowered, and the eyes closed, the countenance suspended, with the neck twisted or the hands joined . . . and other positions according to the affect of the worshiper" (371).[26] Mexican artist Miguel Cabrera's luminous "Jesus Accepts the Cross," in the Puebla Cathedral, is a particularly well-phrased example of the symbolic corporeal vocabulary suggested in Loyola and codified by Carducci. Christ, his eyes tearful and upturned, opens his hands in silent obedience as two Roman guards lead him to his death (*Arte y mística del barroco*, figure 11).[27] Arguing for Sebastiana Josefa de la Santísima Trinidad's sainthood, her biographer employs a very similar version of Ignatian corporeal rhetoric to describe his subject in accordance with the consecrated iconographical image of sanctity: "with her hands in devout gestures of adoration, with her arms, placing them in the form of the cross in his cherished presence, with her knees bent submissively, with her head, humbly inclined, with her eyes always on the ground, with all her body and soul, forming a mystic and pious ritual, forever held in her hands" (Valdés 264).[28] Saints were typically presented with their eyes raised to heaven; religious women, on the other hand, often were depicted either with their eyes directly engaging the viewer, or, when stylized, with their eyes humbly cast to the ground or in half-profile. Modeled perhaps after the *Mater Dolorosa*, this position also was a more effective means to involve the viewer, whose gaze could meet that of the portrait from below.[29] The repression of physical sight was, moreover, an admirable sign of humility, as the frequent references in Sebastiana

Josefa's biography suggest: "Eyes to the ground, hands crossed over her chest, as if she were in heaven with her thoughts and with God in her heart" (Valdés 331).[30] In contrast to the uncontrolled movements of the medieval mystic, prayer became a ritualized performance in which personal experiences were given meaning by being placed in a symbolic order with cultural, religious, and even political implications. In a less literal sense, to meet the expectations of her reader, the writing subject was also obligated to assume a posture, a pose, to transform herself into an object of art. Worship was thus integrated into the larger historical condition of constraint.

Even as artistic representations could be used to frame the body in viceregal Spanish America, they also had the capacity to liberate the mind. The eyes of the imagination were contaminated and enriched by artwork that trespassed into every corner of the convent. Constructed at the height of baroque sensibility, sensuality was played out in concrete form in the colonial church, with golden altars, velvet robed saints, and the scent of incense. Arenal and Schlau hypothesize that the non-lineal nature of women's personal narrative is related to their daily exposure to artistic expression ("Stratagems of the Strong" 35). In fact, Melchora de la Asunción (Mexico, 1585–1631) notes that the nuns in the choir were *instructed to fix their eyes on the images* so they would not look at the public assembled (Loreto 544). As mentioned in the discussion of the hagiographic model of bodily torment in chapter 3, the baroque "passion for the outlandish" noted by Maravall "developed monstrously among peoples who found their ways blocked to a rational criticism of social life" (*La cultura del barroco* 461/229), and churches were no exception. Of the Temple of Santa Clara in Bogotá, Germán Franco Salamanca comments that by the early eighteenth century paintings had come to fill every blank space on the walls not covered with wood and sometimes even there when no room remained on the walls (84).[31] Murals, altarpieces (*retablos*), and elaborate woodwork could be observed by nuns not only through the bars of the upper choir loft but in the interior of the choirs themselves. Among the more striking examples of artwork within the walls of the convent are the Churrigueresque *retablos* in the choir lofts of La Concepción in Puebla, and of Santa Clara and Santa Rosa in Querétaro, which included statues and life-size representations of Christ crucified (Maza figures 36–38, 53–58, 59–64, 86). Although usually not elaborately decorated, the lower choir and individual cells were adorned with images and small objects of veneration (Viñuales 209); many orders also allowed women to keep some small icon in their rooms. In the convent of Santa Catalina in Cuzco, each nun had a *retablo* of the infant Jesus in her cell; the convent of La Encarnación in Mexico provided each professed woman with a representation of the Nativity, sometimes flanked in triptych style with other scenes from the Bible. Teresa de Jesús, who describes herself as "very partial to images," attributes an experience with an *Ecce Homo* as essential to her religious conversion (*Libro de la vida* IX.1–3, 177–78/54) and advises her readers to carry an image of Christ with them at all times and to speak to him whenever possible (*Camino de perfección* XXVIII, 107–10). Sebastiana Josefa de la Santísima Trinidad carried an image of the infant Jesus with her at all times (Valdés 142); the imagination could be stimulated further by life-size wooden figures of the infant Jesus that could be held in the arms of the devout worshiper; many portraits of nuns show them holding such icons (Viñuales 200; Franco Salamanca 84; Petroff 6; Ruiz Gomar "Retratos" 29–40). These objects of veneration were explicitly intended to encourage spiritual meditation (Vargaslugo "La obra de arte" 122).

The centrality of Christ's body as a focus of *visual* desire in devotional literature and hagiography was translated into a self-conscious meditation of the power of images. In a chapter of the hagiography of Lutgard of Aywières (d. 1246), Lutgard conjures Christ's presence by gazing at his image until, "rapt in spirit," she ascends to suck from the bloody wound in Christ's side (Thomas de Cantimpré 22); the painting by Gaspar de Crayer (1653) explicitly alludes to the power of images as Lutgard is embraced not by Christ on the cross but by what clearly is an *image of Christ* in the Church. This intimate allegorical relation with a representation of Christ was a common theme in the *vida*. María de San José describes a similar experience in which her contemplation of a portrait of Christ is transformed into an intimate embrace. Mysteriously detained at the foot of a staircase in the convent with a painting of Christ above it, she suddenly levitates toward the image: "I saw myself rise from the ground and I was rising to the top until I reached the image of our Crucified Lord. . . . I put my lips and mouth on the wound in His side" (II.29).[32] In this reciprocal correlation between visual image and spiritual communication, the image itself becomes the object of adoration; and, in turn, it is precisely in response to visual images that corporeal rhetoric makes itself most manifest.

Gerónima del Espíritu Santo is particularly explicit regarding the use of images to activate spiritual contemplation: "I asked them to bring an image of Jesus the Nazarene to my bed. . . . They put it before my eyes . . . and I fixed my gaze on the eyes of this sovereign image that, speaking lovingly to my soul, said: '*Venite ad me omnes qui laborati et onerati estis et ego refitiam vos*' [Come to me all of you who are burdened and overwhelmed and I shall renew you]. Hearing these words, I observed the loving benevolence with which those pious and compassionate eyes seemed to speak louder than words" (Nava 62).[33] This is not the only episode in which Gerónima interacts with a visual representation. The Colombian nun's "pictorial" imagination includes a portrait of the Virgin Mary that invites Gerónima to nurse from her breast (115, 130); paintings of Christ and Saint Francis that speak to her (131, 140, 172, 187); Christ removing his arm from the cross to point Gerónima out to the Virgin Mary, entrusting her to be Gerónima's mother (143); a painting of Christ with the sacred heart transformed into a living heart (145); and the image leaving the frame, removing his crown of thorns, and placing them on her head, pointing to his wounds and instructing her to *see and read* his doctrine (155). Gerónima's visionary repertoire—likely also influenced by emblem books—synthesizes a remarkable variety of allegorical images.[34] Christ appears as a slave with his hands tied (73, 175); as a king, with her soul as his kingdom (76); as "Capitán General" [commander in chief] (77); as a head of household (79); as a peddler (85); as a hunter, with Gerónima as a bull (89–90); as an orange tree (100); as a knight (114); as a warrior (172); and as a lamb eating grass from her heart (183). In one vision Christ dresses Gerónima and braids her hair (74–75); in another, he gives her a ring and dresses her in silver; they marry with Joseph and Mary as godparents (82). Gerónima envisions herself as a tortoise, pushed by her confessor (92); as a blind woman (94); as a "little piece of land" Christ wishes to cultivate (100); as a spider trying to climb a mountain peak (115); as a basil plant cultivated by Christ and tended by her confessor (147); and as two Gerónimas: one of clay and the other of sand (148), or one as a large dry tree, representing a time when she was in the power of the devil, and the other as a small tree full of fruit, when Christ became her gardener (171).[35]

Gilles Chazal asserts that it was no longer enough to read about visionary experiences; it was also necessary to *see* (23). At the very least, the number of episodes recounted in the *vidas* in which the power of images is manifested directly from a work of art illustrates the close connection between the visionary realm and art. At the same time, it suggests that if any aspirant, through an intense act of faith, can convert the sign into embodiment, then the presence of the divine in this world is somehow made more palpable. In an episode in the life story of María de San José, the image of Mary with the infant Jesus above her bed speaks to her, asking her to draw closer. María dramatically falls to her knees, directs her hands to the picture, and weeps uncontrollably (*Word* 97–99). As Freedberg notes in relation to the worship of images of the Virgin Mary: "Perhaps the suggestion will run that one cannot believe that the Virgin is in the picture—or *is* the picture—unless one believes, to begin with, in the Virgin. Then, wanting her to be there, to exist (because of the love we bear her), we willingly concentrate on the image, and what is represented on it becomes present again. She is, quite literally, re-presented" (28).

In the biography of Lutgard of Aywières, her encounter with Christ is described in this way: "Lowering his arm which was nailed to the Cross, He embraced her . . . and pressed her mouth against the wound in His right side" (Thomas de Cantimpré 21); similarly, in an episode of the life of Bernard of Clairvaux (1090–1153) that appears in Ribadeneyra's *Flos Sanctorum,* Ribadeneyra relates: "one time weeping before a crucifix, the crucifix stretched out an arm and cast it about him, embracing him and caressing him with singular favor" (632).[36] Religious art and devotional literature became intertwined in baroque Spanish painting, which often reproduced such scenes from hagiographic literature.[37] The striking image of Christ lowering his arm was repeated insistently, most notably in Francisco Ribalta's "Christ Embracing Saint Bernard" (1620–25). Bartolomé Esteban Murillo's "Saint Francis Embracing the Crucified Christ" (1668) adopted Ribalta's image for Francis of Assisi, and in the numerous imitations commissioned by the Franciscan order, it is this saint who dominates (Knipping 459). In Murillo's painting, Christ detaches one arm from the cross to embrace the devoted saint; Ribalta's rapturous composition brings Christ's humanity closer still, as Bernard rests his head on the savior's chest. The embrace of Christ on the cross became a common motif in the visionary imagination of religious women. Sebastiana Josefa recalls: "I saw my Lord on the cross. . . . he lowered his arm and embraced my soul, which was to the side of his heart, with great assurance, and the other arm remained hanging on the cross" (303).[38] María Marcela not only imagines herself as the subject of Christ's embrace but plays with the sensual trappings and adornments she has provided: "One day . . . the Lord revealed himself to me resurrected with unspeakable beauty, adorned with jewels and flowers I had provided for him with my exercise of virtue. He also wore a crimson tunic and a blue mantel like a choir cloak; he sat at my side, covered me with the cloak, and putting his right arm around me, leaned me against his side, communicating unspeakable favors to my soul, between an ardent fire and lights brighter than the midday sun" (139).[39] Through art, this world and the next are combined as spiritualized experiences are summoned through images that are a part of the nun's everyday existence. At the same time, the power and attraction of such episodes for the writing subject are that here she is able to place herself in the center of the visual representation and in the center of her narration in an idealized mystic vision.[40] The speaking image of Christ engages the gaze of the observer, taking her on a visual tour of his tortured body until she integrates herself into the frame. As Stanbury notes, the increasing erasure of boundaries between Christ and his audience is performed through a "doubled language": Christ's speech not only invites the viewer's gaze, his body also facilitates the reader's empathetic transformation. Christ asks the viewer to perform two "turns"; the first, "a turn of the body to reveal that blood is everywhere" and the other, "a turn of his or her own empathy toward that bleeding body" (269; see also Kristeva 120).

* * *

Peter Stallybrass observes that "there can be no simple opposition between language and body because the body maps out the cultural terrain and in turn is mapped out by it" (138); Loyola's "corporeal rhetoric" was part of a wider trend in which Christian cosmology mapped the world as a human body, or as Christ's body in particular (see Mignolo 230). María Manuela envisions the mysteries of Christ illustrated "as in a map" (4), as does María Marcela (170). The female body was, however, a more ambivalent referent: as Stallybrass notes, it could represent both the "symbolic map of the 'civilized' and the dangerous terrain that had to be colonized" (133). Since chastity was framed in terms of bodily enclosure, the cloistered space of the convent was also imagined as a metonymy for female virtue. Foucault asserts that by the seventeenth century the conventional trope of the body imprisoning the spirit had been inverted so that the body was subjected to the spirit (*Discipline and Punish* 30). This reversal, as Tambling points out, "suggests that the concept of the soul reduces the body to a mere instrument or machine, territorialises it, and licenses a textualising of its movements and instincts" (85). In the Hispanic world, however, with its distinctive combination of medieval and modern world systems, body and soul remained ambiguously intertwined. Nowhere was this more evident than in religious women, since their expression of spirituality retained the stereotypical notion of woman's corporeality. The religious woman had two bodily spaces or, as Drid Williams aptly describes it, two "maps": "one which locates her in ordinary geographical space-time, and another consisting of an interior 'territory' of a spiritual and psychological nature in which she is located *at the same time*" (115, emphasis added). Williams calls this dimension "liturgical space-time," in which "above" is also "inside," and devotion to God is associated with "inner efforts towards greater self-awareness" (114–15), or, as Teresa de Jesús explains: "[T]here are many ways of 'being' in a place" (*Las moradas* I.2, 33/31).[41] As Gilmore affirms, while the body was "written" and "read" within a particular discursive network of power relations, the mystic *remapped* the body, unleashing a network of possibilities that in one way or another always return to an image of embodiment (118). Mysticism activates a radical use of the body as a vehicle for salvation. As women attempt to map out their own corporeal and discursive space, the desire to frame and confine the female body makes it the site of contestation and control.

While not questioning the authority of the priest directly, the writing subject could posit an alternate authority whereby Christ spoke through the "weaker vessel." This is particularly true when this allegory extends to encompass an alternate visionary space. In *Las moradas,* Teresa explains that the soul is like a castle, "made of a single diamond or of very clear crystal in which there are many rooms, just as in heaven there are many mansions.... if this castle is the soul, there can clearly be no question of our entering it. For *we ourselves are the castle* and it would be absurd to tell someone to enter a room when he was in it already!" (31–33/29–31).[42] The application of architectural analogies is not, of course, Teresa's invention.[43] Nevertheless, for the cloistered woman whose every movement is delimited and codified, the use of spatial correlations is particularly significant and may help explain the complex interaction between representation and imagination. Teresa used the mystic symbol of the "flight" of the soul from the prison of the body as a metaphor for removing the body from the walls of the convent. The "interior castle" of *Las moradas,* with its imagery of movement and of winged figures such as doves and butterflies, had a special importance for the cloistered woman, as Teresa notes in her epilogue: "Considering how strictly you are cloistered, my sisters, how few opportunities you have for pleasure and how your houses are not always sufficiently ample as would be fitting in some of your monasteries, I think it will be a great consolation for you to take your delight in this interior castle, for you can enter it and walk about in it at any time without asking leave of your superiors" (212/234, translation revised).[44] This interior space, like the text, although still subject to the *authority* of the confessor, was a place *power* could be negotiated. Antonopoulos suggests that this experience of the body "functions both in resistance to and in collusion with conditions of constraint" (188); it is a flight out of the body *through the body.* As Jean Franco observes, although the limitations on discourse affected both men and women, "men had authority and the freedom to occupy *public space* whereas women had not. And this, in turn, helps to explain why the *mystical journey* that took women out of their enclosure, at least in the imagination, held such attractions for them" (5).[45] This also explains why mystic space is so often expressed in contrast to the cloistered physical space of the convent.

Perhaps this was the reason Spanish-American nuns found the idea of an imaginary inner space so attractive. María Manuela de Santa Ana invents a series of "interior chapels" that include a dense profusion of pictorial and sensorial elements (164–65). Gerónima del Espíritu Santo evokes her heart as a "humble little house" where the Lord dwells: "And I saw the Lord who dwelled within it and he said, 'in this humble little house I will make my room because it has been given and devoted to me alone. . . . I do not want the rich and sumptuous palaces offered me because in them I will not be alone'" (120).[46] The space in Christ's heart is infinite: in it she can move freely; whereas the "narrow cloister" of the convent is described as a cage in which Gerónima flutters about in frustration (125). Christ's heart is her dwelling place, where he invites her to "enter these spaces and walk about" (139).[47] In her own private theater, she had the freedom to project herself as heroine of a visionary narrative.

Teresa realizes the eyes of the soul are higher but wishes she could see with the eyes of the body so her confessor would understand her (*Libro de la vida* XXVIII:4, 337/172): similarly, interior space can never escape completely from the realities of exterior space: no matter how far and high she flew, she eventually would return to the confinement of the cell and the confessional. This entrapment was also seen as an impediment to sainthood. Mary Magdalene of Pazzi uses the imagery of obstructed flight to express her frustration: "I have envy against the Birds of the air, who can fly up and down where they will, and make every body hear their sweet notes; and they can everywhere renew their delightful music, without ever resting. O thou Word, so would I be able to do; I would fly throughout the world, and make myself to be heard by everyone, that so I might imprint this love and this delight, in the hearts of thy creatures" (Puccini 189–90). In Spanish America, the continued press for evangelization of indigenous communities during the seventeenth and eighteenth centuries had resulted in the sometimes violent deaths of several priests. These exploits were widely publicized through the regular distribution of missionary reports and the publication of more comprehensive *relaciones*, histories, and biographies.[48] Unable as women to participate in missionary activity, many authors nonetheless allowed their imaginations to literally take flight in pilgrimages to other parts of the world. María Manuela envisages her spirit "flying throughout the world" (folio 10, *Vida* 18)[49] to spread the Word of Christ. María de Jesús Tomelín travels to Ethiopia, Spain, and France in her mystic raptures (Pardo 137–40); María Manuela sees herself in Guinea and China (folio 28, *Esquela* 227); Gerónima del Espíritu Santo in an unspecified

Asian land (83); and Úrsula Suárez, informed by God that he wishes for her to preach like Saint Paul (202), goes to China (219) and "Arab lands" (231). Such visions are doubly transgressive, because not only do they place the female author in a role women were not permitted to pursue; they take credit for the missionaries sent there.

* * *

Beatriz Pastor has suggested a correspondence between the utopic vision of space in the chronicles and the female visionary experience (204). In a less literal sense, the utopia of the female visionary experiences lies in the ecstatic union with Christ and its contrast to the subordination of woman in this world. In the preface to *Súbida del Monte Carmelo,* Juan de la Cruz (1500–1569) states that his purpose was to write the book for men and women who sought someone to listen to them. It is an arduous and painful trial for a soul, he writes, "when it cannot understand itself or find anyone else who understands it" (87/58).[50] Similarly, an important part of Loyola's exercises is to imagine speaking to Christ "as one friend speaks to another, or as a servant speaks to his master . . . making known his affairs to Him and seeking His advice concerning them" (*Ejercicios* 108–9/56). Reiterating the Ignatian notion of dialogue, Gerónima del Espíritu Santo describes her conversations with Christ in these terms: "as one close friend speaks to another, so [the Lord] was conversing with me and comforting my heart with the sweetest of caresses" (103).[51] Sebastiana Josefa, who spoke to no one except her confessor, finds her only consolation in her dialogues with Christ and the Virgin Mary: "I speak volumes with my God and with the Mother of my soul, with such . . . simple confidence and with such an intimacy that I can think of no comparisons to help you, Reverend Father, understand what occurs" (3).[52] This communicative impulse also reflects directly on the role of the confessor. María de San José frequently alludes to her isolation without a confessor, and that in this absence, she spoke to God with Anthony of Padua as mediator/confessor: "There at his feet, I opened my heart and unburdened myself, revealing my soul and all that occurred within it to him. Very frequently I transmitted to him my doubts and my fears. So great was the light and consolation that the Lord communicated to my soul at the feet of this glorious saint through his intercession that I found the cure and solution to all my difficulties, which were great because I had no confessor with whom I could share these things" (*Word* 128).[53]

Teresa de Jesús integrates the Ignatian image of two friends with the Song of Songs, describing her conversations with Christ as if between "two friends," observing: "Just as in this life if two persons love each other dearly, seem able to understand each other without making any signs, merely by their looks" (XXVII:10, 329/174).⁵⁴ And Francis de Sales (1567–1622) remarks: "Prayer is called mystical, because of the hidden nature of the conversation: God and the individual speak heart to heart, and what passes between them can be shared with no one else. So personal is lovers' talk, it has no meaning outside the two who engage in it. 'I lie asleep,' said the mystic bride, 'but oh, my heart is wakeful! That is because 'my true love's voice is calling me'" (219; see also Song of Solomon 5.2). This disembodied voice and the written word of exchange also associates the object of desire with the confessor. It is, after all, the confessor to whom she communicates her most intimate secrets, and it is the *dialogue* with Christ and the saints that constitutes the focal point of mystic discourse (Certeau *Heterologies* 88). In the construction of self, Christ is the ideal interlocutor, because only he gives her the answers she wants to hear; he is part of her soul and so helps her understand herself. This genuine encounter of complementary subjects is what she seeks in a confessor.

Francisca Josefa Castillo often plays precisely with the doubled mediation of the confessor as Christ. She differentiates between divine and earthly guides through the subtle manipulation of pronouns (using "vos" for the confessor and "tú" for Christ); intercalated dialogue further displaces the voice of the speaking subject: "And so the Bride who truly loves knows no other will than that of her Lord and master; and if he were to ask her 'Where do you want to go?' 'Where do you want to be?' she would only respond: 'What do I know, Lord, what do I know, take me wherever you want. I have no other homeland than you. I left my people and the house of my father behind... all I have and all I am I gave up for you'" (*Afectos* 141).⁵⁵ Because she was obligated to put her affective and corporeal experiences into writing, the author had to "convince the confessor in 'his' language" (Gilmore 109). Any attempt to represent the unrepresentable, to speak the unspeakable, would have to settle for a partial representation through language. De Certeau contends that because of this unrepresentability, mystic space is thus constituted outside the fields of knowledge (*Heterologies* 89). At the same time, as McKnight illustrates in her discussion of the *Afectos* of Francisca Josefa Castillo, it is Christ's *Word* that resonates in her expressions of mystic rapture (264–68, *Afecto* 46, 124–25). Francisca emphasizes that her experience of this knowledge and this Word is passive and, indeed, outside earthly experience: "because it seems as if this knowledge is like a word, or a secret language, not like that articulated or formed with the voice" (*Afectos* 58). The voice of the confessor could overwhelm hers, if she listened, but her voice, as one with Christ, could also seduce him. Francisca writes: "The gentle speech / Of the lover I adore / Drips milk and honey / Amidst roses and irises" (*Afectos* 124, translation McKnight 174).[56] The image of milk and honey, derives, of course, from the Song of Songs; as does the allusion to the *voice* of the beloved (2.8, 4.11). Among the exceptional characteristics of the Song of Songs is that the audience is expected to identify with the feminine, and not the masculine, voice; and that this voice responds to God on the affective level of the bride, rather than as a subordinate servant, student, or son (Astell 10, 37). As McKnight concludes: "this desire-filled interiorization of the divine word as milk and honey resonates with a eucharistic quality; Christ is the living Word of God, he is the Word made flesh. The divine and material word moves the soul to the affect of burning desire, and penetrates it with the light of God's wisdom in divine union with her beloved" (176).[57] Bernard of Clairvaux interprets the request of the bride in the Song of Songs that she be kissed "with the kiss of his mouth" (Song 1.2) as a prefiguration of Christ as the Word: "the mouth that kisses signifies the Word who assumes human nature; the nature assumed receives the kiss; the kiss however, that takes its being both from the giver and the receiver, is a person that is formed by both, none other than 'the one mediator between God and mankind, himself a man, Jesus Christ'" (II,2,iii). The kiss of his mouth is, then, a request for spiritual union based on love, as Bernard explains: "it is not for liberty that she asks, nor for an award, not for an inheritance nor even knowledge, but for a kiss," a token of love (VII,2,ii). Francis de Sales confirms, "the kiss has always been used as a symbol of perfect love—[a] union of hearts" and this is the one aim of the bride in the Song of Songs (22–23).[58]

The sixteenth and seventeenth centuries witnessed a renewed emphasis on affective prayer, in which aspirations of love toward God replaced discursive reflection (Cross and Livingstone 23). With sexuality increasingly associated with the demonic, to speak openly of an intimate union with Christ was a calculated risk; but it was a time, as Maravall observes, in which people longed for miracles, illusions, and extraordinary events (*Cultura del barroco* 462/230). Moreover, as Arenal and Schlau point out, as the brides of Christ, women's role in the Church, their relationship to sexuality and power, "moved along a different axis than religious men's" (*Untold sisters* 11). Male discourse often referred to the beloved as the Church itself; whereas women were able to interpret the Song of Songs in a more literal manner, situating themselves in the position as the "most beloved" bride.

Textually mediated by the Song of Songs, Christ appears to María Manuela de Santa Ana "as he was in the world," lying on her pillow, as was the bridegroom, "sick with love" (Song 2.5): "Suddenly, his face came to mine and he kissed me on the cheek. He remained lying there despite my fearful pleas that he leave" (folios 3, 18, *Esquelas*, 235, 255). The "fears" mentioned here symbolically represent María's anxiety of submitting to the mystic experience, but the allegory of erotic submission remains: Christ is a man and he is in her bed. Fear is also mentioned by María Marcela, although Christ gently calms her soul: "The Lord kissed me with the kiss of his mouth and the soul, trembling with fear . . . tried to enter the wound in his side to hide, until the Lord realized what she was trying to do and laughed to see her so frightened" (139–40).[59] Desire for the kiss of his mouth, then, represents a desire for direct union, unmediated by theological meditations. If, in fact, discourse and sexual pleasure may be affiliated, as French feminists Luce Irigaray and Hélène Cixous suggest, then the linear "phallic" discourse of the devil and the multiple centers of "female" eroticism in encounters with Christ, paralleled in a narration that denies temporal and spatial coordinates, imply an alternative narrative of desire in women's writings that escapes the demands of the reader/confessor. The bride and her beloved look at each other in a relation of absolute reciprocity: an expression of mutual desire. The one-way male gaze on earth is superseded: Christ loves only his equal.

The eroticized language of mystical union glorifies the human heart, a physical and spiritual dwelling place where "love . . . binds everything together in perfect harmony" and the peace of Christ rules (*Colossians* 3.15). One of the key images of this ethics of love was the devotion to the physical heart of Jesus. The sacred heart, and particularly the exchange of hearts, had long been favored by mystics and those who sought an ascetic path, and was one of the most cultivated symbols in seventeenth-century emblem books (Praz 151–56; Knipping 98).[60] As a symbol of mutual love, the exchange of hearts appears both in Mary Magdalene of Pazzi and Catherine of Siena, and it is a favored symbol of Teresa de Jesús, particularly in the *Camino de perfección* (see, for example: 271, 275, 282, 307). Its most prominent feature was reparation for affronts committed against divine love (Cross and Livingstone 1437); for women writers, it also had a discursive significance as representative of the authority of direct experience of God in contrast to abstract theological treatises.[61]

The altar of the holy family in the Templo de Santa Clara in Bogotá, where Gerónima del Espíritu Santo was cloistered, depicts Christ with an illuminated heart which he holds forth in his hands (Franco Salamanca 89, figure 31). The sacred heart is the single most important image in Gerónima's narration, and, ultimately, a source of uncommon discursive authority. In one episode Christ is unable to enter her heart with the cross, and he enters alone, leaving the cross outside; she begs him to put the cross in her heart, but he only shows it to her. Finally she convinces him to share his cross with her, and in an act of love, he inserts it himself (64). Like Lutgard, Catherine of Siena, and Mary Magdalene of Pazzi before her, Gerónima literally exchanges hearts with Christ in a series of visions: Christ removes hers from his chest and replaces it with his own (65); Christ removes her heart and finds written on it the last words of Saint Francis Xavier: "Oh my beloved Lord God!"; Christ removes her heart and shows it to her, revealing his presence there. In a variation on the often-cited episode in Teresa's life in which she tells Christ that she is "Teresa de Jesús," to which he replies that he is "Jesús de Teresa," Christ confirms: "Gerónima is my heart and I am the heart of Gerónima"; Christ gives her a piece of his heart (87); the infant Jesus enters her heart and makes her a little cross (89); Christ knocks on her heart as a door, and she lets him in (138); Christ constructs invisible bars around her heart so no one else may enter (117).[62] Gerónima envisions Christ with a tablet on which the ten precepts of the Decalogue are written: the first, that we love, was written in gold and the remainder in ink (81).[63]

It was a common belief that "while on the cross, Christ surrendered to absolute love as well as to absolute pain" (Petroff 11); love is also an essential part of Pauline doctrine (1 Corinthians 13–14). As the empowering discourse of corporeal pain is transmuted into a suffering of the soul, the author is free to express herself in the language of longing and of desire. Sebastiana Josefa de la Santísima Trinidad feels as if the love of Christ "releases the deepest recesses of my soul with a gentle sweetness . . . that consumes and overwhelms me and my heart, throbbing painfully, no longer fits in my body and my breath is taken away with such loving longing that life itself ends in this suffering, so inflamed are the desires to please my soul's beloved" (1).[64] María Marcela, after taking communion "felt as if an arrow had stopped my heart, causing a pain so fervent that it forced me to moan and this was heard in the chorus loft. . . . I was left with such violent longings to love God that the fire that continually burned within me and the flame that endlessly blazed proved insufficient" (145–46).[65] Francisca Josefa recounts: "throwing his arms around my shoulders he set upon me a weight, though so immense, so sweet, so gentle, so strong, so tranquil, that my soul wished only to die and deliver myself to him and with him, but it could only receive and consume itself" (65).[66] Violence and suffering is projected upon the figure of *Christus patiens* or upon his attributes: blood, the sacred heart, and the Passion. In the image of the wounded heart, love and pain are combined, as Francis de Sales notes: "When a man realizes that love for him wounds the heart of God, he immediately receives a mutual wound in his own heart.... Can we not think of our Savior wounded by a love for us 'which brought him to death, death on a cross' and not be wounded for his sake?" (257, see also Philippians 2.8).[67] By emphasizing the love of Christ, these authors displaced the symbol of the cross while focusing on a part of Christ's teachings they could practice with complete happiness. This passionate discourse of desire and domination may be constructed for the male reader, but clearly the woman has embraced it as her own. As de Certeau affirms, to engage in mystic speech involves a *willing subject:* the mystic must actively seek such an experience (*Mystic Fable* 166). Gerónima del Espíritu Santo describes the presence of Christ as a process *she controls:* "I tried to remember"; "I surrendered myself more; I strived to submit more"; "I felt an interior impulse calling me and I went"; "my heart remained imprisoned there because that is what I sought" (62, 65, 104).[68] Jessica Benjamin has suggested that "the impulses to erotic violence and submission express deep yearnings for selfhood and transcendence" (281). If the ecstatic surrender of the body to Christ parallels the resignation of her body and will within the walls of the convent, then agency is asserted as the female subject rewrites her subordination as something she has actively chosen.

* * *

Teresa de Jesús asserts that words composed by the intellect have no effect: Christ speaks both words and works (*Libro de su vida* XXV.3, 310/157). And Thomas à Kempis maintains that "it is not learning that makes a man holy and just, but a virtuous life makes him pleasing to God.... what would it profit us to know the whole Bible by heart and the principles of all the philosophers if we live without grace and the love of God?" (2).[69] The assertion of the affective realm over the intellect was not a particularly radical position since the idea that knowledge breeds conceit was deeply rooted in the Christian tradition (1 Corinthians VIII.1). At the same time, the direct experience of God afforded in visionary encounters was an important means of defending the act of writing, since the claim was made that women were not actually "authors" of the text: God was writing through them. By crediting God as the producer of the text that follows, the writer hopes to prove that at worst she could be accused of an inadequate transcription; doubts about demonic interference are, for the moment, suspended. Francisca Josefa Castillo explains the messages she received as "a light that was imprinted upon my heart" (130); and Christ instructs María de San José: "Write everything as it happened, without omitting or adding a single letter, not even a tilde more or less, of the pure and simple truth" (*Word* 151). María Marcela appeals to the visionary realm not only to communicate through her but to help her translate what she has seen into language: "I spent three days struggling . . . and on the fourth my mind was illuminated, my will was inflamed, and as in a map, the Lord revealed all the mysteries and teachings that he has shown me and that are written. . . . This revelation served me in two ways: first to console me and protect me from the fear that I am wasting time, the other to allow me to write" (170).[70]

The language of mysticism is expressed through the space of the body, and this space asserts its own alternative authority. In the same way that representation reflects and reinforces ideological differences, the symbolic use of space may be interpreted, as Henrietta Moore asserts, as the meaningful construction of a representation (90); in other words, the spatial domain also produces an ideological discourse of personal realization and access to power. If human activity can be read as a text and interpreted as a process, "action, like texts . . . possesses an internal structure as well as an ability to project an interpretation of being in the world" (80). Precisely because the mystic space is textualized, visionary power puts discursive hierarchy into question. As de Certeau comments, the place from which the mystic author speaks is legitimized neither by discursive authority and canonized texts nor by the position of the speaker within institutional hierarchy. Its authority derives exclusively from "being produced in the very place in which the Speaker, the Spirit, *el que habla,* speaks. It is authorized solely by being the locus of that 'inspired' speech act, also designated by the term 'experience'" (*Mystic Fable* 178).

Visionary authority could be used not only to defend the act of writing, but, in some cases, to assert authority in more worldly matters. Gerónima del Espíritu Santo and Úrsula Suárez invoke the support of Christ to consolidate their positions in convent administration, positing themselves as the only ones who love him sufficiently to assume such authority. Gerónima comments: "an image was induced in me that told me that if I was the Mother Superior, so, too, would be the Lord God" (111, 152, 165); while Úrsula alleges that Christ had promised "I will favor your convent if you accept its governance" (239). When the words of the Gospel are mysteriously reproduced by Úrsula, God affords her a most unusual privilege: "'I put the words of Saint Paul in you because I want you to preach as he did'" (202).[71] Although she continues to state her unworthiness of such a gift, and does not report the response God gives her, Úrsula takes the extraordinarily daring step of opening a door in the convent so she may instruct a group of

African workers in Christian doctrine (231–32). Gerónima also contests official Church doctrine by instructing on matters of faith, confidently asserting God's approval: "I had clear knowledge that God was pleased that I instructed ignorant people, because there were many souls lost for lack of light and so I tried and did enlighten some people by instructing them.... And I am certain that many souls would have been lost had they not come to communicate their faults to me" (71).[72] In one passage Gerónima affirms she has no doubt that her visions are divinely inspired; in the episode following she admits to some doubt but is vacillating between divine works and her imagination: the question of demonic deception never arises (55–56).[73]

Teresa de Jesús boldly asserts the authority of Christ over both her confessor and "those whom we call lords on earth, all of whose power rests upon a [false] authority conferred on them by others" (XXXVII:5, 437–38/263).[74] More impertinent still, María Manuela de Santa Ana often uses her visionary primacy to make requests to authorities in this world. In a conversation with the Three Kings, she asks them to try to convince the pope and the king of Spain to officially recognize the Immaculate Conception and the cult to Joaquim and Anne, her patron saint. She argues for the validity of her visions, concluding: "May the Lord be served and may it be for His greater Glory that *I alone have been chosen*" (folio 3, *Esquelas*, 234–35, emphasis added). In another section, María Manuela declares that God, Mary, and Jesus "urge me to proclaim that [the mercies] conceded and given me are innumerable and *greater than those given to many Saints,* because He wishes . . . that I again declare that His mercies and gifts are innumerable." Fearing accusations of excessive pride, she immediately follows this statement by deferring to the confessor's authority: "I have always told you all I can recall. You will know what to do. I want nothing more than the glory of God . . . and to remain hidden" (folio 11, *Vida* 188).[75] Nonetheless, by asserting the divine will to "publish" her gifts from God, more plentiful than those of "many" canonized saints, María Manuela clearly insinuates that she hopes her confessor will share her writings, even as she reiterates her wish to remain concealed.

There is a similar disparity between the modest self-representation that María Manuela presents in her *vida* with the substantial legal and political acumen of her professional correspondence. Although it is likely that the language María Manuela uses in official documents was standardized (and indeed it is notably more refined in terms of orthography), it is clear that she was actively involved in the management of her properties. When financial and administrative matters are discussed in her autobiographical account, however, María Manuela diverts attention from her role by situating herself as the mediator for God's will. In an episode in which Christ asks her to build a golden altar that would cost 60,000 pesos, she downplays her role in raising funds, contending she was able to secure the money "with no more maneuvering nor intercession than a few little papers written by this paltry little ant with no education nor social contact beyond that inspired by the Lord God." She further absolves herself from worldly matters, insisting that divine intervention is responsible for all the convent's successful fund-raising: "It seems to me that I can say that not even half the money spent was collected, but rather that it multiplied from that acquired by the Lord God" (folio 3, *Vida* 166).[76] María Manuela goes on to take the extraordinary liberty of abandoning the cloister to solicit funds from wealthy benefactors, including the viceroy himself, a particularly notable transgression since she belonged to the Discalced Carmelites, a reformed order. To justify her aberration, María Manuela alleges that she was acting only as the mediator for God's will, and that he instructs her, moreover, to criticize the government for its lack of economic support: "In the desire and light that Our Lord gave me to enter the house of the Countess Del Portillo, the Lord God stood . . . at my side and put before me Viceroy [José Antonio] Manso, who governed then. The Lord told me to tell the Viceroy . . . to use a year of his revenues to build a house for His brides with a wall around it. And that in return he would free him from a great hardship. . . . And the Lord would have freed [the Viceroy] from the difficulties he suffered in Havana if he had done this task for him" (folio 7, *Vida* 176).[77]

Gerónima del Espíritu Santo's discourse also borders dangerously on arrogance as she asserts authority in unusually self-assured interchanges with Christ. In one episode, seizing Christ's heart, she refuses to return it to him: "The Lord looked at me and said 'Gerónima, give me my heart.' 'What do you mean, give you your heart,' I replied, 'I will not release it.' Turning to me with unspeakable love he said, 'Gerónima, give me my heart,' and I held it closer still to my chest. . . . He insisted again: 'Gerónima, give me my heart.'. . . I did not want to, and I got my way. Seeing that I did not want to return his heart, he said, 'Keep it and you will practice what I practiced'" (104). In a later vision, this subversion of conventional roles (and codified physical positions) is more remarkable still, as Christ falls to the ground in front of Gerónima, declaring, "'What do you want of me? Here you have me, prisoner of your love'" (135); and in another occasion, putting *his* mouth to *her* heart: "you are my mother, nourish me with your heart" (136).[78]

Although, as Pascal notes, the "truth" of spiritual autobiography may be the truth of belief rather than of experience (61), the account of visionary experience takes truth one step further by transforming the confession of sin into a confirmation of faith. In baroque representations the imaginative journey could be conceived as just as real and more than what was perceived as reality; as Maravall notes: "the baroque placed little trust in strictly intellectual arguments. . . . It preferred to appeal to extrarational means that moved the will" (*La cultura del barroco* 458/228). On the other hand, as Arenal and Schlau indicate, to see mysticism in opposition to intellectual activity "obscures the richness of women's thinking in this period" (*Untold Sisters* 218): although authors may not have had access to theological treatises in Latin, their creative merging of images from sermons, liturgy, devotional works, and religious iconography does not represent so much an antithesis to intellectual activity as an alternative. The vocabulary these women used was from their devotional books and the Bible; thus it was not only an imaginative synthesis but an intellectual one. It was precisely through this process that women were able to assert their voices and sometimes even wrest interpretative authority from their confessors.

Because women were defined primarily in terms of their bodies, the appropriation of corporeal rhetoric and a theatricalized sign system allowed them to manipulate the patriarchal perspective with which they were expected to identify. On the one hand, by admitting female subjectivity through the subordination of the body, authors trespass into a dangerous territory of complicity that perpetuates a rigid codification of social attitudes. On the other hand, once they gained access to speech and discourse through the frame of male desire, they could then put a game of mutual seduction into play, through which they could manipulate his vision and his language to their advantage. Although mystic discourses may not always have challenged the orthodoxy of Church teachings, their discourse had the potential to subvert divisions of gender and class hierarchy as well as the gender-inflected dichotomization of body and soul. As Jean Franco affirms, in the visionary realm, women could transcend the original demand of the confessor—confession as recuperative discourse—to become active agents in the "feminine equivalent of the heroic journey of transformation" (16).

6

The Unimprisoned Mind

Úrsula Suárez and the Self-Fashioning Heroine

> Ya de tu imperio callaré forzada.
> Lope de Vega, "La vengadora de las mujeres"

Sor Úrsula Suárez y Escobar (1666–1749) was born in Santiago, Chile, to a family whose fortune was in decline. Her mother's progenitors had descended from the earliest conquistadors of Chile, while her father's ancestors were Spanish functionaries and merchants. Úrsula's entrance into the convent was ensured by a *capellanía* [chantry] from her father's great-uncle, Alonso del Campo, who, like many wealthy merchants, sought to legitimize his family's social standing through a generous donation to the Church. In his will, del Campo directed his inheritance to the construction of a Clarissan convent in Santiago that would cover the expenses of twenty black-veiled and ten lay nuns without dowries. In exchange, as was customary, his relatives were given priority; in 1678 alone, eight members of Úrsula's family were admitted to the newly constructed convent.[1] Úrsula rapidly rose within the religious community to assume important administrative positions. Upon taking her vows in 1684 she was immediately admitted to the inner council and appointed *escucha*; a year later, *portera*; and in 1687, she was made *definidora* [secretary] to the abbess.[2] She became vicaress in 1710 and abbess in 1721, despite controversial defeats in the 1710 and 1715 elections.

The original title of Úrsula's life story, *Relación de las singulares misericordias que ha usado el Señor con una religiosa . . . mandada escribir por su confesor y padre espiritual* [Account of the singular mercies the Lord has used with a religious woman . . . ordered to write by her confessor and spiritual father], was revised when the text was reprinted in 1984 as *Relación autobiográfica*. The manuscript remains in the archives of the Clarissan convent in which Úrsula lived. A second copy of the narration, now in the Chilean National Archive, was made in the mid-nineteenth century by order of José Ignacio Víctor Eyzaguirre. María Inés Lagos discovered a third copy of the autobiography, made in 1914 (353). As was often the case, the version that survived was not the first, and the narration was directed to more than one confessor.[3] How many versions preceded this final copy is not clear. As Mario Ferreccio Podestá suggests, the existent manuscript was composed over a long period—from at least 1708 to 1730—however, Úrsula does not discuss her life in detail after 1715 (14, 16). This suggests that there could have been one or more intermediary texts, likely written sometime between 1708 and 1715, and that the final version, which notes the death in 1729 of Tomás Gamboa, her addressee for most of the text, revised the earlier version with limited additions.[4] In fact, given the unusually "literary" development of the text, it seems likely that Úrsula may have gone through various drafts, at least of her secular life, a hypothesis that Ferreccio Podestá and Armando de Ramón both support (19–20, 36–37).

* * *

Although she credits the spiritual writings of María de la Antigua and Marina Escobar as her primary literary models, Úrsula's textual self bears little similarity to the hagiographic paradigm (208, 230).[5] She insists, in fact, that she is ignorant of devotional readings, confessing not only that she has enjoyed prohibited literature, but that she read the lives of the saints primarily for pleasure and not for moral edification: "I have never even read an entire book," she protests, "but only a few pages of those I did. . . . when I would take up a book it would be for entertainment and not to make good use of it, and I looked for books with histories and stories, novels and comedies. . . . I also read . . . some Scripture and the lives of saints [but] if they were not tragic, I left them" (148–49).[6] Though Úrsula does not posit a penitential life from early childhood, she does incorporate cursory references to certain expected elements of hagiographic narrative such as divine intervention through the resolution of a series of childhood illnesses (92–93), her position as the "best-loved" daughter of her father (93), childhood vanity (94), and familial opposition to her entrance into the convent (118–19, 138). An initial horror of confinement (140–42), prophecies (146–48, 152–53), illnesses, and penitence (143–44) are further elements from the hagiographic paradigm. Nonetheless, the first manifestation of her future vocation, in which she makes the sound of church bells as a small child, takes place in the unlikely setting of the bathtub; and, rather than focusing on the tortured or fragmented body of a future penitent, little Úrsula takes center stage, naked and standing up for the entire household to see, as she noisily moves her body back and forth in the motion of a bell (92). Indeed, as Úrsula herself admits, she does not conform well to the penitential model of sainthood, with its harsh prescription of self-discipline: "Since I do not engage in nonsense like eating foolishly nor in many penances, they used to say to me, 'How then will you become a saint?'" (246); and, although she expresses a desire for the cloistered life as a child, it is with unmitigated pride that she tells her skeptical aunt that she will be "the crowning glory of my generation" (92).[7] Úrsula in fact radically inverts the hagiographic paradigm of having "acquired virtue with the mother's milk," when she blames her "perversity" on a series of wet nurses—ten in all—who were likely black or mulatto (the nurse she blames for her unruly character is explicitly identified as a slave) (91).[8] This admission, as well as her marginalized position in the house (raised by her grandmother, she foresees becoming the "dog of the house" after her death) further sets the stage for Úrsula's use of comedic elements to narrate her life story.

Myers suggests that Úrsula's conflictive relationship with her mother is cast according to the conventionalized positions of master and servant in picaresque narrative ("Miraba las cosas" 160).[9] Flourishing during a period in which religious and juridical discourse had merged under the Inquisitorial confession, picaresque narratives and the spiritual autobiography share, as Edward Friedman notes, "a point of origin in the spiritual confession, which gives them a formal model to emulate and an ethical course from which to diverge" (124). Simultaneously directed to a single addressee and a multiple reading public, picaresque narrations, like the *vida*, skillfully negotiate subversive social messages through strategic plays of language and the artifice of a marginalized self who spoke not in the terms of the educated hierarchy but in popular language.[10] Notably, there are several examples of female rogues (*pícaras*), who resort to masks, disguise, and denial of identity to expose the masquerade of male authority and inherited wealth.[11]

Combining the picaresque image of the tyrannical mistress (or evil stepmother?) with the hagiographic leitmotif of familial opposition, Úrsula masterfully recreates her mother's physical and verbal threats through dialogue and apostrophe. When twelve-year-old Úrsula expresses her desire to become a nun, her mother threatens her verbally and physically: "so furious that her eyes, mouth and nostrils dilated like a lioness, and speaking to me with harsh words . . . she grabbed the silver salt-shaker, threatening to cut my face to pieces with it" (118–19).[12] Maravall writes of a lack of love in the picaresque narration, a reality sadly echoed by Úrsula as she attempts to rationalize her mother's abuses (*Literatura picaresca* 95, 101). Much older, she has a dream in which God consoles her by reminding her that it was by his design that she was distanced from her parents and that she was born with those "longings to understand" that had so frustrated her confessors (228). Úrsula thus absolves herself from responsibility for her indomitable character, since this is how God had wished her to be.

While Maravall correctly points out the irony that strong women appear in literature at a time when women's rights in Hispanic society had actually been circumscribed and misogyny reasserted (*Literatura picaresca* 652, 658), Úrsula's strong-willed mother is just one example of commanding female characters that dominate the narrative. In addition to her mother, Úrsula is influenced by her paternal grandmother, who exercises economic control over the household; an aunt who teaches her to read; and a supporting cast of female servants and slaves, who, along with the nuns in the convent, all overshadow the almost negligible presence of Úrsula's father, who soon is erased completely following an apparent stroke that leaves him physically and mentally incapacitated.[13] Although, as Anne Cruz points out, "literary constructions of women have little to do with reality and *everything to do with ideology*" (203, emphasis added), Úrsula's dominant female characters and silenced, feminized father remind her readers that male and female roles do not always divide as neatly as conventional gender codes would have it.

Women's place in colonial society is perhaps summed up in an incident from Úrsula's childhood in which, in search of "una varilla de virtud" [a magic wand], she narrates repeated visits to a house of prostitution where she witnesses couples engaged in "such shameless acts that it was scandalous" (108).[14] When the discovery is reported to her mother, Úrsula is severely reprimanded, but this does not stop her visits since, she recounts, she believed her error had not been watching the couples but talking about it. She explains, moreover, that she did not realize the women were prostitutes, believing she was witnessing weddings. As Ramón notes, it was a typical social custom at the time to include the marriage bed in wedding festivities and that occasionally the guests remained in the room after the newlyweds had retired for the evening, separated from them only by a curtain (76).[15] At the same time, for Úrsula, marriage in her mother's terms is not so removed from prostitution, since it implies to her the selling of the woman's body. And, effectively, it is neither reluctance to submit to male dominance nor fear of childbirth but dread of the corporeal commodification of her body in marriage that most horrifies the young Úrsula: "that I must allow them to bed me with a man? I would rather hang myself, slit my throat with a dagger, or run a knife through my chest (123–24)."[16] At a wedding, Úrsula differentiates between "the other unmarried girls" and the bride as an object of exchange, "a separate thing," sold by her parents to the highest bidder: "And I had great pity for her ... and saw her with the same extreme [grief] with which we view the dead who are separated from us" (126).[17] In Úrsula's view, marriage is a death sentence for women, who are converted into objects of exchange by their parents.

According to Úrsula, as a small child she overhears a tale that leads her to despise men and vow to dedicate her life to avenging their betrayals of women: "They related some case of a woman who had been deceived by a man and they were enumerating all those women men had deceived. And I, attentive to this, took an abhorrence to all men and, with that, the desire to avenge women by deceiving them. And I longed to vindicate all women.... I vowed not to miss a single opportunity to use my talent on as many men as I could, and this with great decency as if I were doing God a great service" (113–14).[18] Punishing men for their indiscretions with women would seem to be an unusual calling for a future nun; yet Úrsula's speeches conform to the baroque literary figures of the *mujer esquiva* [disdainful woman] and the *mujer varonil* [masculine woman].[19] Averse to marriage and, usually, to men in general, the *mujer esquiva* was, as Melveena McKendrick affirms, the most popular as well as the most important manifestation of the *mujer varonil* (142). Significantly, although comedies had their own version of the *pícaro* [rogue] in the figure of the *gracioso* [comic fool] or the *criado* [servant], in theater, humor was not limited to these marginal figures; main characters often participated in the comic action and deceptions (Arellano 108).[20] The *mujer varonil*, moreover, represented not only a more attractive model for the upper-class cloistered woman than the sharp-tongued, streetwise *pícara*, but, as was discussed in chapter 4, it was the same term conventionally applied to saintly women. A reading of some of the plays in which this figure appears makes immediately clear to what extent Úrsula's speeches had to be influenced by works from this genre. In Lope de Vega's "Los milagros del desprecio" [Miracles worked by scorn] (1603), Juana declares: "Universal vengeance / to his broken promises / and frustrated hopes / I declare, with deadly rigor" (I.IV, 1032); and in "La vengadora de las mujeres" [The avenger of women], Laura proclaims: "I have only wanted / to satisfy my desire: to abhor men ... / I want to avenge, if I can / offenses from here on / toward women, since I am one" (I.1, 1571–72).[21]

* * *

When Francisca Josefa Castillo asks her confessor if it is a sin to read *comedias*, he replies that although it is not sinful, "many people would not be in hell if it were not for comedies" (7).[22] And indeed, as Irving Leonard demonstrates in his study of reading and readers in the colonies, all efforts by the clergy, the moralists, and even the Spanish monarchy to discourage secular reading proved ineffectual in the face of the enormous popularity of lighter forms of fiction. Contrary to popular belief, inventories of books confiscated by the Inquisition in Spanish America demonstrate not only that prohibited literature was widely distributed in the colonies but that this was a deliberate policy of the Casa de Contratación in Seville and other European distributors, more interested in making a profit than in complying with the Church (Leonard *Baroque Times* 93–97; *Books of the Brave* 78).[23] In fact, Leonard speculates, Spanish authorities could well have encouraged the reading of popular literature written in Castilian Spanish as a means of controlling their colonies through linguistic domination and the restriction of regional variations (*Books of the Brave* 105, 329).

By the beginning of the seventeenth century comedies had supplanted prose narratives as the preferred form of entertainment for readers, and it is comedies for which Spanish-American nuns most often confess a weakness.[24] The reasons were often practical: comedies, printed in unbound loose copies, were easier to read, more accessible, and more affordable than most novels (*Books of the Brave* 287, 325).[25] Theater was so popular that plays were even produced within convent walls, to the great consternation of authorities; Guernica confirms that musical and artistic festivals were frequently organized by the nuns in Úrsula's convent (95), and religious comedies (*comedias devotas, comedias bíblicas,* and *comedias de santos*) were produced by the scores (McKnight 88; Morrison 33).[26] With images, manners, and habits of speech from these *libros de comedia* infiltrating popular culture, it is of little surprise that comedies were mentioned in religious women's life stories, particularly since theatrical strategies had long been widely used in spiritual autobiographies, especially in mystic dialogues with Christ. As Petroff suggests, the use of dialogue in mystic texts not only points to the orality of this type of discourse but is a means of self-definition and can provide justification for a woman to write (25–26).

Marginalized from public discourse, women had to find ways to create and convert their textual selves to consolidate their power within the convent and ensure themselves a place in literary history. The laughter provoked by the comic character has a specifically subversive function that can, as Bakhtin affirms, demolish "fear and piety before an object, before a world, making of it an object of familiar contact" (*Dialogic Imagination* 23). Even the usually somber Sebastiana Josefa de la Santísima Trinidad employs humor when, in a struggle with the devil, she grabs his nose and refuses to let go until he cowers away, noseless (290–91). María de San José laughs at the devil's ugliness, commenting that laughter could be "the best tactic in the battles one has with demons" (III.66).[27] Judy Little underlines the subversive power of humor to expose the discourse of power and control and its implied worldview (31). Simultaneously obeying and subverting the confessor's request for an account of her sins, Úrsula uses alternative first-person genres to defend herself rather than adhering to a model in which she would only admit to her guilt.[28] Appropriating elements from the theater, the picaresque novel, and popular oral traditions, Úrsula Suárez, who envisions herself as a "preposterous" but "very happy" saint and is designated by Christ himself as his "holy comedienne" (231, 245–46),[29] chooses to reject being typecast in the hagiographic model in favor of a positive vision of a woman conscious of the liberating potential of laughter.

* * *

Humor and the theatrical device of disguise are underscored the first time Úrsula puts her newfound knowledge to work, costuming herself with makeup and veils so potential suitors will not realize she is a child. Seated at a window, she immediately attracts a passing gentleman from whom she is able to extract a silver coin before loudly rejecting him ("I have tricked you, you fool, what an idiot you are to have let yourself be deceived by me") and slamming the window shut. Supposedly, the caller returns later to the house and Úrsula is revealed; the humiliated suitor attempts to absolve himself, refusing to believe he could have been duped by a mere child ("this girl must either be very holy or very evil").[30] For her part, Úrsula laughs with her aunt, imagining how he had been up all night thinking of her (114–15). Although no longer physically above him (as she was in the window), she has exposed the superficiality of male desire by making him the target of her practical joke. While this incident may be dismissed as a childish prank, it is repeated after Úrsula takes her vows and has been in the convent for six years. Already a professed nun and ostensibly responsible for the supervision of the receiving room, she leads a suitor on for over a month of almost daily visits until he asks her to marry him (159–60). In another episode, she engages in a popular Golden Age comedic device of transvestism when she dresses a male slave as a nun and amuses herself as he flirts with *devotos* (161).[31] Úrsula, in turn, takes on a male role when she takes confession from other nuns and repeats their stories, to her confessor's great amusement (188–89).

Úrsula's games become increasingly daring as the narrative proceeds. She seduces a married man into purchasing a house for her on the pretext that she is tricking him into providing his neglected wife with a new home. This was, however, hardly an insignificant prank, as she claims, since the relationship lasted, by her account, for five or six years. She promises another married man that she will leave the convent to elope with him and berates his simplemindedness for believing her. Repeating the topos that Sor Juana Inés de la Cruz made famous in "Hombres necios," Úrsula comments: "It was his foolishness to believe me, when he said I seemed thoroughly perverse, that I looked as if I could deceive the Devil himself, they said it themselves, and so on them it fell; so that now I think for women the devils are those deceived" (185–87).[32]

Glossing over some details and omitting others ("so as not to tire you"; "the story was long, let us get to the point"; "I do not want to relate such a long story"; "I leave [unsaid] this and other such nonsense that has occurred because it would be a waste of time to write so much" (159, 160, 175, 182), Úrsula justifies her friendships with men to Christ on the basis that he is her one true love, but gives little indication of remorse for her games. "My Lord . . . do you not know that I do not love them, that I am deceiving them and that you alone are my master and my beloved? . . . I do this for self-interest alone, and not for love" (176).[33] When she goes to confess her sins, however, she does not do so to her regular confessor, and for reasons not entirely clear she interprets his invitation to change confessors as a desire to seduce her (184). Úrsula's reaction in retrospect, that she had mistakenly offered her body to someone who had asked for her soul, is a telling commentary of the sublimated erotic impulses beneath the system of *devociones*.[34] Although she excuses herself by alleging she only leads men on to punish them and that she engages in these relationships out of economic necessity—of one *devoto* she affirms "thanks to him I am dressed and fed" (178)[35]—the gifts received clearly provide her with luxuries that go beyond daily necessity. Her favored visitors included a wealthy merchant who dressed her lavishly: "he dressed me from head to toe, and not just in any which way, but with materials he ordered for me from Lima, and not satisfied with what was in his store, he insisted that my dress be of the finest quality, with silver platformed shoes."[36] He pays for her food; provides her with coveted indulgences such as powders, tobacco, and maté; brings gifts almost daily; and even renovates her cell, adding a kitchen and pantry (179). Moreover, it is with genuine affection that she breaks off her friendship with this economic benefactor and sincere sorrow when she recalls him after his death (215, 246).

In her study of Teresa de Jesús, Weber has shown how what readers have described as "irrepressible feminine 'charm' or 'coquetry'" might be better understood as covert strategies of empowerment" (*Teresa of Ávila* 15); indeed, for Úrsula the right to engage her wit and ingenuity in *devociones* is closely associated with the freedom of expression. To God she pleads: "God, grant me permission to enjoy such foolishness in retribution for all the shameless affronts that men do to deceive women: let me avenge them, in the name of those they have deceived I want to deceive them." Framing her activities as harmless pranks, she writes: "And although with those men that I have mentioned I committed lies and mischief, do not take it to be a serious offense, because I did not understand what I was saying any more than would a child repeating senseless prattle" (190).[37] By insisting on the inconsequential nature of her activities, Úrsula downplays the seriousness of her transgressions while at the same time unleashing subversively aggressive laughter at the expense of her male targets. Other infractions are similarly dismissed. Citing her success in converting a group of African workers she has instructed, Úrsula's laughter defuses not only the original offense but also her report of the incident. She recounts, with barely concealed pride: "I laughed at their foolishness in saying they had not been able to learn from the Fathers but from me" (232).[38]

Following Henri Bergson's notion of laughter as a social phenomenon, Maravall suggests that laughter may also be a factor of social *integration* and that this is the novelty of Lope de Vega's *gracioso*: "Unlike the fool and the rustic, at whom everyone else laughs without his realizing, the *gracioso* is aware of his skills as a wit, and of his position, the others laugh and he with them" ("Relaciones de dependencia" 24). Laughter, when shared, is also a medium of communication that, unlike the confessional mode, does not depend on the subservience of one person to another.[39] The laughter Úrsula shares with her sisters (245–46), her wealthy suitor (180), her confessors (188–89, 229, 231, 245, 251), and even the bishop (243–44) has a liberating quality that breaks down hierarchical power relations. She even charms Christ with her humor instead of employing the saintly rhetoric of tears, excusing herself by reminding him that she is only playing with language, which should not be considered a grave sin: "If a married man and noble lord trusted his wife entirely and knew that even when he was not at home, that she would not dishonor him, that she was only talkative and mischievous," she reasons in one of many discussions on the subject, ". . . he would not be offended that she played tricks or made jokes of which she would inform him herself; in fact, it seems to me that he would commend her" (190–91). "Women," she concludes, "have only words with which to defend ourselves" (195–96)[40]; and it is language that Úrsula manipulates most skillfully. Through colloquialisms, cliches, colorful expressions, deliberately ambiguous pronominal references, and sometimes even barely defused bragging, Úrsula's hybrid discourse allows her to create a narrative self that transgresses boundaries of gender and social hierarchy. Like the *gracioso*, who despite his lower social position often voices truths not evident—or, sometimes, inadmissible—to those above, Úrsula is equally assertive in her relationship with Christ, questioning his judgment even on such controversial subjects as the Inquisition (252). Úrsula goes so far as to hypothetically put herself in God's place to complain of his inefficiency in converting the "unenlightened": "Ay! If I were God for half an hour . . . I would create new worlds with creatures able to love you. . . . and if I would do this for you in just a half-hour as God, what could you, who are really [God] not do?" (205–6).[41]

Like the *mujer esquiva*, Úrsula glories in her power over men and her untouchability. She describes her satisfaction when, denied her hand, a respectable and elderly suitor kneels before her and kisses her sleeve (180); and can barely contain her laughter as another admirer weeps brokenheartedly at her feet (186).[42] At one point she has three devotees, and she delights in playing off their jealousies and firing their fantasies. Juggling various men turns into an entanglement worthy of the best comedy of errors (174–75), and she dedicates many more pages to these transgressions than to her divine dialogues with God (with whom she shares a similarly unconventional relationship). Úrsula confronts men by actively appropriating the voyeuristic gaze for herself, as when she spies at length from the chorus loft at a suitor whom she finds "handsome and gallant" (176), and an awareness of her own body—an awareness that she is being "seen"—is expressed in a prolonged argument with God in which he insists she remove her headdress on the absurd pretext that the wings on the side frighten him.[43] Although she denies her sisters' accusations that she uncovered herself to catch the attention of her confessor, Antonio Alemán, she ambiguously recalls that he compliments her appearance and then leaves the incident hanging in mid-sentence at the end of the twelfth notebook (246–48). While writing about such episodes clearly is an enjoyable task for Úrsula, there is no question that she is also aware at all times that these texts are destined to be read by her confessor. As such, Úrsula's relative lack of remorse and provocative discussions of worldly matters suggest a complicated game of misrecognition and seduction between author and addressee in which she asserts her superior position as the center of attention in the text.

* * *

Úrsula's wit and intelligence caught the attention of Bishop Luis Francisco Romero during his weekly visits to the convent and soon they began to have long conversations in private: "he called for me specially, speaking to me with great affection and enjoying the jokes I would tell him . . . he was so amused by my cleverness that when I was not at the door he would say 'Where is the philosopher? Call her,' and he would remain alone with me" (243).[44] Úrsula states that she is sought out to alleviate the "hypochondria" of the bishop (243); indeed, sixteenth-century medical treatises extolled the "curative powers of witty conversation" (Mariscal "A Clown at Court" 70). However, she also comes to enjoy his company, and is obviously flattered by his gifts and attention.[45] In one particularly unusual exchange Úrsula complains of her difficulties in dressing and undressing, and the bishop, commiserating with his own discomfort in that respect, has her remove his shoe and feel his foot to verify how many socks he has on (244). Although the scandalized mother superior, warning Úrsula that bishops have been known to have children, intervenes to separate them, their meetings apparently continue: "It was said that the bishop had illicit relations with me, and one of the founding mothers went so far as to tell me . . . not to speak with the bishop because it dishonored me" (234).[46] Úrsula continues to deny the insinuations of the women in the convent but immediately follows the narration of her friendship with the bishop with a convoluted story of a secret pain in her abdomen that she shares only with a girl she had raised in her cell. The girl later escapes the convent, returns pregnant, and finally becomes a woman of the street (236–37). Úrsula begins to suffer a strange condition in which she bleeds from the mouth so severely that "God permitted that the vicaress would find me flooding the cloister with blood" (244, 259).[47]

As is evident in this episode, the tone of the narration undergoes a dramatic change in the last two notebooks of Úrsula's life story: she speaks less confidently, less coherently, less authoritatively. Literally deprived of her mask when she comes to the confessional without a veil, with Alemán, Úrsula is not able to play the role of the *gracioso*, although she continues to use dialogic techniques from the theater. In one particularly intense exchange with the priest, after she has left him for another confessor, he summons her to the locutory and apparently reproaches her for leaving him: "He told me 'sit down, we must get to work.' I said to him 'what?' He responded: 'the bridegroom with the bride.' This ashamed me so much that I wanted to bury myself in the ground. . . . Lifting my head, I said to him, 'You are driving me mad'; he said, 'What have I said?'; I responded, 'Damn your games!' and I said this as if I were out of my mind, laughing loudly and furiously hitting and striking the bars between us" (251).[48]

Although Úrsula continues to insist on a disjunction between her self-image and that projected onto her by the confessor, she eventually is seduced into conformity. When God tries to convince Úrsula to definitively leave Alemán, she tearfully resists: "I started to cry for Father Alemán. Hearing this, he said, 'Do you not want the confessor I give you? You will be detained.' 'For how long?' I responded, 'a year, four or twenty? What does it matter! I want my confessor,' and I cried inconsolably" (253).[49] However, on the following page she gives another version, stating that her confessor remembered the circumstances of their parting differently: "Later the Father said that I had told him . . . he was not worthy to be my confessor, which not even in my wildest dreams would have occurred to me to say . . . that would have been very arrogant" (254).[50] In contrast to the emotional details provided regarding her earlier struggles, the relation of her actual abandonment of Alemán is indicated only when she records: "Having changed to Father Tomás and informed my confessor, he advised me not to confess with him nor with Father Roque Arbildo, giving me his reasons that I omit here" (258).[51] The explanation that follows is suggestive: although Úrsula refuses to write what was said ("I told him this and that . . . things I do not want to recount here, having given my word to keep this silent"), she provides the response of the priest: "I will be denounced" and her complaint, that he did not believe—and possibly feared—her conversations with Christ following holy communion (258).[52] Whatever the true nature of the irreconcilable hostility toward Alemán may have been, the responsibility in Úrsula's account lies squarely with the confessor, with her own role never fully defined.[53] No longer able to use language to put herself at an advantage with the priest, Úrsula at first cuts short her narration on the pretext that she has written it elsewhere: "I think there is something about this in the other notebooks, if not, it will remain in the inkwell, so as not to bother you, Honorable Father" (254)[54]; however, in the following paragraph she returns to the subject, commenting first on her resentment of two other women who were "like owners" of the priest and pushed her away from the confessional, then on a jealous Christ's intervention to mete out discord between Úrsula and her confessor (255). Apparently, "inappropriate" rumors about the priest had been circulating in the convent for which Úrsula is inexplicably punished after the abbess reads her papers (256–57).

* * *

Although polemical, the temporary role reversal of the *mujer varonil* was not a model for social change. Ultimately, these strong women were punished or in some way made conscious of their erring ways, usually capitulating to their "proper" place in the social order through love and marriage, or, on occasion, to the convent or to death if their transgressions in defense of women crossed the lines of decency. The literary figure of the *mujer varonil* may have been devised, in fact, as a safety valve for social change, her rebellion being recast as the *cause* rather than as a *symptom* of class struggle (Freedman 134, 140). In Úrsula's narration, divisions and political intrigues in the community began to spiral out of control beginning in 1710 following a controversial election. Úrsula describes this period as one of continual battle (239). According to Úrsula, she had not only won the election but was recognized by Bishop Romero as the winner; yet she was passed over in favor of María de Gamboa, who had the support of Church hierarchy (240).[55] While the reader may doubt Úrsula's version, political machinations seem to have been operative, since the bishop bypassed the privilege of the abbess to select her own vicaress, the second in command, by appointing Úrsula to this important position. What Úrsula does not elaborate on here is the apparent contradiction between the rumors in the convent and her own testimony about her friendship with Romero and his refusal, on two occasions, to intervene on her behalf.[56] Úrsula's close relation with Romero begins to deteriorate in 1710, the same year he prohibited *devociones* and ordered the complete enclosure of the convent (Guernica 221). Úrsula conflates the two incidents without explicitly establishing any sort of causal relation between them. Nonetheless, and even in retrospect, she can barely contain her anger as she recalls her reaction to the bishop's pastoral on enclosing the convent: "I am so impudent that I became angry with His Eminence [the bishop] after his sermon at the chapter of faults, treating us like harlots . . . I assure you, Reverend Father, that I was the most shamed of women, and everyone was, even the priests covered their faces with their hats, there are no words I can think of to recount this" (241). After this humiliating speech, the bishop meets with Úrsula, where they exchange a series of sarcastic barbs that lead back to the election: "'What did you think of the sermon?' [he asked] and I, reproachful and almost malicious, responded, 'Good, but it had its faults.' 'They all have their faults and their merits, but that is to be expected'; 'for that very reason I omit my opinion.' The others in the window turned around and looked, and he turned to them and said 'Such a fine philosopher.' I finished with the list of nominees and when it came time to vote, he asked me, 'For whom?' . . . I said, 'for the greater honor of this religion.' He said, 'The name of the individual?' I said, 'Your Most Holy Lordship has already decided'; he said to me: 'Speak!' 'Does not your most Holy Lordship say it must be doña María?' and I left the window" (241).[57]

Why this talented storyteller would end the narration of her life story with events occurring some fifteen years before it was written (and some thirty-four years before her death) is not entirely clear. Ramón speculates that there were later notebooks that were destroyed (39).[58] This explanation is not entirely satisfying, however, since we know she wrote this version in or around 1730; yet she barely mentions any events between 1715 and 1730. Another plausible interpretation is that from 1715 on Úrsula was no longer able to recount her story, or was no longer interested in doing so. The year 1715 was crucial for Úrsula: she was defeated, for the second time, in a controversial election for abbess and subjected to an uncommonly harsh sentence by her old friend Romero and the Ecclesiastical Tribunal. The situation was more painful and complicated than Úrsula admits in her narrative. Santiago had become the center of one of the most controversial cases in the Inquisition when Juan Francisco Ulloa, a Jesuit priest, was accused posthumously of leading a heretical sect in which several religious women were implicated. Bishop Romero intervened and relieved a Clarissan nun from her administrative post; Úrsula's confessor, Antonio Alemán, and an uncle, Ramón de Córdoba, were also involved (Medina *Historia del Tribunal del Santo Oficio de la Inquisición en Chile* 476).[59] In addition, Romero was having problems of his own: accused of disloyalty to the king of Spain, he was stripped of his position and transferred to Quito in 1718, where he died in 1729 (Silva Cotapos 112).

No longer protected by Romero, and feeling abandoned after her confessor's death in 1729, it is a broken and defeated Úrsula who ends the 1730 narration. In the final notebooks, Úrsula's account begins to include more traditional elements of hagiographic discourse. She expresses a desire to suffer, comparing her torment with that of Christ by setting it during Holy Week. In a passage with confusing logic and chronology, Úrsula describes a period of "illness," which seems more likely to have been solitary confinement, during which the bishop is called on to intervene.[60] Harshly reprimanding Úrsula for her behavior following her electoral defeat and accusing her of fomenting rebellion, the bishop refuses her communion for forty days and imposes corporal punishment (261). Although the sentence is relaxed because of Úrsula's ill health, she is forced to eat on the ground, kiss the feet of her sisters, and remain confined to her cell. There is no explanation of the connection between her problems with her confessor and the sentencing that followed the elections. But in the final pages of her narration, Úrsula pleads with her addressee to take care with her notebooks, "so that nobody ... may know what for so many years I have kept silent"; and refers, again enigmatically, to Bishop Romero's having told her secret "to two or three people," after which she falls gravely ill (268–69).[61]

Peter Berger asserts that comedy, like Christian faith, overcomes the tragic perspective through the promise of redemption: "redemption promises in eternity what comedy gives us in a few moments of precarious liberation—the collapse of our walls of imprisonment" (128).[62] Úrsula uses her wit and intelligence to challenge traditional structures of authority with the liberating power of laughter, but her liberation proves to be precarious. In the end she remains marginalized by the male voice; the walls of his discursive authority remain intact. When Christ proposes to make Úrsula his "santa comedianta," her confessor, Tomás de Gamboa, curtly responds: "As queen, comedienne or fool?" (230–31)[63]; and when she describes her spiritual conversion to an earlier confessor, Miguel de Viñas, using the words of Paul, she is instructed to reword her confession in a way more appropriate to a woman: "He told me not to repeat what Saint Paul had said, but to quote Samuel, and also the words of the Holy Virgin" (201). Even Christ eventually chides her for her unruly tongue. When Úrsula asks when she will learn to become a saint, he responds, "'When you are silent,'" to which Úrsula replies, "'I have a long way to go, because I can not be silent'" (245).[64]

In the final pages of the text, defeated and seriously ill, Úrsula reproaches Bishop Romero for revealing her "secret," to which he responds: "Daughter, all I have done to you has been for your own good, so do not speak to me in Latin and do not quote Saint Paul and do not recite the Bible to me" (269).[65] As George Mariscal explains in his discussion of the role of the court jester: "while the potential for manipulating language was obviously very real, the system itself . . . was jealously maintained by the ruling elites" ("A Clown at Court" 63, 67). When the bishop reasserts his authority to Úrsula, it is no laughing matter: she feels betrayed and hurt, because she has overestimated the power of her mind and wit to equalize deeply entrenched social hierarchies. Ultimately, in real life, power relations remain unchanged and unchangeable.

This episode is followed by a dream from many years earlier in which Úrsula finds a deformed snake inside the confessional, which she kills by putting it in her mouth and tearing it in half. Her face covered with blood, she hears the bishop enter the confessional; he is somehow already aware of what has transpired. Although the serpent is of course associated with Eve and original sin, its destruction is a paradoxical symbol since the Virgin trampling on the snake had been an emblem of the Immaculate Conception since the fifteenth century (Knipping 249). Moreover, bleeding was often associated with the cleansing of those who shed it as a parallel with Christ on the cross and, as was observed in the case of Francisca Josefa Castillo (chapter 2), the explosion of blood in her mouth may be interpreted simultaneously as redemption for her verbal excesses and as a sign that the accusations against her for transgressive speech were unfounded. That Úrsula finds a "deformed" snake instead of a priest in the confessional, and kills it with her mouth, perhaps suggests that it is the confessor who is imagined as evil and that Úrsula is implicated somehow by her speech. Indeed, her uncontrolled bleeding from the mouth always occurs in those periods in which she suffers most; and it is through intentional bleedings that the doctors attempt to "cure" her after she is accused of fomenting rebellion (269).[66] The fact that the recounting of her dream is immediately preceded by her reproach of the bishop for revealing her "secret," to which he responds with a reprimand for transgressive speech ("no me tomes en la boca la Biblia"), further underlines the centrality of sin and the mouth. Figuratively "tomar en boca" means to mention or refer, but literally it translates to *take or put in the mouth*. While others may take the condition to be a sign of her punishment, in her dream she is simultaneously sinner and *victim* when the serpent bites the inside of her mouth. Perhaps the serpent in her mouth is the bishop himself, whom she holds responsible for her fallen state. Or perhaps the snake is her own tongue, her intellectual defenses, her cleverness, her independence, all crushed by the overpowering force of patriarchal power.

Rather than help her decipher the strange vision, the only reaction of her confessor, Miguel de Viñas, after this painful account is to brusquely remark that snakes have no bones; she tries to insist, but eventually is silenced by his logic. Her words have no place: ultimately it is the confessor who controls her experience and her text. Like the *mujer varonil,* Úrsula in the end is forced to defer to male authority, although with a decidedly unhappy, if not tragic, ending. Úrsula Suárez's decision to end her narration with a dream that predates the time of writing by at least twelve years suggests the enormous pain of realization when this "very happy saint" was forced by circumstances into silence.[67]

Epilogue

And the Rest Is Silence

The Reply to Sor Filotea and Other Random Thoughts

As I was making the final revisions to this manuscript, I could not help but feel the burden of an overwhelming sound of silence: Úrsula Suárez, punished by the Ecclesiastical Tribunal for transgressive speech; Francisca Josefa Castillo, tormented by those around her for not knowing her place; Gerónima del Espíritu Santo, María de San José, María Manuela de Santa Ana, María Marcela: for all their daring negotiations of visionary experience, they always returned to their enclosures. For all their imaginative storytelling ability, ultimately they learned, as did María Marcela, to suffer in silence. Sebastiana Josefa de la Santísima Trinidad, silenced by her own slow self-torture, the embodied protest of a situation in which no other control was possible; and María Coleta de San José, charged by the Inquisition, dying before judgment could be pronounced. All of them, silenced by the structures of authority, because they were too intelligent, or too dangerous, because they made the people around them feel uncomfortable.

When thinking about silence it is inevitable that I mention, if only in passing,[1] perhaps the most tragic case of all: Sor Juana Inés de la Cruz, one of the brilliant minds of her time, who, pressured to abandon her humanistic pursuits, renewed her vows of obedience and humility and died soon afterward. But before her voice was finally muted, Sor Juana wrote a remarkable essay in which this tension between silence and the word resonates: *La respuesta a Sor Filotea de la Cruz* ([Reply to Sor Filotea de la Cruz] 1690). Without describing in detail this fascinating document, I would like to underscore that in this, perhaps the best example we have of autobiographical writing by Sor Juana, the author has clearly appropriated discursive strategies from the *vida* to structure her argument: the rhetoric of humility and obedience, her repugnance toward writing on demand, the use of positive female models, the paradigm of Christ and her own martyrdom. Make no mistake: Sor Juana was an exceptional woman and, as Kathleen Myers has noted, although her essay is framed by conventions from women's spiritual autobiography, she also subverts these formulae "to insert her own story, to satisfy her own need for self-revelation and self-justification" ("Sor Juana's *Respuesta*" 461). And yet, I would suggest, although Sor Juana may have expressed it more eloquently, argued it more ingeniously, and felt it more profoundly, her experience and her final anguished decision to renounce learning were not so different from those of many intelligent women who found themselves caught between the structures of power and their own will.

As is well known, Sor Juana had been asked to write a theological commentary by the bishop of Puebla, Manuel Fernández de Santa Cruz; he published the treatise, titled the *Carta atenagórica* [Letter Worthy of Athena], without her permission and then added a preface signed with the female pseudonym "Sor Filotea de la Cruz," censuring Sor Juana for having written it. It was 1690 and several circumstances had made the Mexican nun's already precarious position especially vulnerable. She had lost the support of the viceregal government that previously had protected her from higher Church authorities; Francisco Aguiar y Seijas, an archbishop with an almost pathological disdain for women, had assumed power; and one or possibly two volumes of Sor Juana's secular poetry, published in Madrid, had made their way to New Spain.[2] One theory is that the bishop was using Sor Juana to advance his own political position, jeopardized by the archbishop. Others speculate that it was an attempt to gently reprimand Sor Juana before Aguiar y Seijas attacked her. Finally, as implausible as it might seem, Fernández de Santa Cruz, like Antonio Núñez de Miranda before him, could have put Sor Juana to the test for what he perceived to be her best interests. As Asunción Lavrin points out, the bishop considered himself a protector of women, but his perception of them remained tied to his time and his situation: he felt obligated to assist Juana on the path of perfection and obedience ("Sor Juana Inés de la Cruz" 618–19). It is not clear whether Sor Juana knew her treatise would be published, but if her "Reply" is any indication, she apparently did not anticipate that it would be accompanied by a preface that reprimanded her not only for the "Letter" but for all her secular pursuits.[3] At any rate, two points seem certain: first, that Juana knew who was behind "Sor Filotea," and considered it an act of betrayal; and second, that she realized it was only a matter of time before she would be completely silenced.

As Josefina Ludmer observes, although everything addressed to the bishop in the letter implies full acceptance of her subordinate role and intention to remain silent, the autobiographical passages of the essay underscore a different perspective on silence: that of a strategy of resistance, a "not saying that she knows" that subverts forbidden practices while at the same time revealing the mechanisms of power that restrain her. "Public saying," Ludmer notes, "is a space occupied by authority and violence: the other grants and retracts the word. The bishop publishes (and she, while expressing her gratitude, protests: I don't want to publish, I'm forced to do so); the bishop writes (and she: I don't know how to respond to you); the bishop orders the study of sacred matters (and she: I don't know, I'm afraid). *Juana, as a woman, says that rather than she being its mistress, the word is granted, retracted and demanded (as is confession) from her*" (88–90, emphasis added). If all this sounds contradictory, it is: and so is Sor Juana's reply, vacillating between intellectual self-justification and deference to ecclesiastical authority. Yet ultimately the "Reply" is *not* apologetic: Sor Juana politely declines the bishop's (apparent) offer to repent; she considers, but ultimately decides against, remaining silent. She *answers* the bishop and, transgressing all lines of propriety, does so with a poignant and public defense of a woman's right to pursue an intellectual vocation.

If Sor Juana had been a man, Octavio Paz suggests, none of this would have happened: "the zealous Princes of the Church would not have persecuted her. Deeper than the incompatibility between secular and religious pursuits was the . . . *contradiction between writing and being a woman*" (607-608/470, emphasis added). We can only speculate what a tortured decision it was for Sor Juana to admit defeat and surrender herself to the will of those in power. The silencing of Juana's voice after the "Reply" was actually a more gradual process than popular legend would have it: for two years, she continued some literary activity, albeit limited, including revising her books and even writing some new texts. Her final poem, a discourse on fame, was mysteriously left incomplete. But if it was not the last work she wrote, the "Reply" clearly marked the beginning of the end. Shortly after writing it, Sor Juana reconciled with her confessor, gave all her books to the archbishop (with the notable exception of a few left for her sisters in the convent), sold her musical and scientific instruments, and renewed her vows. A pact, signed in blood: "I, Juana Inés de la Cruz, the worst of all." And the rest is silence.

And the rest? Silent, *silenced*, made invisible, by history and by literary history, by scholars who begrudgingly admitted Sor Juana's genius on the condition that she be seen as an aberration outside other women's experiences: an anomaly at best, a hysteric or monster at worst. Silences that cannot be filled, losses that can never be restored. If conventional standards of what is historically or politically significant and what is of literary value preclude or isolate women's experiences, then maybe we should reevaluate these standards. As Joan Wallach Scott notes, women's writing can tell us a lot about unequal distributions of power: how they are established, contested, and maintained. History needs to recognize "the often silent and hidden operations of gender that are nonetheless present and defining forces in the organization of most societies. With this approach women's history critically confronts the politics of existing histories and inevitably begins the rewriting of history" (27). If the power relations exposed through *private* experiences of these (invisible) women cannot be divorced from hierarchies of race, class, and ethnicity, then their writings and what was *made* of their writings may also bear witness to Spanish America's very *public* struggle for national identity.

Silent. Or not? By understanding historical representations of gender and how writing subjects negotiated (or attempted to negotiate) voices for themselves within such representations, we may begin to understand how hierarchies of gender are constructed and how they are legitimized and interrelated by codes, contexts, and value systems determined by a social order from which women have historically been excluded. Beyond the silence, strategies of resistance: Sor Juana's legacy, and that of all her forgotten sisters and multiple heroines. Silence as subversion, as disguise, as duplicity. Silence as model.

Notes

Preface

1. Elaine Showalter and others have used this term to refer to writing that "embodies the social, literary, and cultural heritages of both the muted and the dominant" (*The New Feminist Criticism* 263).

Introduction

1. Mariscal cites the example of Huarte de San Juan, who, in *Examen de ingenios* (1575), devotes an entire chapter to how to prevent the birth of female children. As Ronald Surtz points out, Castilian Spanish literary culture differed from that of other European countries in that the Castilian tradition of writing women did not begin to take hold until the fifteenth century (2). It is, however, important to distinguish Castilian literature from cultural production in other parts of Spain. Arabic women writers whose work has survived include Wallada (fifth century), María Alphaizuli (eighth century), Labana (tenth century), María Abi Jacobi Alfarsuli (eleventh century), and Aisha (twelfth century). Oral traditions such as the Hispano-Arabic *kharja* (*jarcha*), the Galician *cantigas*, and the Castilian *villancico* probably also included female *jongleurs*.

2. In fact, in emblem books, sin is often depicted as a woman.

3. Laqueur notes, moreover, that the male body is the "measure of all things" and all representations of female corporeality are assessed from this perspective (62).

4. Strict enclosure was normally limited to black-veiled nuns. Lay nuns and *beatas* (beguines) had more mobility but less protection. As Inquisition records demonstrate, they were also more susceptible to charges of heresy.

5. *Cratícula* seems to be the most commonly used term in Spanish America, although Úrsula Suárez, in Chile, uses the peninsular Spanish *comulgatorio*.

6. As Ahlgren points out, to speak of an "openness" in fifteenth-and sixteenth-century Spanish society is relative. This period, in which a more democratic approach to theological discussion was admitted, was also the time when the persecution of Jews and Moslems was at its height (9).

7. Among the works translated to Spanish under Cisneros were the texts of Augustine, Gregory the Great, Cassian, Bernard of Clairvaux, and Angela of Foligno.

8. These dates correspond to books censored by the Spanish Inquisition only. Since only one book was censored in 1551, most historians cite 1559 as the first year of the *Índices*. Eckenstein hypothesizes that it was the rigid control of theological treatises that led to an increase in mystic literature (528) and its radical expression based on the symbolic union of the female body with that of Christ.

9. Even vernacular translations of the Bible were prohibited beginning in 1492 after the expulsion of the Jews.

10. Ironically, the method of prayer advocated by the *alumbrados* was similar to what had once been an accepted practice and was used by Teresa de Jesús in her discussion of mystical experience, the Franciscan exercises of *recogimiento*. *Alumbradismo* was officially denounced by the Inquisition in 1525. In the late sixteenth century, a second series of *alumbrado* circles, unrelated to the earlier groups, emerged in southern Spain (Ahlgren 12–15, 38).

11. The Viceroyalty of New Granada, which included what is now Venezuela, Colombia, and Ecuador, separated from Peru in 1739. The Viceroyalty of the River Plate (Argentina, Uruguay, Paraguay, and part of Bolivia and Chile) was declared in 1776. Six of the eight women studied here were affiliated with the Franciscan order: María Marcela and María Coleta de San José were Capuchine nuns and Francisca Josefa Castillo, Úrsula Suárez, Gerónima del Espíritu Santo and Sebastiana Josefa de la Santísima Trinidad belonged to the Clarissan order. María Manuela de Santa Ana was a Discalced Carmelite and María de San José, an Augustinian Recollect.

12. Guernica's detailed examination of convent records in the Chilean Clarissan convent in which Úrsula Suárez professed lists several cases of "redimidas" [re-deemed] and "rescatadas" [rescued] women allowed to enter for about 300–400 pesos, in comparison to the 2,250 minimum for black-veiled nuns. The term *recogimiento* is also used to refer to the Franciscan exercise of meditation widely practiced in sixteenth-century Spain.

13. According to McKnight, in Colombia, mestiza or quadroon women (mulattas whose ancestry was one-fourth African) could be admitted as lay nuns (89). Wealthy patrons sometimes "donated" slaves in their wills in addition to or instead of funds, and Guernica notes at least one case in Chile in 1723 in which a slave was used in lieu of a dowry (55).

14. Not only were mestizos whose ancestors had married into indigenous nobility considered criollo but, at least through the end of the sixteenth century, any mestizo born in wedlock would be registered as a *Spaniard*. "By the beginning of the eighteenth century," Pagden concludes, "there were few criollo families who were entirely without Indian blood" (68–69).

15. [Han sido, y fueron Españoles, Cristianos Viejos, limpios de toda mala raza, sin mezcla alguna de moros, judios, rénegues, recién conversos a nuestra santa fe Católica, ni de mulatos.]

16. Three granddaughters of Moctezuma (Catalina and Isabel Cano Moctezuma, Ana Sotelo Moctezuma) and one great-granddaughter, Leonor Sotelo Moctezuma, professed in Santa Clara. Marie-Cécile Benassy-Berling also cites the case of a great-granddaughter of Cuahtémoc who took her vows in La Concepción. Of course, as

Benassy-Berling notes, indigenous nobility enjoyed certain privileges denied the general population (41).

17. Although this experiment ended in failure, there were cases of mestizas who were allowed to profess as black-veiled nuns in Santa Catalina of Arequipa (Burns 51, 107).

18. The Dominicans, who did not come to the Americas as a reformed order, also adopted reforms in the late seventeenth century.

19. [Criollas regalonas y chocolateras.]

20. [Haciendo fiestas, no estando yo para tenerlas.] Úrsula's grandmother had promised her a life of comfort, with "a furnished cell, decorated with sumptuous cloth, with an armoire, fine silver from Peru and linens from Cuzco; one slave within and another outside, and four-thousand pesos of rent." [Tu celda alhajada, muy bien colgada, escaparate y tu plata labrada, que del Perú se traerá, y los lienzos de Cuzco . . . tu esclava dentro y otra fuera y cuatro mil pesos de renta] (101).

21. [Fue muy afligida nuestra Gerónima con necesidades de los subsidios corporales, con desamparos y soledades, de suerte que llegó al extremo de estar sin una criada.] [Pues de sus criadas (cuando las tuvo, sé lo que es esta gentalla) fuera de muchos y graves sinsabores, jamás le asistían a tiempo, ni en cosa que hacían le daban gusto. . . . Todo esto llevó con gran paciencia.]

22. The role of convents in the education of young girls varied. Muriel notes that reformed orders did not accept young girls as pupils. McKnight reports that there is little evidence of convent schooling in New Granada, although young girls were often placed in convents to be raised by the nuns after the death of a mother (88).

23. After a controversial electoral defeat Úrsula was charged with fomenting rebellion in the convent and was sentenced to be whipped daily for nine days by all members of the community; she was also made to kiss their feet and eat dirt. In addition she was placed in solitary confinement and denied communion, except for twice during holy week (261–62). See chapter 6 for further details.

24. For more on economic activity in the colonial convent, see Reyna, especially 71–75 and 79–83.

25. [Por él me visto y sustento.] Burns notes that in some cases *devociones* may actually have been business transactions (185).

26. In 1606, Archbishop Bartolomé Lobo Guerrero of Santa Fe in New Granada threatened severe punishments for nuns who received devotions; the practice was ended in Santiago in 1710 by Bishop Luis Francisco Romero. In Lima, reforms were passed in 1785 by Archbishop Antonio de Parada, followed by a similar measure in Arequipa in 1786 (Martín 236).

27. Sor Juana Inés de la Cruz's early training was apparently from such an institution (*Obras completas* 445).

28. It should be noted that organized schooling for women was for the most part an urban phenomenon and distance from urban centers could preclude an adequate education. Indeed, most autobiographies that allude to childhood education (those of Francisca Josefa Castillo, Úrsula Suárez, and María de San José, for example) recount that they were educated at home by their mothers or other female relatives.

29. As Surtz notes, women did have indirect access to Scripture through sermons; documents further suggest that readings for nuns during mealtimes included the Bible, devotional texts, and hagiography (13).

30. The influence of Juan de la Cruz seems apparent in many women's texts; María de San José also mentions reading Pedro de Alcántara's *Tratado de la oración,* another on the list of prohibited books. Because women's readings were in principle limited, imagery from the Scriptures or mystic texts usually was integrated as if it had arisen spontaneously from their visionary imaginations; indeed reading and writing were themselves commonly attributed to divine intervention.

31. Palafox, who published a commentary to Pedro de Alcántara's work, had his own difficulties with Inquisitorial authority and was temporarily excommunicated.

32. Manuscript copies of books also circulated in Spain. Copies of Teresa de Jesús's life story as well as her *Meditaciones sobre los cantares* were distributed in convents even as the first was under investigation by the Inquisition and the second ordered burned by Teresa's confessor. It is likely that Teresa herself ordered copies made to preserve her work in the event it would be destroyed (Ahlgren 51, 75).

33. Although *vida* may refer to several kinds of autobiographical writing, I use the term here to refer to spiritual autobiographies and biographies only.

34. Leigh Gilmore, distinguishing between formal autobiography and other forms of self-representation, uses the term "autobiographics" (144). Although I do not use this term in my study, it is consistent with my notion of the *vida* as a hybrid genre.

35. Fifty-five of these texts were biographies and autobiographies, plus sixty-six funeral sermons, collective biographies, chronicles, and visionary works. My own count of biographies published in New Spain between 1640 and 1800 totals thirty, plus seventy funeral sermons and collective biographies, two unpublished biographies, and twelve unpublished autobiographies, not including Inquisition records. Thirty-four biographies of men were published during the same period. Notably, although in New Spain women's and men's life stories seemed to generate an equal amount of interest, biographies published in Spain and Rome about men and women from the colonies were clearly centered on male experiences: thirty-five were about men, only nine about women. However, this may have as much to do with the time frame as with anything else, since most of the aforementioned biographies from Spain were published in the seventeenth century, whereas the majority of *vidas* in Spanish America appeared during the eighteenth. Six biographical works and eighteen funeral sermons about women were published in Lima between 1640 and 1800: notably, three of these biographical accounts were by other women: Sor María Ángela on María Catalina (1767), Sor María Antonia de la Natividad on Melchora de Jesús (1781), and Sor Josefa de la Providencia on Antonia Lucía del Espíritu Santo (1793). Most of my figures are from Medina.

36. Of nine Spanish-American biographies about male subjects from both the seventeenth and eighteenth centuries that I have examined, none included autobiographical excerpts by the subjects, and descriptions of bodily mortification generally covered no more than one and a half to six pages. Only one, about Nicolás de

Guadalajara, includes writings by the subject, some "notes" on his life, and four devotional treatises. Of these nine life stories only that of Domingo Pérez de Barcia, described at length the visionary experiences of the subject. See Villavencio, Faria, Mayora, Eguiara y Egurén, Espinosa, Florencia, Gutiérrez Dávila, García de la Concepción.

37. Bakhtin notes a similar abstraction of time in the chivalric romance (*Dialogic Imagination* 151).

38. Although by the eighteenth century most of the clergy in New Spain was criollo, well into the seventeenth century there had been some reluctance, even among the Jesuits, to admitting criollos to any level of the church or state bureaucracy because of their "dubious sanctity" and their permissive attitude toward women (Moraña 238; Pagden 81–83). New World saints such as Martín de Porres (1579–1639), Rosa of Lima (1586–1617), and Mariana of Quito (1618–1645) could also be used as rallying points for criollo interests, though Rosa of Lima was the only one of the three canonized during the colonial period (1671).

39. Sigüenza cites as evidence the transcripts of mestizo historian Fernando de Alva Ixtlilxochitl. His attitude toward contemporary indigenous communities was considerably less utopian, particularly following the uprising of 1692.

40. [Tiene en México un Relicario, en que pueden venerarse, no ya reliquias de cuerpos, sino cuerpos enteros.] Although it is possible that Valdés is referring to Mexico *City* here, the term "Mexico" had been used by criollos as early as 1570 and was explicitly identified with nationalistic ends by Francisco Clavijero in 1770, just five years after the publication of Valdés's text. Like Sigüenza y Góngora, Valdés was a native of Mexico.

41. The title of Agustín de la Madre de Dios's 1649 history is *Mina rica de ejemplos y virtudes;* Setagolo's text, *La nueva mina del Perú,* was published in Lima in 1669 (Medina *Biblioteca Hispano-Americana* vol. 3, 165).

42. [Pues de este modo no sólo tributaría la nueva España a la antigua lo precioso de sus metales, sino que la enriquecería con el oro con tan celestiales ejemplos; debiéndoles tanto más en esto que en aquello, cuanto es mejor la edificación que la opulencia.]

43. For a provocative discussion of the commodification of indigenous women during the early years of colonial encounter and conquest, see Keller.

44. In the biographical notes that I have been able to locate regarding the authors of biographies of saintly men and women, fifty-three were criollo and twenty-one Spanish, with a noticeable increase in criollo presence from the beginning of the seventeenth century through the eighteenth century (see Medina; Beristain de Souza). Convents under episcopal jurisdiction could have confessors appointed from any order. Jesuits were the preferred counselors for Teresa de Jesús, Juana Inés de la Cruz, Francisca Josefa Castillo, and Úrsula Suárez, among others. Antonio Núñez de Miranda, confessor to Sor Juana and an influential figure in his own right, wrote an application of Loyola's *Ejercicios espirituales* to religious women (*Ejercicios espirituales de San Ignacio de Loyola aplicados a las Señoras religiosas*) that was published in Mexico in 1695. In Spanish America, nearly all biographies of

male subjects were written by and about Jesuits. My research does not detect any one religious affiliation that predominates in women's biographies, although Jesuits and Franciscans outnumber authors from other orders.

45. Slade has also detected a relation between this hybridity and the theories of Bakhtin (12–13).

46. Paz is perhaps referring to "literature" in a more limited sense to emphasize the exceptional situation of Sor Juana Inés de la Cruz in the seventeenth century: indeed, of the thirteen books by women published in New Spain between 1640 and 1700, ten of them were by Sor Juana.

47. According to Antonio Márquez, when translations are included, the number of editions of María de Ágreda's treatise reaches 168.

48. Arenal and Schlau point to the use of Mary as a symbol of wisdom (*Untold Sisters* 220). The *Mística Ciudad de Dios* takes Mary as a central figure in its narrative. Francisca Josefa Castillo mentions the Virgin's milk as a transmitter of doctrine (*Afectos* 55, 297, 301, 304) and, in a radical inversion of expected roles, speaks of the milk of God himself (396). Of Teresa de Jesús, María de San José says: "I am very fond of this saint and she is my beloved, although I serve her little and imitate her less." [tengo gran afecto a esta santa y es muy mi querida aunque le sirvo poco y la imito menos] (V.23).

49. [Sentí que con una violencia se me ponía delante Santa Teresa . . . y parece que entendía o me decía tan claro como decía sus cosas que le pasaban a los confesores que así lo había yo de hacer.]

50. McKnight affirms that we may speak of "an increasing codification of the generic form" established by Teresa. In fact a complicated *interrogatorio* was made up along the lines of Teresa's discourse, in which witnesses were asked to respond to certain details that could later be used to argue for sainthood. This formulaic document, in turn, seems to have been used by biographers to frame their versions of the life stories of their subjects. Initially based on ten topics, by the early eighteenth century it had expanded to include forty-seven, each with three to nine questions (52–53).

51. [suplico por amor del Señor, lo que he dicho hasta aquí de mi ruin vida y pecados lo publiquen (desde ahora doy licencia, y a todos mis confesores, que ansí lo es a quien esto va), y si quisieren, luego en mi vida. . . [para] que no engañe más el mundo, que piensan hay en mí algún bien.] References to Teresa de Jesús's works include the chapter and section numbers, followed first by the page numbers in the Spanish editions I have used and then by the page numbers in the English translations.

52. [Como la mujer sea naturalmente animal enfermo y su juicio no esté de todas partes seguro y puede ser ligeramente engañado, según mostró nuestra madre Eva, que por muy poco se dejó embobecer y persuadir del demonio: por todos estos respectos y por otros algunos que se callan, no es bien que ella enseñe.]

53. For more on the relation between the Althusserian subject of ideology and gender representation, see de Lauretis *Technologies of Gender* 6–11.

Chapter 1

1. The *capítulo* or *capitulo culpis* (chapter of faults) refers to the public reprimand of a religious in the presence of the community. It is mentioned in women's texts through the eighteenth century (see, for example, Castillo I.91; Suárez 241). Penitential exercises and public confession have been retained in some orders to this day (Warren 3; see also Curran).

2. Juan Gerónimo was prosecuted and severely reprimanded by the Inquisition of Toledo for a 1594 sermon on the subject; Henríquez's treatise, in which he suggested written confession and oral absolution, was prohibited by the *Índice* in 1603; and Manuel Sa's essay had the passage censored. For a detailed discussion of the debate over written confessions, see Lea I.362–67.

3. Further aberrations are recorded in Inquisition cases such as those of Mariano Antonio Múnive in Puebla, who was accused of resting his head on the laps of his female penitents, holding their hands, and embracing them (Archivo General de la Nación ms. 1177, exp. 1, folio 20); and José Ignacio Dávalos, also from Puebla, who touched women through the bars (Archivo General de la Nación, ms. 1045, exp. 1, folio 2). That most of these incidents took place outside major urban centers perhaps suggests that policy was more difficult to implement and enforce in outlying areas.

4. Francisco Aguiar y Seijas, archbishop of Mexico, was particularly vocal in his denunciation of the licentiousness of both secular and religious society. The threat of excommunication was revived through treatises such as Raymundo Lumbier's 1694 *Destierro de ignorancias,* commissioned by Aguiar y Seijas with Núñez de Miranda.

5. Sor Juana commented ironically: "Not ignoring the veneration and great esteem which Your Reverence . . . receives from everyone, for they listen to you as to a *divine oracle* and value your words as though dictated by the Holy Spirit, so that *the greater your authority, the more my reputation suffers.*" [No ignorando yo la veneración y crédito grande que Vuestra Reverencia . . . tiene con todos, y que le oyen como a un *oráculo divino* y aprecian sus palabras como dictadas del Espíritu Santo, y que *cuanto mayor es su autoridad tanto más queda perjudicado mi crédito*] (*Carta de Sor Juana Inés de la Cruz a su confesor* 26; Scott 433, emphasis added).

6. [No tuvo ejercicio alguno con acto nacido de su propia voluntad, porque todas sus naturales, y prenaturales operaciones, eran hechas por orden de la obediencia antecedente o concomitante de sus confesores.]

7. [He reconocido que su Majestad quiere que sea muy fiel a Vuestra Merced, y con razón, pues está Vuestra Merced en su mismo lugar.]

8. [como a santo que está en su lugar y obedezca a ciegas en todo cuanto me mandase y ordenase.] María has a vision of Christ on her bed, and he says a single word to her: "obey" (III.96).

9. The notion of the confessor as a "physician of the soul" was suggested by Augustine and incorporated in Giovanni Battista Scaramelli's manual. See Stockman 132.

10. See also Gómez Moriana on the double bind in the *Lazarillo de Tormes* (82).

11. [Esto he escrito con grandes temores de perder mi alma con escribir estas cosas ... yo no hago más de obedecer a costa de muy mucho trabajo por no saber bien escribir y por las grandes tribulaciones que en esto padezco.]

12. [Esta ... parte ... está muy mal escrita porque cuando la escribí estaba actualmente con aquellos tres demonios que tenían asistentes que me lo impedían fieramente y no me dejaban escribir si no era con indecible trabajo y eso muy mal escrito.]

13. In emblem books, the figure of humility was usually depicted as a little *girl* (Knipping 106). See also Lerner 51.

14. [Declaro ... que cuando digo que medito y pienso, hablo de lo pasado porque al presente ni medito ni pienso porque no puedo y sólo veo a Dios con una sencilla vista poseída toda de su Majestad.]

15. For more on the distinction between mind and intellect, see Teresa de Jesús *Las moradas* (4.1, 8/76–77).

16. [Todo esto y cuanto declare lo vi con el entendimiento porque con los ojos ... nunca he visto nada.]

17. [Por el entendimiento no me vino la luz, el incendio de amor, y lo infinito que me dio Dios a conocer, fue sólo por el amor con que me encendió el corazón.] [No me deje Usted de avisar si todo esto que he creído lo puedo ver. Yo mi Padre no me sé explicar porque soy una bestia.]

18. [Lo que Vuestra Merced verá por este escrito, es lo que tengo impresionado; sin dejar cuidadosamente cosa ninguna, ni haber ponderado ni exagerado lo que llevo dicho; y con la gracia de Dios no saliera un punto de las reglas de la verdad, ni me parece que equivocadamente dijera ninguna cosa. Y porque soy una pobre ignorante y mi sexo es tan ruin digo casi en todo que me parecía. Van con mucho gusto sujetas a la lima de su entendimiento.]

19. [no veía al santo, más me parecía estaba presente en mi alma.] [me pareció verlo (esto no era en sueños). ... y quejándome yo con todo mi corazón a Nuestro Señor, en esta su santa imagen ... del rigor de mis penas, sudó ... y yo entendí que era mostrando acompañarme en mis penas.] Unless otherwise indicated, all subsequent references to Castillo's autobiography will be by page number only.

20. [De cosas pudiera decir acerca de las mercedes que este señor me hacía y hace, mas de suyo son dificultosas de darles lenguaje y no para escritas.] [No hay palabras para explicar el amor de Dios para con esta pobre, no tengo palabras para las mercedes que estoy recibiendo de todos los misterios divinos.]

21. [Escribo sólo una u otra cosas, porque fuera nunca acabar decirlas todas.] [Quererlo declarar todo será nunca acabar.] [Díjele yo tal y tal cosa que le referí, que no quiero referir en éste por haberle dado mi palabra lo callaría.] [Era necesario gran volumen.] [Pudiera escribir y decir mucho más de lo que tengo escrito si no fuera por el trabajo que me cuesta.] [Si quisiera decir que en esto sólo padecí era menester hacer un libro aparte.] [Pudiera haber escrito otros dos tantos de lo que he escrito si tuviera facilidad en hacerlo.]

22. Sandra Gilbert and Susan Gubar have adapted the term "anxiety of author-

ship" to refer to the mark of textual self-consciousness in women's writing (18–19).

23. [Sólo por la Santa obediencia,] [Dulce Jesús, es posible, que padezca tantas ansias y para mayor tormento me mande la obediencia, que escriba, y que lo haga yo a fuerza y con desconsuelo tanto, que mejor . . . padecer un tormento, que tomar la pluma y más experimentando tanto susto, y embarazo, que poniéndome a ello ni papel, ni tinta servía sólo para mancharme, y no parecerme, que me convengan estas cosas. Pero por obedecer a Vuestra Paternidad me olvidaré de todo lo que me viene al pensamiento.]

24. [Estas cosas . . . no me dan a entender que no es del agrado de Dios que venga.]

25. Sherry Velasco observes that the devil's silencing of the female voice is often expressed in terms similar to those used with the threat of patriarchal authority (81).

26. [Yo había querido quemar aquellos papeles . . . y por otra parte, como en leyéndolos me alentaban y consolaban, no me determinaba. Díselos, para que me dijera lo que había que hacer. Díjome: que eran de Dios, y que lo que había que hacer era ser agradecida a sus beneficios. . . . Nuestro Señor abrió los ojos de mi alma y conocí que esto era lo mismo que vuestra paternidad me había dicho siempre, y el padre Juan de Tobar, el padre Francisco de Herrera y el padre Juan Martínez.]

27. [Padre de mi alma llevan a Vuestra Merced los papeles si le parecieran mal quemarlo que no hay nada perdido.]

28. [Cuando Vuestra Merced me escriba, no me envíe a decir cosa que se entienda que yo le escribo, sino que sea con todo disimulo, que no se entienda nada, porque no se sabe que estoy escribiendo, y en el instante que lea ésta, la rompa o la queme y esto se lo ruego por el amor de Dios.]

29. María Coleta died during the trial and her case was suspended.

30. For more on the relation between judicial and penitential confession, see Slade and Gómez Moriana.

31. [Si algunas cosas parecieron increíbles me obligo a dar juramento dentro del tribunal de la confesión o fuera de él así de parte como del todo lo que aquí he referido y también de lo que voy a decir y de cuanto diré adelante.]

32. Conversely, as Darcy Donahue observes, the biography could be used as a confession manual "case study" for "dealing with 'problematic women'" (233–34).

33. [Sé que hay . . . personas a quien el Señor hace estas mercedes, y si los que las gobiernan no han pasado por esto, por ventura les parecerá que han de estar como muertas en arrobamiento, en especial si no son letrados, y lástima lo que se padece con los confesores que no lo entienden.] See also *Camino de perfección,* especially chapter VI.

34. [Siempre he creído sólo en lo que el confesor (bien informado) dice.]

35. [Aquí callo porque sólo quien ha pasado por ello puede saber lo que es.]

36. Among the other factors that could render a confession invalid: if the priest was deaf, did not speak the same language as the confessant, or fell asleep during confession. The *vidas* imply that the abbess could also be persuaded to intervene in extreme cases (María Marcela 163; María Coleta carta 28, folio 151).

37. [Beneficio grande de Dios pues conozco vino de su mano poderosa que sin

despedir yo al confesor . . . se despidió de mí por escrito para no volver más al confesionario.] In an earlier volume, María has a prophetic vision of her confessor two months before his arrival in the convent, proof of God's will (II.30–31).

38. [Le hice la propuesta de que le hablaría al . . . Padre Fray Plácido, fue tanto el sentimiento y enojo que tuvo de esto que no contento de lo que me había dicho en el confesionario luego que entró en su celda me escribió una carta despidiéndose para no volver más al confesionario.]

39. [Aunque hubiera sido la más santa no hubiera dejado de quedar muy espinada. . . . Me dijo que ojalá estuviera en su mano traerme otro, entonces le dije, Sr., si yo no le digo jamás que quiero otro, y aunque lo quisiera no se lo había de decir, y entonces me dijo no te entiendo ni tú me entiendes y así no me quiero calentar la cabeza ni calentártela, que yo estoy enfermo y tú también.]

40. [Me parece ocioso ir con Vuestra Paternidad que no me ha de entender, ni me ha de sufrir, cuando yo no me puedo aguantar.]

41. [Este Santo Religioso . . . [me] decía . . . de mi engaño, que todas mis cosas le parecieron malísimas. . . . No me valían razones que lo pudieran mudar del mal juicio. . . . De tanto que me decía, llegué al extremo de perder el poco quicio y la paciencia. . . . Ni le di oídos a lo que me decía, y lo dejé muy acongojado; llamándome no volví, quedándome estampadas sus palabras para muchos tiempos.]

42. [Cuando se lo contaba, no decía más palabras que "Bien va." Yo decía para mí: "¡Hay tal! ¿qué entenderé yo de 'bien va'? ¿qué tiene que ver eso con lo que voy a contar?; cierto que este padre no debe de estar atento a lo que le estoy diciendo."]

43. [Y cuando vine el padre todo se lo conté, y dijo, "Bien va, ¡ea, pues paciencia!" Yo dije para mí, "Estas son otras quinienta[s]: vengo al padre afligida y sale con 'Bien va' y 'Paciencia.'"] "Estas son otras quinientas" is a colloquial expression that refers to an absurd reaction to something else said or done previously.

44. [El consuelo que me daba era decirme paciencia, paciencia, y de ahí no salía. . . . esta fue la Cruz más pesada que tuve porque creo que si hubiera tenido confesor [que] me entendiera todo me hubiera sido llevadero. . . . Me había retirado de él y tenía intención de no ir hasta que viniera otro con quien poder desahogarme porque con él digo era imposible . . . no sólo estaba yo mal con él sino también él mal conmigo.]

45. Actually María Marcela apparently had two addressees in her narration: she states that drafts of her text were approved by her current confessor, Diego de Segovia, as well as José Ignacio Cabrera, the priest she mentions here (124).

46. [Me mostró Nuestro Señor el alma del sacerdote luego que consumió hermosísima y blanquísima, mostrándome también lo mucho que este señor sacerdote le agrada (No lo nombro por no mortificarlo porque esto ha de ir a sus manos), yo quedé llena de gozo.]

47. [Nuestro señor. . . . me daba a entender creyera que nuestro padre me dice.]

48. [Con el amor [y] la caridad que te asistí en vida lo hago ahora aquí.]

49. [Conociendo yo que por el papel de Usted me había venido este bien, me removió el corazón al agradecimiento para pedirle a Dios mucho por Usted . . . de Usted es el cielo, que allá estuvo mi espíritu ayer y me volvía a asegurarlo.]

50. This condition might be compared to what would later be called "analytic transference" when female patients fell in love with another representative of fatherly wisdom, the psychoanalyst.

51. As William Taylor points out, solicitation in the confessional was actively prosecuted not because it was a violation of the priest's vow of celibacy or even an offense to the woman's honor but rather as *a crime against the sanctity of the act of confession* (185–88). Notably, Lavrin's extensive investigations in the Inquisitorial archives of Mexico have yielded only *one case* in which a women denounced a priest and later recanted her testimony ("Vida conventual" 81).

52. In contrast, the cases in Lima had dropped to less than one a year during most of the seventeenth and eighteenth centuries. Cases there had peaked in the late sixteenth century, especially between 1595 and 1603. These figures are from Medina.

53. Nonetheless, Lavrin has found at least one case in which a priest charged with solicitation was allowed to confess women until he was charged again ("Vida conventual" 79).

54. On the other hand, Lavrin points to the case of Juan Plata and Agustina de Santa Clara, in which the relation between confessor and penitent went on for some six years before the Inquisition intervened, and this was for charges of heresy and not for illicit sexual relations ("Vida conventual" 77).

55. [Hombre soy, y confieso que me acobarda el pensarlo solamente. . . . Ya querida mía hemos jugado bastante, vamos ahora con las ganancias.]

56. Although Medina does not always provide details on the plaintiff, he counts only 5 of 72 cases in Lima and 9 of 162 in Mexico in which confessors were charged with solicitation by religious women.

57. Among the eighteenth-century cases I have reviewed in the General Archive of the Nation in Mexico are those of María Guadalupe de San Antonio, "Sobre lo acontecido con el confesor Juan Crisótomo de Victoria" (1732); María Manuela de Guadalupe, "Denuncia al confesor" (1788); and Isabel de la Santa Trinidad, "Denuncia al confesor" (1753). At the time of my research there, archives for the sixteenth and seventeenth century had not yet been catalogued.

58. [En una ocasión dijeron que yo le había levantado un testimonio a un sacerdote y sobre eso me dijeron tales injurias que no me atrevo a escribirlas.]

59. [No hay entrañas tan piadosas, como las suyas, que si conmigo las tiene, como las tendrá con las otras sus queridas almas. ¿Qué bien experimentarán la dulzura de su amor? Que verdaderamente es el mejor tesoro, que se debe desear con todas las fuerzas del Alma, que a mí me ha confundido muchas veces, como nos da gusto, y lo agradecemos el saber que nos tengan amor.]

60. [Ha sido mi Padre y mi amparo, y el remedio de mi alma, y así más que sea yo, no hija, porque no lo merezco, ni ya del corazón de vuestra merced, pero me contento con ser la criada de sus hijas, y señoras mías. . . pídale vuestra merced mucho a Dios de caridad hágalo pídale digo que sea yo toda suya, y que sepa yo corresponderle, porque soy muy ingrata para con mi Dios. La Madre María me dio la queja que vuestra merced ya no la cuenta en el número de las suyas. La Madre F. me ha reído mucho con su corrida, porque me dice que ya vuestra merced es suyo,

y que por ella ha de echar vuestra merced a todas, que las ha de reempujar y que yo sola ha de ser la querida.]

61. [Conmigo parece quiere endevotarse.] [cuán distante iba de lo que el padre quería: queriendo mi alma, yo al cuerpo lo acomodaba.]

62. [Sólo a uno lo quería mucho y era en quien tenía la mira porque desde muy chiquita le conocí inclinación y yo también se la tuve.] [Pero dejémoslo aquí que después veremos lo que Nuestro Señor hizo con él sólo porque yo lo quería y vamos a ver lo que su Majestad empezó a hacer conmigo.]

63. [Dio en venir al torno a oírme, lo cual me sirvió de gravísima mortificación porque como antes me había conocido tan altiva y vana me causaba sonrojo que me viera en traje moderado y con las sumisiones de pretendienta.] [Me retiré unos día del torno y con eso el hombre se volvió a su casa y se me quitó el sobregüeso.]

64. [No me declaro aquí por no manchar el papel con inmudicias ni atraer a la memoria torpezas.] [Porque quería componer las cosas y hacer mis causas y lo que salía era ponerlo peor todo y dar margen a las otras para mayores cosas.] [Quererlo declarar todo será nunca acabar. Sólo digo que el padecer fue general en todo y por todo en cuantas materias se puede imaginar y declaro . . . [que no] hallo en mi conciencia haber dado el menor motivo a las religiosas para que me persiguieran ni les tuve nunca mala voluntad.]

65. [Apúrela más en que diga lo demás que le pasó en los veinte años del siglo, pues no es posible que no tenga más; y con ocasión de que refiere, si tuvo tentaciones, u otros trabajos interiores, y socorros espirituales de Dios, se acordará para decirlos.]

66. One way to view the male fantasy of lesbianism is as a means to defuse the threat of the unknown, private, and exclusionary nature of women's friendships with other women.

67. [Soy un miserable pecador. Lo demás que ella me hace a los [sic] que el Redentor debo atribuirlo a la misericordia del Señor y a las oraciones de esta su sierva.]

68. This hypothesis is supported by at least three passages in which she mentions Loayza in her letters, some of whose lines have been crossed out and are illegible. It is possible that Loayza censored these portions for his own protection (folio 9, *Esquela* 242; folio 9, *Esquela* 243; folio 12, *Esquela* 247).

69. [Le dijeron al padre algunas cosas de mí, que le causaron un grande enojo: decíame cosas muy sensibles, y me dejaba en el confesionario y se iba sin oírme, hasta paró de confesarme. . . . [B]ien veo ahora que el camino hubiera sido rogarle con humildad . . . mas lo que hice fue disculparme y *dar mis razones, y a cuatro o cinco veces que me reprendió, callar y retirarme.*]

70. I have found no record of formal charges of solicitation, although it is possible that he was reprimanded by his order.

71. Teresa de Jesús also experiences particularly reciprocal relations with some of her confessors, most notably with a priest she meets as a young woman who "took an extreme liking to me" [se aficionó en extremo a mí] and whom she convinces to leave his lover (V.4–6, 143–44/27–29), and with the addressee of her autobiography, the much younger García de Toledo, who, as she notes, is both her "son" and her "father" (XVI.6, 237–38/99).

72. [Llegó a hablarme con tanta lisura y llaneza las cosas de su interior y de su alma. . . . Se dio en venir al confesionario sólo [a] hablar conmigo y a decirme sus ahogos y aprietos que los pasaba harto grandes.] [Sentía mucho el modo con que me trataba. . . . El modo con que me hablaba era como si estuviera hablando con otra que no fuese yo cuando me decía que hiciera alguna cosa su término era "la Madre María haga esto no haga lo otro. . . ." y le dije "¿Padre quién es esa Madre María?" y me respondió "la Madre María con quien estoy hablando.". . . en siete años que fue mi padre espiritual no oí de su boca palabra en que se pudiese entender que yo era su hija de confesión.] [Hallé los cuadernos todos encuadernados de sus santas manos que me había dicho el gran trabajo que le había costado el ponerlos en orden por los que se perdieron. . . . Entre todos los confesores que he tenido no ha habido otro que tanto se había esmerado en el cuidado y solicitud que tenía el venerable Padre Fray Plácido Olmedo en recoger estos escritos y tenerlos tan en orden . . . estando ya para morir se los remitió todos juntos a mi madre priora.]

73. [Estando con Nuestro Señor, me veía a mí misma con la significación o semejanza de un huertecito, con la puerta muy angosta y cerrada, aunque algo maltratada. . . . Estaba el huerto con muy abundante agua, mas ésta sin corriente ni orden, y así lo tenía como empantanado. . . . Estaba adentro aquel padre, que con mucho ánimo y desembarazo abría camino al agua, arrancaba aquellas yerbas y trabajaba a vista de Dios, que estaba allí asistiendo y mandando como señor y dueño de aquella pobrecita tierra.]

74. [Sin saber yo cómo, al cabo de un mes me hallé confesándome con aquel padre, de tal modo que me decía después: que se ponía a pensar qué lo movió a venir contra la determinación que tenía de no venir a monjas.] As will be seen in the next chapter, Francisca often continued long epistolary relationships with former confessors who occupied positions of power within the local ecclesiastical establishment.

75. [Mi confesor me mortificaba cuanto alcanzaba su industria. . . . Tratábame mal, cuanto se podía, de palabra, y me respondía asperísimamente. A veces, y lo más ordinario, se enojaba tanto y tan de veras, reprendiéndome sobre cosas que a mí me parecían buenas, que me quedaba temblando y temiendo, y después me decía que las prosiguiera, y que bien iba. Algunas veces me echaba del confesionario, con tal enojo y desprecio, que parecía le había dado alguna grave causa; en particular en algunas ocasiones me escribió: "Que ya había echado de ver que yo y todas mis cosas sólo para quemadas eran buenas y que estaba determinado a huir de mí, porque mi camino era de perdición," y otras cosas muy duras. . . . Pero luego venía y me volvía a reñir y reprender, porque no había sabido llevar bien aquella mortificación y cruz. . . así, aquel rigor era lo que más me animaba.]

76. [Solía decirme después: que aunque se sentía inclinado a ayudarme a llevar mis cruces, mas que por otra parte no podía menos de tratarme de aquel modo . . . pero que él sólo deseaba mi mayor bien y que se limpiara y purificara mi alma para Dios. . . . [M]e parece me metiera en hornos de fuego por conseguir esta dicha.]

77. [Lo que deseaba de mí era el que mi nombre no se oyera en el mundo y que padeciera mucho.]

78. [Vi al Señor que caminaba un camino muy fragoso y de grandes atolladeros. Me llevaba de la mano y al lado siniestro iba mi Angel Custodio y mi confesor, los cuales iban como sirviendo de despejar el camino. Y en algunos malos pasos que había le mandaba el Señor a mi confesor que me alzase en brazos y me pasase, y él así lo hacía, quedando el Señor muy contento y pagado.]

79. [Un niño pequeñito que apenas podía dar paso aunque quería caminar no tenían fuerzas mis pies para andar.] [Si no era con aquella ayuda no podía andar.] [El dolor de su falta atravesó mi corazón.] Francisca Josefa Castillo has a similar vision in which she follows her confessor/addressee, Diego de Tapia, up a steep peak, catching herself on his cape when she stumbles (153).

80. [Me lleno de temores, con tan penosa amargura. . . . que sólo deseo a mi Padre, pero con un temor de pensar que me aborrece . . . y que ya no me quiere confesar. . . . [E]s mucho lo que padezco allá dentro . . . y todo me lo causa Vuestra Paternidad que me podría dar una puñalada, que fuera menos.] [Su hijita que desea obedecerle.] [El examen de conciencia lo traigo continuamente Padrecito mío: mi deseo es de la más mínima respiración darle cuenta.]

81. [Le ruego a Usted no me deje de escribir . . . para poder proseguir. . . . Pida Usted mucho a Dios por mí. No puedo más.] [Mi Padre postrada a sus pies le ruego me perdone lo que le molesté ayer. . . . A las seis me sentí con las profecías muy descaminada y con mucha torpeza. Con la ayuda de Dios empecé con mis ejercicios interiores y al instante llovieron las misericordias de Dios.] [Mi padre yo quedé ayer muy consolada con todo lo que Usted me enseñó y me habló las verdades. . . . Quedé tan alentada . . . que luego me puse a rezar y pude rezar todo, y hacer todo los ejercicios que hago todos los días.]

82. [Tres días antes de la ruina se me representó la capilla interior de mi alma media caída. Y me parece representaba su Majestad, que no sería todo arruinado sino la mitad como lo vimos.]

83. [Ayer por la noche nació de mí el deseo de volver a desatar a Nuestro Redentor en el paso de la Coronación de espinas. . . . Al instante le rogué me trajera a Usted en espíritu y me lo concedió para que Usted me ayudara a desatarlo. Lo vi a Usted con mucha claridad con una vista sobrenatural hincado de rodillas con mucho amor a usted por un lado y yo por el otro desatando a Nuestro Redentor.]

84. [Te daré las llaves del reino de los cielos; lo que te ates en este mundo también quedará atado en el cielo, y lo que tú desates en este mundo . . . quedará desatado en el cielo.]

85. [Comencé a temer y a dudar si esto había sido algún engaño del enemigo o imaginación de mi cabeza . . . "No temas hija, que no es engaño del enemigo. Y para que veas lo mucho que te amo y cuánto te quiero, te muestro el alma de tu padre gloriosa."]

86. [no dudaba que no era engaño del enemigo.] [aunque siempre con temor me digo estas razones.] [ya es tiempo de que des cuenta a tu confesor de lo que yo he obrado en ti . . . no quiero que se queden en silencio mis grandezas.] [Padre y Señor mío, por lo que deseo obedecer a Vuestra Merced me hace proseguir lo comenzado

por la gran repugnancia . . . e imposible que en ello tengo aunque por otra parte *no puedo dudar que lo que digo es así como lo digo y así le digo.*]

Chapter 2

1. Achury states that in Santa Clara alone there were more than one hundred black-veiled nuns (xiii–xiv); McKnight, however, finds that at the time Francisca was writing her life story, the number of black-veiled nuns in the convent had dropped significantly: from ninety-two in 1644 to between twenty and thirty from 1691 to 1730 (90).

2. This unusually high figure may be due to her brother's difficulties with the authorities (177).

3. Because Cartagena, along with Veracruz, was one of the first stops from Seville, access to prohibited literature was available even in as a remote a region as Tunja (Achury cxv).

4. Apparently most of this correspondence has been lost, with the exception of brief notes attached to some of the *Afectos*. Most of the correspondence published dates from 1724 and later; two letters from Diego de Tapia and four from Felipe Arguindegui, who does not seem to have ever confessed Francisca but with whom she apparently had a close relation, judging from the affectionate tone and numerous references to future visits (*Afectos* 537–42).

5. Sor María Antonia del Niño Dios, the twentieth-century author of an unpublished biography of Francisca, also believes that the text was written for Tapia, and that it was written between 1713 and 1724; McKnight confirms that clearly the events described predate her second term as abbess in 1729 (131).

6. [A este modo, he pasado lo más de mi vida. Escribo sólo una u otra cosas, porque fuera nunca acabar decirlas todas, que casi han sido unas mismas.]

7. [Así le pido, padre mío, que pues con el favor de Nuestro Señor yo me he vencido tanto y pasado tantas tribulaciones en escribir esto y darle cuenta de toda mi vida, la mire bien, y los pasos que lleva mi alma, para que no se pierda; pues de nuevo la vuelvo a poner en sus manos.]

8. [Fiada en las promesas y palabras de aquel Señor que dijo: que quien obedeciere a sus ministros, obedece a Su Divina Majestad; y viendo que vuestra paternidad me manda esto, y el padre Diego de Tapia (a quien descubrí todas mis tribulaciones y trabajos de mi alma) viene en ello, y me escribe obedezca a vuestra reverencia en esto.]

9. [He escrito [los papeles] por muchos y repetidos mandatos de mis confesores, y los han visto y registrado.]

10. This could either be due to the visionary nature of her poetry or to the fact that many *Afectos* were written during an earlier and more insecure period of her life.

11. [Si en algún tiempo pudieran venir a noticia de alguna alma, pudiera alentarse a amor a tan benignísimo Dios.] [Con estas cosas y otras que escribí en aquellos

papeles, consoló y animó la infinita piedad de Dios entonces mis desconsuelos, y me detuvo a que no quemara lo que había escrito, según yo había muchas veces propuesto y pedido a vuestra reverencia.]

12. The *Divine Office* refers to daily public prayers recited orally.

13. Achury counts 1,087 references to Psalms in her work, 143 to the Song of Songs, 89 to the Epistles of Saint Paul, and 82 to the Book of Job (cliii).

14. [Solía mi madre referir que teniéndome en brazos, cuando apenas podía formar las palabras, le dije con mucho espanto y alegría, que una imagen de un Niño Jesús . . . me estaba llamando.]

15. [Leía mi madre los libros de Santa Teresa de Jesús, y sus *Fundaciones*, y a mí me daba un tan grande deseo de ser como una de aquellas monjas, que procuraba hacer alguna penitencia, rezar algunas devociones.]

16. [Púsome una determinación y ansia de imitar a los santos. . . . dejé todas las galas y me vestí una pobre saya. Hacía muchas disciplinas con varios instrumentos, hasta derramar mucha sangre. Andaba cargada de cilicios y cadenas de hierro, hasta que sobre algunas crecía la carne. Dormía vestida, o sobre tablas.]

17. [Mi padre, en hablando en eso, empezaba a llorar, con ser hombre muy serio; y si estaba en la mesa, hacía quitar la comida. Parece que aquellos últimos tiempos que estuve en su casa, me cobró mayor amor, o me mostraba más el que me tenía. Solía esperar mucho tiempo a la puerta de mi aposento hasta que yo acababa mi ocupación y abría. Entonces entraba, saludándome con palabras muy tiernas. . . . Algunas veces me decía: que si yo no estuviera en casa, no entrara él en ella, porque no tenía otro consuelo.]

18. [Dios . . . por medio de vuestra paternidad hizo que entrara un día acaso, a su confesionario, a reconciliarme, y no se me olvidan las primeras palabras que me dijo, que fueron: "¡Ea, tenga ánimo, que ahí nos alentaremos a servir a Dios!" Hicieron tal impresión en mi corazón que de allí a adelante me dejé toda a su disposición y puse mi alma en sus manos para que la encaminara a Dios, no pudiendo ni queriendo apartarme de su parecer.]

19. The work was attributed to the editor, José Cassani. For summaries of these missionary expeditions and their casualties, see Pacheco 381, 390–91, 404, 412–16, 454–64, 486–90.

20. Before the 1715 election Francisca has a vision in which the devil informs her that all the condemned souls who accompany him were once prelates (158). Francisca herself notes that her rivals are slowly dying off; McKnight's comparison of rosters in the convent reveals that by 1720, of the twenty-two black-veiled nuns only six had professed before Francisca. Of the remaining fifteen, two were likely contemporaries and thirteen had professed later, at least six of whom were novices under Francisca (112, 118, 122).

21. Nuns' cells, at least the desirable ones, were purchased (45).

22. Around 1693, when Francisca had completed two years as a novitiate, some reforms were instituted: most nonreligious women were asked to leave the convent by the archbishop, and outside communications were prohibited (33). However, as was typical of many convents, these changes were contested, ignored, or at best accepted grudgingly by female communities. Francisca herself brought two servants

with her to the convent and received letters from a *devoto,* both actions clearly in violation of the 1693 reforms. It was important, however, that she express her support for the policies because her *vida* was directed to a member of the Church hierarchy who had instituted them.

23. [Con el pretexto de dar gusto.] [El enemigo . . . le puso que me escribiera muchas veces, y solicitara para conmigo esto que llaman devociones, que había entonces muchas. Yo hice mal, pues que a la primera, entendiendo lo que contenían, recibí la segunda y la tercera, aunque siempre respondía que no alcanzaba por qué me escribía a mí.]

24. [No cesaban los cuentos y cosas muy pesadas que me decían, en particular, algunas que me parecían deshonras, como decir: que me enamoraba de sus devotos, y los solicitaba, etc.] [Llamaron al vicario del convento y le dijeron tales cosas que no sé yo cómo las diga aquí. Algunas eran: que comía de balde la ración del convento, que me salía con cuanto quería. . . . que yo fingía aquellas enfermedades, y que lo hacía para tener abierto a deshoras el convento y que entraran los padres.] [Yo me veía hecho escándalo del convento. Hacían y decían contra mí cosas intolerables. Si leía en el coro un libro que trata de las amistades particulares y el daño que hacen, decían que yo fingía aquello para quitarles sus amigas y que me fueran a ver a mí.] [Esta, pues, se había arrimado a mi confesor . . . y esto me fue causa de grandes trabajos e inquietudes.] Perhaps the book Francisca is reading is Teresa de Jesús's *Camino de perfección,* which gives advice on this topic.

25. [De la cólera que tuvo contra mí.] [Fue cosa rara lo que se vio corromper el cuerpo.]

26. [Mi vileza, mi vanísima vanidad y ruindad.]

27. [Dispuso Nuestro Señor que una religiosa antigua en los claustros, siendo yo escucha, tomara tanto furor contra mí (*sin saber yo la causa*), que dando voces y dándome palmada junto a los oídos, repetía a grandes voces: "perra loca perra loca santimora, que has de ser aquí eterna para tormento de todas; comulgadora, que te he de quitar de la cratícula y del confesionario: ¿por qué me deshonras tanto?"]

28. Teresa de Jesús uses a similar strategy in her *Libro de la vida,* see, for example, chapter VII. See also Weber 60–63.

29. [Sólo [el enemigo] . . . pudo prorrumpir en algunas cosas que allí se dijeron; como era: que yo metí discordias entre Fulana y Fulana; que de la otra dije esto, y lo otro, cosas en que yo, por la misericordia de Dios, no me hallaba comprehendida.]

30. [Me dijeron que . . . había desviado una cama de una mulata, que había hallado casi sobre la mía en el dormitorio, y que a aquella religiosa le habían dicho que era de su china la cama que yo aparté, etc.]

31. [La madre abadesa respondía: "darle unos cordeles bien fuertes, que la hagan reventar." Otras veces decía: "ya he estado amolando muy bien un cuchillo para enviárselo que se lo meta, y le enviaré soga para que se ahorque."]

32. [Sólo el rato que estaba en el confesionario, sentía yo alivio, y así contaba los días hasta que volviera.]

33. [Como en un desierto y noche oscura.] [Como en una noche oscura, como el que pierde su guía en un áspero camino por donde anda ciego.]

34. [Nunca la vieron . . . decir palabra injuriosa ni de murmuración.]

35. [Yo me hallaba del todo ignorante, ni aun el estilo de hablar con los seglares sabía.]

36. Although the first draft of this chapter was completed prior to the publication of Kathryn McKnight's *The Mystic of Tunja* (1997), the final version is clearly indebted to McKnight's detailed and well-documented analysis of Francisca's consolidation of power. Likewise, I have omitted detailed discussion of some parts of Castillo's life story to avoid repetition with McKnight's study.

Chapter 3

1. Although the *vidas* often include direct prayers to saints, this kind of worship was not officially recognized by Church hierarchy, since dialogue without the mediation of the Church in general or the confessor in particular could be seen as a challenge to its authority.

2. There were at least six hagiographies of Catherine of Siena published in Spain. Other holy women represented in the library studied by Sánchez Lora included Elizabeth of Portugal, with six hagiographies; Catherine of Genoa, with five; Mary Magdalene of Pazzi, with four; Anne, with four; Mary Magdalene, with four; Gertrude, with three; and the Virgin Mary, Librada, Leocadia, Eulalia, Engracia, Rosa of Lima, Isabel of Monte Policiano, María Reggi, Ana de Jesús, and Juana de Jesús María, each of whom had two (Sánchez Lora 377, 400–401).

3. See also Pascal 24–25.

4. Every summary of Loyola's life includes two books that influenced him, Ludolph of Saxony's *Life of Christ* (*Vita Christi*) and Jacopo de Voragine's hagiographic collection, the *Golden Legend*. Teresa was influenced by the letters of Saint Jerome and other "good books." Books were also essential to the Teresian reform of the Carmelite order. Among the books recommended for nuns in the *Constitutions* of the Discalced Carmelites are the Spanish version of Ludolph of Saxony's work, the *Flos Sanctorum*, and Thomas à Kempis's *The Imitation of Christ* (Ahlgren 38).

5. Although *libros de romance* can be used to refer to books written in the vernacular, I believe that here the author is referring to secular texts, perhaps chivalric novels.

6. [El entretenimiento o peste de las almas con los libros de comedias.] Francisca Josefa mentions *Fundaciones* and *El camino de perfección* (5–6, 116) but curiously fails to credit *El libro de su vida*, emulated in the early chapters of her autobiography.

7. [Me holgaba de leer aquellos martirios que pasaron y deseaba yo también padecerlos por amor de Dios como ellos. . . . cuando hallaba oportunidad me ponía algunos cilicios y ayunaba todos los días que podía.]

8. [era muy inclinada a la lección, leyendo cuantas vidas de santos podía conseguir] [En no siendo trágicas las dejaba.] [A mi parecer todo cuanto se puede pensar bueno viene de la oración y lección de buenos libros.]

9. Beginning in the early seventeenth century, Pope Urban VIII established three basic requirements for candidates for sainthood who were not martyrs: doctrinal purity, heroic virtue, and miraculous intercession after death.

10. I am using the idea of "discourse of virtues" as elucidated by de Certeau: "hagiography is a discourse of virtues. But the term has only secondarily a moral meaning—and not always. It borders instead on extraordinary and marvelous deeds, but only insofar as they are signs. It designates the exercise of 'powers' linked to the dunameis of the New Testament and connects the order of appearance to an order of being. 'Power' represents the relation between these two levels and upholds their difference" (*Writing* 279).

11. Although estimates varied, seven was the age most cited by confession manuals as the appropriate time to begin confession, communion, and religious education. By the time of the Renaissance this age became the accepted standard prescribed (Tentler 70; Lea I.400–404).

12. [Le amaneció el uso de la razón.] [Que [no] era nada.] [El uso de la razón ... me amaneció muy temprano ... fue a los tres años.] [Desde mis tiernos años pues desde que tuve el uso de la razón y supe usar de ella luego tuve tan grandes deseos de amar a Dios.]

13. [Padres virtuosos y temerosos de Dios.] [Padres cristianos y temerosos de Dios.] [Nieta e hija de padres muy cristianos.]

14. [Era mi padre aficionado a leer buenos libros.] [ambos eran amigos de la virtud y de buenos libros.] [Leía mi madre los libros de Santa Teresa de Jesús, y sus *Fundaciones*.]

15. [Era mi padre hombre de mucha caridad con los pobres y piedad con los enfermos, y aun con los criados.] [Mis padres ... eran muy amigos de los pobres.] [mis padres ... eran buenos en extremo, muy caritativos y limosneros.] [Con los ojos llenos de lágrimas ... daba limosna a los pobres ... y aun con los animales enfermos tenía mucha piedad.]

16. [Era de gran verdad, jamás nadie le oyó jurar ni murmurar.] [A mi padre jamás se le oyó una palabra menos compuesta, ni se le vio acción que no fuera.] [Conocí en él un continuo silencio, un no hablar mal de nadie sino bien de todos.]

17. The symbolic repercussions of being her father's favorite are seen in an author's desire for favored status with her confessor and justifies her assertion that she is the most beloved bride or daughter of Christ.

18. [No me permitían ir sino a partir muy decentes, porque ... mi padre era muy rígido y enemiguísimo de que saliera.]

19. [Era naturalmente muy piadosa y caritativa.]

20. [delante de mí no se había de hablar cosa mala ni palabras livianas. ... Me decían que me daba a respetar.]

21. The narrative of beauty was common to the virgin martyr tradition, since it was the heroines' striking appearance that put their honor in danger.

22. [Dotó Dios Nuestro Señor a nuestra Gerónima de realzadas prendas naturales. Pues tuvo un cuerpo muy alto [y] muy proporcionado; su rostro fue muy hermoso, sus ojos fueron muy bellos y vivos. Correspondía a esto que su entendimiento fue muy claro, sutil, delicado y vivo.]

23. [Comenzaba a gustar ... componerme con cuidado para parecer bien ... en especial del pelo, que lo tenía muy lindo.] [Fui amiguísima de seda y aseos desde niña.] The emphasis on hair is perhaps a reference to Bathsheba, who was often

depicted in books of feminine conduct as bathing and *combing her hair* in front of a window, a symbol of the sin of exhibitionism (2 Samuel 11.2; Régnier-Bohler 353).

24. [Comencé a traer galas, y a desear contentar en parecer bien, con mucho cuidado de manos y cabellos y olores, y todas las vanidades que en esto podía tener, que eran hartas, por ser muy curiosa. No tenía mala intención, porque no quisiera yo que nadie ofendiera a Dios por mí.]

25. [Tratando de divertirme, y poniendo más cuidado en las galas y aliños; de modo que ya no trataba de otra cosa que de cuidar el cabello, aunque no con intención de cosa particular, sino sólo con aquella vanidad y estimación de mí misma, que me parecía todo el mundo poco para mí.]

26. [Quedé llena de vanidad, de amor propio, con deseos de ser vista.]

27. [Era . . . celebrada y me llevaba las atenciones de todos.] [Yo me pensé dueña de todas las estimaciones, hermosa, con todos los adornos de la naturaleza y riqueza de la tierra, muy conocida y alabada.]

28. Furthermore none chooses to follow Rosa of Lima, Catherine of Siena, and other saintly precursors who disfigured themselves.

29. [La rara hermosura y belleza . . . arrebataba las atenciones de cuantos lograron verla.] [Vio en su rostro tal hermosura, tal claridad, y tanto golpe de belleza, que iba a prorrumpir en voces. Arrebatado del ímpetu, . . . con el corazón dio gracias a la Majestad Divina que para apacentarse entre hermosos lirios cria esas castas honestas bellezas.]

30. [A breves días se demudó en el aspecto, pues habiendo entrado robusta, se vio después muy macilenta, pálida y extenuada. Continuaba su caritativo celo el confesor, alentándola ferveroso, y la hija correspondiendo y puntual, obedecía a Dios y a su ministro.]

31. [Fue increíble el sentimiento y llanto de mis padres y hermanos, cuando tuvieron la noticia de mi entrada. . . . Mi padre estuvo tres días, sin que hubiera quien le hiciera ni beber un trago de agua ni lo quitara de llorar, en la puerta de mi aposento. Mi madre enfermó mucho de gota coral, y así todo.]

32. [Me parecía estaba en el infierno, o en una cárcel de Inquisición.]

33. ['Si monjas me coges en la boca te he de matar . . . ¡te ahogaré entre dos colchones o al pilar de la cuja te daré garrote!']

34. [Una lanza que traspasaba mi alma y partía mi corazón de dolor.] [Dagas . . . clavadas en el corazón.]

35. [Entrando por las puertas de la clausura me pareció entraba por las del cielo . . . me encogí todo e hincándome en el suelo pedí que me permitieran ir de rodillas al coro; causóles muchas ternura a las Madres y no me lo permitieron.]

36. [Mi maestra . . . me hacía varias preguntas de si estaba contenta, yo le decía que sí, porque aunque estaba tan tentada, lo disimulé y callé de tal suerte que nadie lo supo y eso que estaba que el hábito me abrasaba la cama y no la podía sufrir, la comida me dejaba vacía y hastío y así nada comía, las horas de coro se me hacían siglos; batallaba conmigo misma y me decía ¿qué es esto que por mí pasa? ¿Qué es de aquellos deseos, aquellas ansias de entrar, aquel atropellar con todo que no fue bastante hacerme desistir, ni el disgusto de mi padre, no los halagos y ruegos de mi

hermano, ni las lágrimas y sentimientos de mis hermanas, ni las solicitudes de los mundanos? ¿Qué es esto? ¿Si me salgo, qué se dirá de mí? . . . Me encerré dentro de mí y dije . . . ya entré y no he de salir . . . sola y callada he de padecer y así lo hice.]

37. [Como que llegaron y me arrancaron del corazon la raíz del amor que siempre había tenido a mis padres y hermanas. . . . comencé a dar de sollozos y . . . sentí . . . como si cada parte y cada miembro de mi cuerpo hiciese particular sentimiento y resistencia al apartar de mi corazón este amor que yo tenía a los míos.]

38. [Este día que estaba ya para entrar en el convento . . . no hallaba ni tenía otra cosa que dejar para ofrecérsela a su Majestad que este amor que tenía a los míos. . . . [D]esde este día he vivido y vivo como si no hubiera nacido ni descendido de personas humanas.]

39. [Huelgue de ser reprehendido . . . no se defienda con soberbia; mas imitando a su Señor, quiera más sufrir y callar.] [Demos, pues, mil saltos de placer cuando fuéremos maltratados con injurias y sinrazones.] See also Stockman 415.

40. *The Imitation of Christ* was recommended reading for religious women by Teresa de Jesús and had two editions published in Mexico.

41. For male religious, martyrdom remained an option. Living examples of dying for God were recounted orally and in written missionary chronicles. See also Weinstein and Bell 158–59 and Gilmore 142 on persecution as martyrdom.

42. Confessors who accuse women of delusions are evoked in negative and sometimes even demonic terms; however, since the narrative of persecution recreates the Passion of Christ, it is logically other women who collectively torment the writing subject.

43. [Que había tomado con mucho empeño labrarla una corona y hacerla santa a su costa.]

44. [endemoniada, que todo nacía de hipocresía y soberbía.]

45. [Me trataba como si fuera una indita.] [Como se me juntaba todo me era la vida insoportable.]

46. Seventeenth-century texts embraced the ideal of "blessed solitude" of Ignacio de Loyola, Pedro de Alcántara, and Juan de la Cruz (Knipping 441–44).

47. To name just a few of the most frequently cited examples from other national traditions: Francesca Bussa d'Ponziani burned her genitals with hot wax, so that she would feel pain whenever she moved; Margaret of Cortona mutilated her face with a razor, Christina the Astonishing jumped into an oven on one occasion and hung herself on another (King 122–23; Bynum 210).

48. [No tenía sino la piel y los huesos y no parecía sino un retrato vivo de la muerte. Aparecían en su cuerpo los cardenales, y las señales de los azotes, y golpes que el demonio le daba.]

49. [Prenda que enriquecía su vida.]

50. Sigüenza y Góngora's description is suspiciously similar to Juan de la Presentación's *La corona de Madrid: Vida devota de la Beata Madre María Ana de Jesús* (1673): "They discovered a formidable cilice of chains and points of iron so incorporated [into her flesh] that they could only be removed with great effort, tearing out with them not only chunks of flesh but also affects of the heart"

[descubrió formidable cilicio de cadenas, y puntas de hierro, tan incorporado . . . que se le quitó con mucho trabajo, arrancando no sólo con él pedazos de carne, sino afectos del corazón] (104).

51. See also Puccini on Mary Magdalene of Pazzi: "her understanding was to be dead without troublesome considering of anything which might concern either herself or others" (38).

52. On similar spectacles in Spanish America, see Cesareo.

53. Although confessors were no longer required to interrogate their spiritual daughters on matters of the flesh in graphic detail, the number of treatises dedicated to the subject suggests that the danger of suggestive interrogations remained a concern well into the eighteenth century (Lea I.370–73, 379–80).

54. [Desnudo, grande, y muy tosco . . . me oprimió todo el cuerpo con tanta fuerza que me reventaba.] [Todos los huesos se los desmigajaban en menudos pedazos.] [Apretándola entre sus brazos con tanta fuerza, que todos los huesos de su cuerpo parecía haberse desencajado y hecho pedazos.]

55. [Con un grave e insoportable peso, con que como presándola la martirizaba.]

56. [Me amenazó que se me metería en el cuerpo.]

57. According to Jean Franco, blacks, mulattos, and indigenous men and women "were perceived to be the dangerous guardians of the erotic arts" (xiv).

58. Of course in some cases the nightmares could have been the result of an actual sexual trauma; it would not have been particularly unusual that a daughter was placed in a convent after a sexual violation made her unmarriageable.

59. [moviendo su imaginativa con horribles sugestiones, y arrojando furiosas llamas de fuego sensual.] It is interesting to note that in a biography of a male visionary, Domingo Pérez de Barcia, the devil appears in the form of a *woman* (Gutiérrez Dávila 223).

60. [La ponían inmobile, sin que pudiese menearse ni huir de allí (aunque quería, y lo procuraba la criatura) y tenían acto con ella.]

61. Weinstein and Bell's statistics show that although women constituted only 17.5 percent of canonized saints between A.D. 1000 and A.D. 1700, they represented 53.2 percent of the cases of painful illness. Disparity was also noted in descriptions of extreme asceticism: women represented 29 percent of the saints who engaged in excessive penance and 23.3 percent of those who died from these practices (234–35).

62. [Me clavaba alfileres en la boca y no los sentía; tiraba a arrancarme los cabellos de la cabeza, y me quedaba con la mano pendiente y sumida en aquel letargo. Ponía los nudos del cordón debajo las rodillas cuando me rodillaba, y nada sentía. Tomaba verbena y otras cosas amargas en la boca y me las echaba en los ojos, untándolos de tabaco, y nada de esto era remedio. Hacía a las novicias que mientras rezábamos el oficio, me estuvieran torciendo y apretando los dedos de las manos, mas no aprovechaba, aunque ellas lo hacían con harta fuerza, como yo se lo mandaba.]

63. [Mandábanme hacer. . . varias devociones a los santos, llevar agua bendita, etc., y yo mojada en agua bendita y cargada de cruces, me quedaba como he dicho.]

64. [Una voz que hablaba a mi interior y que me decía que una enfermedad habitual sería el único medio para que me retirase de todo. No puedo negar que esta propuesta me ensanchó el corazón porque me pareció muy a propósito para lo que yo deseaba (que era abstraerme de toda ocasión peligrosa); y así, la acepté con muy rendida voluntad y la abracé con un regocijo grande.] Teresa de Jesús also claimed that she had asked God to send her illness (*Libro de la vida* V.2, 141–42/26).

65. During a case of what Muriel interprets as rheumatic fever, María Magdalena begins to suffer uncontrollable tremors from Sydenham's chorea: once it is determined she is not possessed by the devil, the physicians cut open her thighs and arms and burn the wounds with a hot knife; hot iron cautery is also applied to the crown of her head. Ironically, Sydenham's chorea does not normally cause lasting problems and would probably have subsided with the rheumatic fever.

66. [Dolores de ijada, de orina, del pulmón, de costado, de corazón, de oídos, de estómago, de quijadas, de dientes y de muelas, con inflamación del hígado y bazo, padeciendo juntamente dolores en las espaldas, brazos, pies, y manos, sin que hubiese coyuntura sin especial verdugo y singular tormento, padeciéndole de ordinario en la frente, ojos, cabeza, con fríos y calenturas interminables, con unos sudores copiosísimos de tan mal humor que inficionaba el convento.]

67. Lavrin interprets these attacks as epileptic seizures ("Vida conventual" 88).

68. Teresa de Jesús begs God to send her the torments of the devil so that she may take on the sins of another (*Libro de su vida*, XXXI.7, 369/207). See also *El libro de las fundaciones*, especially chapter 12, and Mary Magdalene of Pazzi (73, 175).

69. [El humor pestilente infeccionaba todo lo interior, de tal manera que causaba podre y materia de pestilencial olor y de color verdinegro por la boca y demás partes.] [Padecía intolerable hedor que las religiosas apenas podían sufrirlo y el mal olor penetró de tal manera las tablas de la cama que tuvieron que quemarlas y el colchoncillo se deshizo fuera de casa por su mal olor.] Isabel was so renowned as a saint that at the time of her death her hands were cut into pieces to distribute as relics (Peña 2; Ramos Medina "Isabel de la Encarnación" 48).

70. [Le consta . . . que no sabe [que] tenga vicios, padezca defectos, deformidad en el cuerpo, enfermedad incurable, contagiosa, mal caduco, gota coral o de corazón que la prive de sentido, ni que haya estado loca, frenética, espirituada, endemoniada, ni excomulgada.]

71. [María, come, que esta vida no se puede pasar sin comer y lo que da la comunidad es para que se coma sea lo que se fuere y no me desagrado de que se coma.]

72. [Como si hubiera cometido una culpa muy grave.] [Me dio a entender Dios Nuestro Señor con mucha claridad cuánto se desagradó que se falte a lo que mandó las reglas y constituciones *aunque sean en cosas muy menudos*. . . . [P]idiéndole a Nuestro Señor me diera modo para ser santa, y me dio a entender diciéndome que *no me afligiera* que era ejercicio en que me había puesto porque era tanto lo que se agradaba de ver con las lágrimas y dolor con que lloraba una falta o una imperfección *por leve que fuera como si fuera una culpa muy grave*, yo quedé consolada]

73. [Que al comer padecía inmensamente, porque cuanto de gusto tomaba, era mayor disgusto y amarguras para mi alma.]

74. [Se me fabricó una capilla interior, donde se colocó su Majestad en la textura de ella, y alrededor, todo su adorno de los pasos de la pasión santísima. Y así ha perserverado hasta hoy ... Y siempre se ha renovado y colocado su Majestad en ella, siempre que lo he recibido sacramentado.]

75. [Entendí que el Santo Apóstol me negoció este padecer, conmutándome en él las terribles penas que me esperaban por mis gravísimas culpas.]

76. In the *compassio,* Mary was believed to have suffered the same torments as her son (Surtz 53).

Chapter 4

1. [Los sesenta argumentos que ofrezco son otras tantas cartas que escribió a sus confesores. Porque cada una es real de su humildad.] For this chapter I have consulted both Sebastiana's original notebooks and Valdés's biography. Although Sebastiana never wrote a retrospective life story, the use of rhetorical strategies of the *vida*, the centrality of the confessor as addressee, and in particular, the application of the hagiographic model justify her inclusion here. It was customary to call the daily entries "letters," an interesting point that underscores the importance of the confessor/addressee in their production, even though they were not always sent as individual documents.

2. [el clarísimo espejo en que pudieran ver las religiosas almas las más heroicas virtudes compendiadas.]

3. The recogimiento of San Miguel de Belén was affiliated with the congregation of the chapel of San Felipe Neri and modeled after similar communities established in Spain by Loyola and his followers. See Muriel *Cultura femenina* 417; *Los recogimientos de mujeres* 88–89, 96.

4. [la servía de cruz muy pesada esta prolongada demora.]

5. [Así consiguió la Venerable Sebastiana ser más pobre de lo que era, habiendo sido pobre en extremo, y viniendo a quedar, como vivo retrato de la pobreza. Lo que vestía era pobre, lo que comía, pobre, lo que usaba, pobre, lo que hablaba, pobre, y pobre en lo que pensaba hasta llegar a lo más fino de la apostólica Pobreza.] The original Spanish uses "poor" in the double sense that includes poverty and humility. I have left the translation literal to emphasize the insistent repetition of the author.

6. [sólo con lo necesario para cubrir honestamente su cuerpo.]

7. Contending that the sense of touch is the most dangerous of the senses because it is spread throughout the body, Scaramelli's manual warns its readers not to touch anyone and to avoid touching oneself (200).

8. Ignacio de Loyola, who had emphasized solitude and seclusion as a means of bringing the soul closer to God, recalls Thomas à Kempis's prescription for the need to set oneself apart from the world in a "small corner with a small book" (22).

9. [estos fueron los primeros pasos de Doña Sebastiana en el camino glorioso de las virtudes.]

10. [puertas a sus sentidos, candados fuertes a sus labios, y grillos a sus pies.]

11. [como una margarita en su nacar, como una paloma en su nido, como en su propio jardín una rosa: tan gustosa quedó en el Recogimiento de Belén, que a pocos días de entrada ya la servían de molestia las visitas de sus parientes, haciéndose violencia, aun para las de sus padres.]

12. See also Catherine of Siena: "If I make my principal desire bodily penance, I build the city of my soul on sand, so that every little wind can blow it down, and no building can be erected on it. But if I build on the virtues, my soul is founding on the living rock ... and there is no building so tall that it cannot stand firmly, nor wind so contrary that it will ever pull it to earth" ("Letter" cited in Petroff 268).

13. [gran medicamento, para curar muchas enfermedades.]

14. [Fue el caso que ... hizo una noche tan cruel, tan sangrienta, y tan rigorosa disciplina, que brotó mucha sangre, de modo que no solamente se tiñeron con su caliente púrpura los jazmines cándidos de su cuerpo sino que mancharon los ladrillos de la recámara en que se recogía] (119–20). Such bloody episodes—related, of course, to Christ's passion—were relatively commonplace in spiritual biographies. See also Juan de la Presentación, whose description of María Ana de Jesús includes a similar scene: "with rigorous disciplines she stained the walls of her room with blood" [con las rigurosas disciplinas había teñido de sangre las paredes de su habitación] (17).

15. [La lengua ... en sí es universidad de maldades.]

16. [Añadiendo dolor a dolor, y tormento a tormento. O lengua dichosa, y qué premio habrás recibido por tan cruda Penitencia! O dichosa Penitencia, y qué gloria habrás alcanzado, como piadosamente creemos!]

17. [después que probó las delicias del espíritu.]

18. [como si fuera un regalado manjar.]

19. [a veces pierdo el sentido y acabado se me revienta la cabeza, y quedo tan desconsolada que me faltan alientos para cosa buena y al cuerpo le faltan fuerzas, y con la flaqueza recuerva tanto el apetito de comer que me violenta a comer lo que en muchos tiempos no probaba, esto es cosas que tuvieran dulce. El verme tan perversa me da tanta pena que estoy como afrentada y con vergüenza delante de mi Dios y de todos, como cosa aborrecida.]

20. [Me sucedió ... que por cena comí un pedacito de semita y un pedacito de panocha, y esto fue bastante para desconsolarme de mi poca mortificación ... hasta cuando me había de ver libre de mis apetitos? Parece que esto no era cosa para que me afligiera tanto ... lo malo fue que no tenía necesidad, y había pensado no cenar.]

21. Noelle Caskey notes the "peculiar oversensitivity" of anorexics to the perceived wishes of those around them (179).

22. In *La perfecta casada* (1583), Luis de León also described the perfect wife as a "mujer varonil" [manly women] (30). In contrast, the indigenous populations of Spanish America were often *feminized* as a means to justify their subaltern status. For example, one of the reasons cited for the rigid control of reading material in the New World was that the native population, with its "torpeza femenina" [feminine depravity] was unable to distinguish good from evil (Adorno "El sujeto colonial" 60).

23. [no era entendimiento mujeril. . . . Tan magnánima y fuerte que, puedo aseverar, pudo competir con la más grande fortaleza varonil.]

24. As is fairly obvious, women who fast for long periods of time begin to lose the bodily characteristics that mark them as females, such as breasts, curved hips, and menstruation. Caskey contends this is also related to a desire to reflect the male body (177–78).

25. [habiendo singularidades (vamos perdidas) en el traje, en la modestia, en el estilo, y en todas las acciones ha de haber igualdad, desde la Prelada hasta la última novicia.]

26. [En ninguna de ellas se descubrirá inclinación a la extraordinaria comodidad del cuerpo, o a la delectación carnal, sino mucha *honestidad* en todas. No se hallará perniciosa inquietud, sino *suave paz interior*. . . . No se descubrirá en ellas *dureza o indocilidad,* sino rendida obedencia, y sujeción al dictamen prudente de sus confesores. . . . No se registrarán . . . simulación alguna, queriendo aparecer Santa, o virtuosa, pues se reputaba por la más indigna de la criaturas todas del Mundo.]

27. [más admirables, que imitables.]

28. [Lo que parece más cómodo y más seguro de la penitencia, es que el dolor sea sensible en las carnes y que no entre dentro en los huesos, de manera que dé dolor y no enfermedad.]

29. As Weber observes, Teresa came to understand the "unfortunate mental consequences" that the rigorous way of life she had promoted could sometimes produce: "The life of asceticism, enclosure, and prolonged periods of mental prayer in the reformed Carmelite convents, a life that she had hoped would open the mystical path for more women, had led several nuns along another path, which Teresa was forced to recognize as illness. She began to acknowledge the difficulty of . . . distinguishing divine communication from the effects of poor diet, self-inflicted pain, and sensory deprivation" (*Teresa* 40).

30. [admirable extrañeza sino el intenso amor a Dios y deseo sólido de agradarle.]

31. [Pero qué ingeniosas trazas no discurre la sutileza del amor divino!]

32. As Caskey observes: "Refusing to eat is supremely defiant and supremely obedient at the same time" (181).

33. Paula's life story in the second edition of Ribadeneyra emphasizes her rigorous disciplines and fasts and her desire to die to be one with God: "'Who will give me the wings of a dove so that I may fly away to rest?'" ["¿Quién me dará alas como de paloma, y volaré y descansaré?"] (249). In his funeral sermon, Ignacio Saldaña adopts the image of the dove to describe Sebastiana. In the "Dedicatoria" to the published version of this oration, her brother, Miguel Joseph de Maya, elaborates on this theme, noting that although doves are the least precious birds they symbolize purity, simplicity, and beauty. It is also the dove, de Maya observes, that cries rather than sings (vi–vii).

Chapter 5

1. The purpose of these bars was not so much to prevent nuns from seeing out, but to keep the outside world from seeing in. Individual variations of the bars also

had symbolic functions: austere reformed orders such as the Capuchines and Discalced Carmelites reinforced the notion of cloister with sharp spikes on the outer sides of the bars dividing the church from the convent; in contrast, the ornate grilles in the Franciscan convents of San Juan de la Penitencia in Mexico City and Santa Clara in Querétaro celebrated the nun's presence in the community (Maza 8, figures 11–15, 50–52).

2. Convents with common refectories also used seating patterns as a means of reinforcing social hierarchy, honoring the superiors as those who guided the community toward the realization of God's will (Curran 111–15).

3. Of course this vertical configuration also suggests the spatial relations between heaven and earth, with the black-veiled nuns symbolically closer to heaven.

4. As Curran's research shows, postures of humility were retained in women's religious communities as late as the early twentieth century, including kneeling or lying at the doorway as penance, begging on one's knees for food, and kissing other sisters' feet during prayers after meals. Although many practices were abandoned after 1921, when constitutions were rewritten in accord with new canon law, Curran reports that in some North American convents kneeling, confessing to the mistress, and kissing the floor were required of all sisters twice a week even in the 1960s (121–25).

5. See Althusser 168–69.

6. I borrow the term from Víctor García de la Concha, who posits a connection between the tears in the works of Teresa de Jesús and Francisco de Osuña's *Tercer abecedario* (121–24).

7. It is this version of the Gospel that is reproduced in the *Flos sanctorum*.

8. This figure is often conflated with that of Mary Magdalene (Ferguson 135). In addition to Mary Magdalene, favored iconographical subjects also included Mary as the *mater dolorosa* and the repentant Peter.

9. Teresa de Jesús frequently refers to her tears, as well as to her devotion to Mary Magdalene. In *Las moradas,* Teresa merges the figure of the fisherwoman in the home of Simon the Pharisee with those of Mary Magdalene and Mary of Bethany (*Las moradas* 7:4.13). It was Mary of Bethany's tears that inspired Christ to raise Lazarus from the dead (John 11.33–37), and Teresa is "dead" for four days before she awakens to her spiritual calling (*Libro de la vida* VI.1–5, 149–52/32–34). The prophecies and lamentations of Jeremiah are also characterized by the recurrent symbol of tears (9.1, 13.17, 14.17).

10. This figure bears some similarity to an image in Cesare Ripa's emblem book [Mourning over the sins], in which the figure holds a ledger book on which is written "absolved from all debts." Significantly, this emblem represents the freedom from sin gained through a good confession.

11. In the biography of Lutgard of Aywières, her affliction for the sins of others provokes a "fountain of tears" (Thomas de Cantimpré 69).

12. [anegada en el mar de mis lágrimas.] [Y decía [Jesucristo]: "los pecados que no fueron llorados serán los que no quedaran borrados." Y se quedaba como esperando a que me doliese de los que no tenía borrados para luego que yo los

llorase, borrá[ndo]los con mis lágrimas.] [eran fuentes de lágrimas continuamente, de noche y de día, y a todas horas estaba hecha un mar de lágrimas. . . . hasta hoy se continúan mis ojos un aguacero de lágrimas.] [Tenía en este tiempo . . . un paño que tenía más de dos varas para enjuagar las lágrimas que lloraba, y a días las dejaba correr hasta el suelo. Y hoy en día hago lo mismo, porque tres paños que me permite tajá los empapo y no tengo bastante, y así las dejo correr sin enjuagarlas.] [un charco de agua de las lágrimas que lloré.]

13. Obviously Francisca and her readers are aware that infants often cry for less consequential reasons.

14. [Decían que aun cuando apenas podía andar, me escondía a llorar lágrimas . . . como si supiera los males en que había de caer ofendiendo a Nuestro Señor.] [para escribirle a vuestra paternidad . . . me puse a llorar sobre el tintero, para mojarlo con las lágrimas que lloraba . . . quise mojarlo con mis lágrimas y escribir con ellas; cosa que podía hacer con facilidad, por lo mucho que lloraba.]

15. [El verbo fundamental es aquí el verbo "ver". . . No es una especulación ilustrada con ejemplos. Es el testimonio de un hombre que ha visto con sus ojos y tocado con sus manos a otro hombre, hombre tan real como él mismo.]

16. "So that scene is imprinted more forcefully . . . Listen as if it came from your own ears, and see it as if it came from your own eyes, with all the passion of your soul." [para que las cosas se graben con más fuerza . . . Escuchadlo como si viniera de vuestros oídos, vedlo como si viniera de vuestros ojos, con todo el afecto de vuestra alma" (ctd. Vargaslugo "Mística y pintura" 34).] Bonaventure's *Mística teología* was widely distributed in Spanish America, and an edition was published in Mexico in 1575. Thomas of Aquinas also advocated images to stimulate devotion (Vargaslugo "La obra de arte" 117).

17. In a meditation on the *Ecce Homo,* Pedro instructs his readers to: "First put the earlier image of the Lord *before your eyes* . . . and then again *look* at the way in which he is here. . . . And after you have *looked and delighted in the vision* of the exhausted figure *turn your eyes to see him* as he is here. . . . Take in the entire scene, from within and without . . . *Put yourself in the place of He who is suffering, and look at what you would feel.*" [Pon primero *ante tus ojos* la imagen antigua de este Señor . . . y luego vuelve a *mirar* de la manera que aquí está. . . . Y después que así le hubieres *mirado y deleitado de ver* una tan acabada figura, *vuelve los ojos a mirarlo* tal cual aquí lo ves. . . . *Míralo* todo de dentro y fuera. . . . *Ponte tú mismo en el lugar del que padece, y mira lo que sentirías]* (76–77, emphasis added).

18. [El primer preámbulo es composición viendo el lugar. Aquí es de notar que en la contemplación o meditación visible, así como contemplar a Cristo nuestro Señor, el cual es visible, la contemplación será ver con la vista de la imaginación el lugar corpóreo, donde se halla la cosa que quiero contemplar.]

19. See introduction, note 44.

20. ["No tengas pena, que yo te daré libro vivo". . . Su Majestad ha sido el libro verdadero adonde he visto las verdades.]

21. [Paréceme a mí que si tuvieran la fe como la tuvieron después que vino el Espíritu Santo, de que era Dios y hombre, no les impidiera.]

22. On each page of these emblem books was an illustration with a brief caption in Latin or in the vernacular, accompanied by a longer explicatory text. At the end of his life, Loyola sought to publish a book in which his compositions of place would be illustrated with engravings. He left the project to his disciple Jerome Nadal, whose posthumous *Adnotationes et meditationes* (1595) became a model for these immensely popular texts.

23. The Mexican Jesuit José Vidal de Figueroa also advocated speaking directly to images as a means of spiritual contemplation (Vargaslugo "La obra de arte" 122).

24. Spanish polychrome sculpture reached its apex in the early to mid-seventeenth century through the work of artists such as Juan Martínez Montañés, Gregorio Fernández, and Juan de Juní, whose work was exported (eight Virgins of the Rosary in Chile were carved by Martínez Montañés) and copied (Freedberg 241–42). It is documented that paintings by Francisco Zurbarán were sent to the New World, and copies of the masters, particularly Bartolomé Esteban Murillo, could be found throughout the colonies, where they exercised an important influence. This kind of art was also promoted by the school of the Sevillan painter Sebastián de Arteaga and his Mexican disciples such as José Juárez, Antonio Rodríguez, Juan Sánchez Salmerón, Pedro Ramírez, and Baltasar de Echave Rioja. Other important figures in the development of religious art in the colonies included Juan Correa, Cristóbal de Villapando, and Antonio de Torres. See also Praz 13.

25. Maravall suggests that the bloody spectacles mounted by the Church in Spain (and repeated in Spanish America) were a way for rulers and their collaborators to terrify people into accepting their places in the social order (*Cultura del barroco* 163/336–37).

26. [de rodillas, las manos juntas, o levantadas al cielo, o al pecho, la cabeza levantada, los ojos elevados, lagrimosos, y alegres, o la cabeza baja, y los ojos cerrados, algo suspenso el semblante, siempre el cuello torcido, o las manos enclavijadas . . . y otras acciones según el afecto del devoto.] Although there were other important manuals written in Spain and Spanish America, Carducci's was the most influential during the later baroque period (Gallego 187).

27. Cabrera, not coincidentally, was commissioned by the Jesuits for several works, including a series on the life of Ignacio de Loyola. Other particularly well-rendered examples of this corporeal rhetoric include "San Francisco con el ángel de la redoma," by Antonio de Torres and Nicolás Rodríguez Juárez's "Transverbación de Santa Teresa" (*Arte y mística del barroco*, figures 75, 78).

28. [con sus manos en devotas posturas para adorarlo, con sus brazos, poniéndolos en cruz en su adorable presencia, con sus rodillas doblándolas rendida, con su cabeza, inclinándola humilde, con sus ojos siempre en tierra, con el todo de su cuerpo, y alma, formando ritual místico, y devoto, que tenía siempre en las manos.]

29. See Muriel's *Retratos de monjas* and Ruiz Gomar's "Retratos de monjas" for examples of portraits of nuns in New Spain. I am of course referring to portraits commissioned at the time of a nun's profession, not those painted after her death.

30. [Los ojos en la tierra, las manos sobre el pecho cruzadas, como que estaba con el pensamiento en el Cielo y su corazón en Dios.]

31. In this convent alone, there were three paintings each of Gertrude and Antonio de Villanueva, four each of Anthony of Padua and Rosa of Lima, two of Roche, and one each of Claire of Assisi, Catherine of Alexandria, Catherine of Siena, and Ignacio de Loyola. The main altar of the church, visible from the choir loft, included life-size statues of Claire, Carlo Borromeo, the Passion of Christ, Mary Magdalene, and Teresa de Jesús.

32. [me vi a mí misma levantada del suelo y me iba subiendo a lo alto hasta llegar donde está esta imagen de Nuestro Señor crucificado. . . . llegué a poner mis labios y boca en la llaga del costado.]

33. [[R]ogué que me trajesen a la cama una imagen de Jesús Nazareno. . . . Pusieronlo a mi vista y . . . fijé en los ojos en esta soberana imagen que, hablándole amorosamente a mi interior, dijo: "Venite ad me omnes qui laborati et onerati estis et ego refitiam vos." Al oír yo estas palabras, estaba observando la amorosa benignidad con que me miraban aquellos piadosos y compasivos ojos (que me parece que aún ellos hablaban más que la voz que yo oía).]

34. See, for example, illustrations of Christ as shepherd and gardener, and the soul as a dried tree in Knipping (figures 15, 21, 22). Sherry Velasco has pointed out to me that many images may also have been derived from listening to sermons.

35. Of course Teresa also developed an allegory around the image of the garden; the enclosed garden was associated with the Immaculate Conception. For more on the long tradition of this trope, see Surtz 94–95.

36. [un día, cuando éste [San Bernardo] estaba arrodillado ante la Cruz, el Crucificado extendió su brazo y lo posó sobre él, estrechándolo y acariciándolo con extremo amor.]

37. Ribadeneyra's *Flos Sanctorum* was the text most consulted for painters commissioned to represent the figure or life of a saint (Gallego 210).

38. [vi a mi Señor puesto en la cruz . . . bajó un brazo y abrazó mi alma, que estaba en el lado del corazón, con mucha seguridad; y el otro brazo le quedó pendiente de la cruz.] Perhaps not coincidentally, both Sebastiana and María Marcela professed in Franciscan convents.

39. [Un día . . . me manifestó el Señor resucitado con indecible hermosura adornado con muchas joyas y flores que yo le había procurado hacer con ejercicios de virtudes. Traía también una túnica carmesí y una capa azul como capa de coro; se sentó a mi lado, me cubrió con la capa y echándome el brazo diestro me recostó sobre su costado comunicando al alma indecibles bienes esto entre un ardiente fuego y unas luces más claras que el sol de mediodía.]

40. In the case of at least one seventeenth-century mystic, María de Jesús de Ágreda, her sisters would open the communion grille and remove the veil from her face when she was in a mystic trance, so the assembled public could see her (Ximenes Samaniego 59).

41. [va mucho de estar en estar.]

42. [todo de diamante o muy claro cristal, adonde hay muchos aposentos, así como en el cielo hay muchas moradas. . . . Si este castillo es el ánima, claro está que no hay para qué entrar, pues si es él mismo: como parecería desatino decir a uno que

entrase en una pieza, estando ya dentro."] The idea of being in the castle is also discussed by de Certeau in *The Mystic Fable*, 194–95.

43. John 14.23 refers to Christ making his home in the disciples; also 14.2 "in my father's house there are many mansions"; and Paul notes his wish: "that Christ may dwell in your hearts through faith" (Ephesians 3.17). Thomas à Kempis alludes to Christ as the soul's "bridegroom" who dwells within the heart (54) and is enthroned there (65). Catherine of Siena also wrote of an "interior cell."

44. [Considerando el mucho encerramiento y pocas cosas de entretenimiento que tenéis, mis hermanas, y no casas tan bastantes como conviene en algunos monasterios de los vuestros, me parece os será consuelo deleitaros en este castillo interior, pues sin licencia de los superiores podéis entraros y pasearos por él a cualquier hora.]

45. As Arenal and Schlau point out, this sense of enclosure was not exclusively experienced in the convent, since women's physical space was extremely confined even in homes of the nobility (*Untold Sisters* 3).

46. [Y vi al Señor que se alojaba en ella y decía: "en esta pobre casilla he de hacer mi habitación porque me la han dado y entregado a mí solo. . . . No quiero los palacios que me ofrecen ricos y alajados, porque en ellos no estaré solo."]

47. [Dentra en estos espacios y paséate.]

48. For more on the aesthetic of martyrdom and its corporeal rhetoric, see Cesareo, especially 29–79. See also Pacheco 381, 390–91, 404, 412–16, 454–64, 486–90; Silva Cotapos 104–5.

49. [que vuela por todo el mundo.]

50. [no entenderse un alma ni hallar quien la entienda.] [como un amigo habla a otro, o un siervo a su señor . . . comunicando sus cosas y queriendo consejo en ellas.]

51. [Como suele un amigo hablar con otro de su satisfacción, así [el Señor] estaba conmigo conversando y alentando, con aquellas dulcísimas caricias, mi corazón.]

52. [Es mucho lo que hablo delante de mi Dios, y de mi Madre de mi alma, con tanta . . . humilde confianza, y con un modo de intimidad, que no hallo cómo compararlo para que entendiera Vuestra Paternidad lo que pasa.]

53. [Aquí a sus pies derramaba mi corazón y le desaprochaba mi pecho, manifestándole mi interior y cuanto en el pasaba. Muy por menudo le comunicaba mis dudas, mis desconsuelos. Era tanta la luz y el consuelo que el Señor comunicaba a mi alma a los pies de este glorioso santo por su intercesión, que hallaba el remedio y salida en todos mis aprietos, que eran harto grandes por no tener confesor con quien comunicar estas cosas.]

54. [Como acá si dos personas se quieren mucho y tienen buen entendimiento, aun sin señas parece que se entienden con sólo mirarse.]

55. [Así la esposa que de veras ama, no conoce más voluntad que la de su Señor y esposo; y si él le preguntara: ¿dónde quieres que vamos, dónde quieres que estemos?, sólo respondiera: yo qué sé, Señor, yo qué sé, llevadme donde quisieres. Yo no tengo más patria que a vos, yo olvidé mi pueblo y la casa de mi padre, yo no

busco en el campo otro tesoro, pues todas mis cosas y a mí misma di por vos.] Recall that Francisca had asked God to provide her with a confessor to take the place of her dead father (27, 29).

56. [porque parece que aquel conocimiento es como una palabra, o una habla escondida, no como la que se articula o forma con la voz.] [El habla delicada / Del amante que estimo / Miel y leche destila / Entre rosas y lirios.]

57. For more on the devotion to Christ as Word, see also the hagiography of Mary Magdalene of Pazzi (Puccini 39, 41, 47, 66, 68, 75). Catherine of Siena also often refers to Christ as Word.

58. See also Teresa de Jesús *Las moradas* VII, 3, xii. This "kiss" also relates to Eucharistic passion: visions followed communion and emphasized a direct relation with Christ that was not mediated through the confessor.

59. [Al instante llegó su rostro al mío, me osculó el carillo. Se quedó echado por más que le pedí con los temores que se fuera.] [el Señor llegó al ósculo de los labios el alma entonces estremeciéndose de temor ... procuraba entrarse en la llaga del costado a esconderse hasta que el Señor se dio [cuenta] de lo que intentaba y como riéndose de verla tan asustada.] Although the language used in such encounters clearly derives from biblical text, it is conceivable that allusions to the Song of Songs were mediated by other authors. Teresa de Jesús, for example, uses imagery from the Song in *Las moradas:* "These effects ... God bestows when the soul approaches Him and He gives the soul that kiss for which the Bride besought Him." [Estos efectos ... da Dios cuando llega el alma a Sí, con este ósculo que pedía la Esposa] (7:3.427/224).

60. Gallego notes the intimate relation between emblem books in sixteenth-century Netherlands and Spain (89).

61. The image of the heart beaten by hammers represents suffering for divine love. See Valdés 353.

62. ["Gerónima es mi corazón y yo soy el corazón de Gerónima."]

63. Mary Magdalene of Pazzi has a similar vision of Augustine, who writes on her heart: "Verbum caro factum est"; the first word is written in gold and the rest in blood, gold for Christ's divinity and blood for his humanity.

64. [me deshace lo más profundo del alma con una apacible suavidad ... que me consume, y me acaba las fuerzas, y el corazón no me cabe en el cuerpo, y da golpes dolorosos, que no alcanza el resuello con ansias tan amorosas, que se acaba la vida en este padecer y son tan encendidos los deseos de darle gusto a este enamorado de mi alma.]

65. [sentí como que una flecha me parara el corazón ocasionándome un dolor tan vehemente que me obligó a dar un quejido el cual se oyó en el coro. ... Me quedaron de esto unas violentas ansias de amar a Dios que me parecía poco el fuego en que continuamente me abrasaba y la llama que ardía sin cesar.]

66. [echando los brazos sobre mis hombros, cargaba allí un peso, aunque grande, tan dulce, tan suave, tan fuerte, tan apacible, que el alma sólo quisiera morir y acabar en él y con él: mas no podía hacer más que recibir y arder en sí misma.]

67. Teresa de Jesús's celebrated pierced heart reiterates an Augustinian motif.

68. [procuré hacer memoria]; [me entregué más, me procuré rendir más]; [sentía un impulso interior que [me] llamaba . . . y fui donde me llamaban]; [quedando mi corazón allí preso porque era mi pretensión.]

69. This was not an uncommon assertion. Francis de Sales reminds his readers of a parable attributed to Bonaventure in which "a poor simple woman can love God every bit as much as a doctor of theology" (228).

70. [una luz que se imprimía en el alma.] [Escríbelo todo como fue, sin quitar ni poner letra ninguna, ni una tilde más ni menos, de la pura y sencilla verdad.] [pasé tres días batallando . . . al cuarto se ilustró el entendimiento, se inflamó la voluntad y me manifestó el Señor como en un mapa cuantos misterios y atributos me ha manifestado y quedan escritos . . . . Esta manifestación me sirvió de dos cosas: la una de consolarme y asegurarme de los temores de que pierdo tiempo y la otra de facilitarme el escribir.]

71. [se me exitó la especie de lo que me dijo de que, en siendo yo Prelada, lo sería también su Majestad.] ["Favoreceré tu convento si admites su gobierno."] ["Yo puse en vos las palabras de san Pablo, porque quiero [que] prediques como él."]

72. [tuve clara noticia de que gustaba Dios que instruyese a la gente ignorante; pues eran muchas las almas que se perdían por falta de luz y así procuré y lo hice ir instruyendo algunas. . . . Y tengo por muy cierto que muchas almas se hubieran perdido si no hubieran llegado a comunicar conmigo sus errores.]

73. [no tengo duda ninguna]; [quedo con alguna duda.]

74. [los que acá tenemos por señores, que todo el señorío ponen en autoridades postizas.]

75. [El Señor sea servido de todo, que sea su Mayor Gloria que *sólo me ha elegido.*] [me instan que publique que no tienen número [las mercedes] y que me ha concedido y dado más que a muchos Santos porque es su gusto . . . que vuelva a publicar que las mercedes y misericordias no tienen número.] [Yo siempre le he dado parte a Usted de todo lo que me he acordado. Usted sabrá lo que debe hacer. Yo no quiero más que la gloria de Dios . . . y estar oculta.]

76. [sin más manejo ni interposición que unos papelitos escritos de esta hormiga ruin sin instrucción ni comunicación más que lo que su Majestad inspiraba.] [Pues me parece que puedo decir que ni la mitad del dinero que se gastó lo cojió, sino lo creció de aquel que adquirió su Majestad.] On another occasion, during her first term as prioress, the author claims ignorance of the origin of 3,000 pesos used to construct a sanctuary (folio 4, *Vida* 169).

77. [En el deseo y luz que Nuestro Señor me dio de entrar [en] la casa de la condesa Del Portillo, se me puso su Majestad . . . a mi lado y me puso al Señor Virrey Manso, que era el que gobernaba entonces. Me decía su Majestad que le dijera al Virrey que . . . aplicase un año de su renta a hacerle casa a sus esposas y cercales al convento. Y que le libraría de un trabajo grande. . . . Y lo hubiera su Majestad librado del trabajo que tuvo cuando se fue en la Habana si hubiera hecho esta obra.] José Antonio Manso de Velasco was viceroy of Peru from 1745 to 1761. Returning to Spain in 1762, he found himself in Havana just as British troops attacked Cuba. Put in charge of military operations there, Manso was court-martialed in Spain for his

role in the surrender of the island and exiled to Granada, where he died shortly thereafter (Barros Araña 160).

78. [Como a hurtadillas, tomé el corazón del Señor.... Volvió el Señor a mirarme y ... me decía, "Gerónima, dame mi corazón." "¿Qué es dar el corazón," le decía yo, "No lo tengo que soltar...." Volvía con amor indecible al decirme, "Gerónima, dame mi corazón." Y yo le apretaba más con mi pecho.... Volvió a luchar conmigo: "Gerónima, dame mi corazón." ... No quise, me salí con la mía. Y viendo que no quería darle su corazón me dijo: "quédate con él. Con eso practicarás lo que yo practiqué."] [¿Qué quieres que haga por ti? Aquí me tienes, aprisionado me han tus amores.] [eres mi madre, susténtame con tu corazón.] In the hagiography of Lutgard of Aywières, the nun asks Christ: "'What use is it to me to know the secrets of Scripture, I who ... am uncultivated and an uneducated nun?' Then the Lord said to her, 'What do you want?' 'I want your heart.' 'No, rather it is your heart that I want,' replied the Lord.... And so a correspondence of hearts occurred from that time on" (Thomas de Cantimpré 20). A hagiography on Lutgard in Spanish was published in Lima in 1694.

Chapter 6

1. *Capellanas* were women selected by a patron of the convent and exempted from dowry payment. Úrsula entered the cloister on April 11, 1678, two months after its foundation on February 7. Only eleven other nuns, including those transferred from existing convents, had preceded her (Guernica 29, 80).

2. *Definidoras* were members of the inner council of the convent. Úrsula's position as "definidora" in this case refers to the highly coveted position as secretary for correspondence between the abbess and the bishop.

3. At one point she directs herself to Tomás de Gamboa (since she refers to María de Gamboa as "hermana de vuestra paternidad" 163); however, she also mentions his death ("murió mi padre Tomás" 238).

4. As Podestá notes, it is likely that she decided to refine the narration in 1730 because she received the earlier version from Tomás de Gamboa shortly before his death in 1729 (22). We know the incidents described end before 1718 because in the final passage she mentions a dream to Miguel de Viñas, who died in 1718.

5. The biography of María de la Antigua (Spain, 1566–1617) was published in Spain and titled *Vida ejemplar, admirables virtudes y muerte prodigiosa de . . . María de la Antigua* (1677). Marina de Escobar (Spain, 1554–1633) was commemorated in Luis de la Puente's *Vida maravillosa de la venerable virgen Marina de Escobar . . . sacada de lo que ella misma escribió de orden de sus padres espirituales* (1665). As was customary, both women make use of dramatic dialogue.

6. [Ni siquiera un libro entero he leído sino de los que hallo, un pedacito.... [S]i tomaba un libro, era por entretenimiento y no para aprovecharme de ello; y los buscaba de historias o cuentos, novelas o comedias.... también leí ... de la Escritura algo, y también vidas de santos, y en no siendo trágicas las dejaba.]

7. [Como yo no tengo de hacer frioneras de comer tonteras ni muchas penitencias, decíanme: "Pues ¿Cómo ha de ser santa?"] [la corona de la generación.]

8. In doing so, however, she reinforces peninsular Spanish stereotypes of *criollo* inferiority.

9. This part of Úrsula's story also bears similarity to Teresa de Jesús's narration of the life of Beatriz de la Madre de Dios in the *Libro de las fundaciones*. Beatriz, the "least-loved" daughter of her parents, spends her first years in the home of an aunt. Accused unjustly of trying to poison her caretaker, she is returned to her home, where she is whipped and tortured daily by her mother. When her parents attempt to marry her off, she replies she would rather be killed than marry; her enraged mother, like Úrsula's, threatens and indeed tries to kill her daughter (216–17).

10. Furthermore, as Gómez Moriana notes, there is a similar division in the picaresque novel and the spiritual autobiography between the past sinner and the present narrator who has had a conversion experience (85). Alison Weber convincingly argues that Teresa de Jesús's *Libro de fundaciones* may be read as "picaresque history."

11. Female rogues, or "pícaras," were represented in several novels, most notably Francisco Delicado's *La lozana andaluza* (1528), *La pícara Justina* (1605) by Francisco López de Ubeda, and *La hija de Celestina* (1612) by Alonso Jerónimo de Salas Barbadillo. Like women's visionary texts, these narratives often also focus on the centrality of the body; however, as Anne Cruz points out, "the purported sexual freedom of the *pícara—male authored for a male audience*—contrasted with the increasing regulation of prostitution throughout the sixteenth and seventeenth centuries" (198, emphasis added). See also Dunn.

12. [con los ojos, boca y narices hinchadas como una leona de enojada, diciéndome malas palabras . . . tomó el salero de plata, queriendo con él deshacerme la cara.] Although the use of apostrophe resonates in Teresa de Jesús's autobiography, it is interesting to note that two of the Spanish-American authors who most often employ this kind of exaggerated theatricality are also those who most passionately defend their predilection for comedies. See María Marcela 58, 70; Suárez 124. Ironically, Úrsula's mother had been raised in the older Clarissan convent in Santiago for twelve years, after the death of her mother (Ramón 58–59).

13. Úrsula's narration suggests that the "dementia" of her father may have occurred around the time she first entered the convent in 1678 at the age of twelve or, as Ramón points out, sometime before 1684 at the very latest, since at that time Úrsula designated her mother as sole trustee of her estate, two years before the death of her father. Úrsula's grandfather, although still living, is also reduced to a minor role in the text. While Úrsula's focus on female characters may be a deliberate strategy, it apparently contains an element of truth, as evidenced by a remark by one of Úrsula's confessors alluding to the infamously bad temper of her mother (252).

14. [tantas desvergüenzas que era temeridad.] Although I would not go so far as to read this scene in Freudian terms, it is tempting to associate young Úrsula's unsuccessful search for the "varilla de virtud" (literally translated as "rod of virtue") with a coming-of-age ritual. It is the search for this "rod" that marks her initiation into sexual knowledge (when she witnesses men and women engaged in sexual relations) as well as her position in society (when her mother's reprimand

teaches her that her role as a woman is one of silence and submission). Cánovas offers a plausible explanation when he suggests that the "varilla de virtud" derives from folk tradition (114). For other examples of folk imagery see 113, 121, 151, 165.

15. Maravall notes that houses of prostitution, increasingly commonplace by the seventeenth century, were euphemistically termed "casas de camas" [literally, bedhouses] (*Literatura picaresca* 676).

16. [¿pues yo había de consentir que con hombre me acostasen?, primero yo he de ahorcarme, o con una daga degollarme, o el pecho atravesarme.]

17. [las demás muchachas que no eran casadas.] [una cosa separada] [Y le tenía notable lástima . . . y con tanto extremo como miramos a los muertos, que ya de nosotros son separados.]

18. [Contaron no sé qué caso de una mujer que un hombre había engañado, y fueron ensartando las que los hombres habían burlado. Yo atenta a esto les tomé a los hombres aborrecimiento y juntamente deseo de poder vengar a las mujeres en esto, engañándolos a ellos, y con ansias deseaba poder ser yo todas las mujeres para esta venganza. . . . [H]ice la intención de no perder ocasión que no ejecutase a cuantos pudiese mi habilidad, y esto con un entero, como si hiciese a Dios en el estado presente servicio muy bueno.]

19. These images appear in works by many Golden Age playwrights but perhaps reached their best expression in the plays of Lope de Vega, who, as Leonard's research indicates, was also the most distributed playwright in the colonies. Of course the image of the unattainable mistress may be traced back through courtly literature and all the way to the classical tradition (Diana, Athena), which not coincidentally was revived in the Renaissance. Teresa de Jesús touches on the theme in her *Libro de las fundaciones* (214–20), and traces of it may be found in many of the short stories of María de Zayas. For a detailed analysis of the *mujer varonil* see Melveena McKendrick's *Woman and Society in the Spanish Drama of the Golden Age*.

20. Obviously, the *pícaro, criado, gracioso,* and other variants of this character are not synonymous and it is not my intention to conflate their identities. However, in terms of linguistic and social function, they are closely related.

21. [La venganza universal / a sus palabras quebradas / y esperanzas malogradas / seré, con rigor mortal.] [sólo que he querido / satisfacer mi cuidado: los hombres aborrecer. . . . yo quiero vengar, si puedo / agravios, de aquí adelante, / de mujeres, pues lo soy.]

22. ["no es pecado, pero muchos no estuvieran en el infierno, si no hubiera comedias"]

23. Spanish authorities could be bypassed altogether by independent booksellers. A single family of German booksellers, the Crombergers, sold thousands of copies of *libros de caballería* in sixteenth-century Mexico. Forbidden books were most accessible in New Spain (Mexico) and New Granada (Colombia), the regions closest to the port cities of Veracruz and Cartagena, although Leonard shows that interior cities of Peru also had a thriving market for prohibited literature. As he notes, decrees discouraging the importation of fiction into the colonies were pub-

lished periodically; however, that they were repeatedly issued suggests the difficulty of enforcing such restrictions. Moreover, although secular books were sometimes censored, "not a single work of the profane variety" was ever placed on the *Index* of prohibited books. Ecclesiastical works continued to constitute the largest percentage of book trade in the colonies, but secular books were more widely distributed from hand to hand than the large folio tomes in Latin that "gathered dust by disuse" in monastery and convent libraries (*Books of the Brave* 83, 96–99, 105). Although Leonard's research (1964) and that of José Torre Revello (1940) have provided ample evidence to the contrary, as recently as 1986 Mario Vargas Llosa reiterated the myth of an absence of secular literature in the colonies (Adorno "Nuevas perspectivas" 23).

24. María Marcela is interested only in reading *comedias* and going to parties (16, 19). She often returns to this model in her narration.

25. Leonard speculates that it is precisely for these reasons—that popular literature often was printed on loose sheets or in pamphlet form, was not as highly regarded as a bound copy, and was regularly passed from family to family—that few copies survived into the twentieth century (*Books of the Brave* 318–19). A 1690 catalog of books destined to be sold in the Americas included *libros de comedias* (Torre Revello 22).

26. Lope de Vega alone wrote at least twenty-five *comedias de santos* (Morrison 33). *Graciosos*—and *graciosas*—appear even in many religious comedies, such as the character Petrona in Lope's *Comedia de la bienaventurada madre Santa Teresa de Jesús* (1604).

27. [la mayor destreza en las batallas que se tienen con los demonios.]

28. Carole Slade, noting the close relation between spiritual and judicial confession, maintains that Teresa de Jesús makes use of alternative first-person genres rather than adhering to a model in which she could only confirm her guilt (14).

29. [santa disparatada] [una santa muy alegre] [santa comedianta]

30. [Te he engañado, tontazo; tan mal animal que de mí se dejó engañar.] [esta niña ha de ser santa o gran mala.]

31. Comic travesties could undermine patriarchal order and its governing assumptions. In Sor Juana Inés de la Cruz's *Los empeños de una casa,* the *criada,* Celia, conceives a labyrinth of intrigue among the seemingly oblivious noble characters, while Castaño, the *gracioso,* makes a fool out of Don Pedro, masquerading in drag as Leonor (*Obras completas* 687).

32. [Suya fue la simpleza en creerme, cuando decía que yo parecía perversísima, que tenía traza de al diablo engañarlo, ellos mismos lo decían, y encima les caía; con que ahora pienso que los diablos, para las mujeres son ellos que han sido los engañados.] Sor Juana may also be alluding to the biblical episode in which women announcing the Resurrection are dismissed for their "idle tale" until Christ appears to reprimand "Foolish men, and slow of heart to believe all that the prophets have spoken!" (Luke 24.10, 25).

33. [para no cansarlo; El cuento fue largo: vamos al grano; No quiero referir tan largo cuento; Dejo estos disparates y otros que han pasado, porque fuera escribir

largo y tiempo malgastado.] [Dios mío... ¿no sabéis que no los quiero, que los estoy engañando y que vos solo sois mi dueño y mi amado?... Eso hago... por lo mucho que les debo y por el interés que de ellos tengo; no por quererlos.]

34. Úrsula's use of dialogue in this episode is especially adept: although she accuses herself in the past tense of misinterpreting the priest's intention, the original accusation is retained by presenting it as dialogue in the present.

35. [por él me visto y sustento.]

36. [me vestía de pies a cabeza, y no como quiera, sino que a Lima enviaba a traer los géneros que yo vestía, no contentándose con lo que en su tienda tenía, que había de ser lo más fino mi vestido, y los chapines... plateados.]

37. [Dios, dame licencia, que gusto de estas tonteras por las desvergüenzas que hacen de engañar a las mujeres: déjame que yo las vengue, que por las que ellos han engañado quiero yo engañarlos.] [Y aunque con aquellos hombres que dejo referido tenía mentiras y enredos, no tenía por grave esto, porque ni sentía lo que decía más como si fuera una niña, que hablan como tarabillas.]

38. [Yo me reí de su tontera de decir que no habían podido aprender de los padres, sino de mí.]

39. Significantly, for Maravall this is the key difference between the *pícaro* and the *gracioso,* another reason I would be disinclined to term Úrsula's role as simply picaresque. The *pícaro,* he contends, "does not laugh in integrated communication, rather, the opposite; he laughs from a position of a radical solitude. He does not laugh over jokes or witticisms, etc., he laughs vengefully, of cruelty, deceit, and evil" ("Relaciones de dependencia" 28). Although Úrsula does occasionally laugh alone, and certainly plays some cruel tricks on her male suitors, she most often describes a laughter shared by others and always a laughter she clearly intends to be shared by her confessor/reader.

40. [Si un hombre casado y gran señor tuviera de su mujer entera satisfacción, y que sabía que, aunque él no estuviera en su casa, su mujer no le agraviara, que sólo era habladora y truhana... no se agraviara de que ella hiciera una burla o tuviera una chanza, que ella misma se la contara: antes me parece la celebrara.] [Las mujeres sólo con palabras nos defendemos.]

41. [¡Ay!, si yo fuera dios por media hora... nuevos mundos te fabricara con criaturas capaces de tu amor.... y si esto hiciera yo por vos en media hora siendo dios, ¿qué no podréis hacer vos, cuando en realidad lo sois?]

42. Indeed, Úrsula distinguishes herself from other nuns who allow men to touch their hands.

43. As we have seen, in the symbolic system of corporeal rhetoric the saintly woman must neither speak nor much less laugh; her eyes must be modestly downcast at all times; Úrsula challenges this image on all counts.

44. [a mí me llamaba en especial, hablándome con gran cariño y gustando de las chanzas que le decía... tanto se divertía de mis frioneras, que cuando no me hallaba en la puerta decía: "¿Dónde está la filósofa?: llámenla": y se quedaba a solas conmigo.]

45. Mariscal notes that from medieval times on, the laughter provoked by the

court clown was considered essential to the ruler's well-being ("A Clown at Court" 70). See also Maravall "Relaciones de dependencia" 24.

46. [Se dijo tenía conmigo el señor obispo trato ilícito; y a tanto llegó esto, que una de las madres fundadoras llegó y me dijo . . . que no hablase con el obispo, porque me quitaban la honra.] It is worth noting that Úrsula was hardly at an age at which such counsel was necessary: since Romero did not become bishop until 1708, Úrsula must have been at least forty-two years old when they first met.

47. [permitió Dios que la vicaria me encontrase regando los claustros con sangre.]

48. [[D]íjome: "Siéntese bien, que hay que hacer.". . . Díjele "¿Qué?"; respondió: "El esposo con la esposa." Diome tan gran vergüenza que quisiera meterme debajo de la tierra. . . . levanté la cabeza, díjele: "No me haga desesperar"; dijo "Qué le he dicho?"; respondíle, "Malhaya su capricho!" y esto como si estuviera fuera de juicio, dando risadas y golpes en la reja y palmadas, hecha una desesperada.]

49. [Yo empecé a llorar por el padre Alemán. Enteróse diciendo: "No quieres el confesor que yo te doy?: tú te estarás detenida." "Cuánto será?—le respondí—¿un año, cuatro o veinte?; ¡qué importa eso!: yo a mi confesor quiero," y lloraba en extremo.] If I am not mistaken, Úrsula employs a double meaning for "detener" here: detained in her spiritual development, but also, more specifically, detained by the Inquisition.

50. [Luego dijo su paternidad que había dicho yo que por desobediente no era digno de ser mi confesor, cosa que por la imaginación jamás me pasó . . . ésta era una gran soberbia.]

51. Although Úrsula's lack of chronology makes it difficult to determine with certitude what provoked her violent outburst, it is more likely that it stemmed from political problems than from sexual tensions, even though she implies otherwise. It seems likely that Alemán's term as Úrsula's confessor coincided with the tense period during the initial Ulloa investigations (Alemán was a confessor for one of the accused and a witness at this trial, which dragged on for more than fifteen years). However, as Úrsula points out, the priest was in his late seventies and in poor health, and Úrsula was likely in her late forties or early fifties. If there is any truth to Úrsula's dramatic exchange, it suggests some interesting role-playing between the elderly priest and his middle-aged spiritual daughter.

52. [Habiendo pasado al padre Tomás y avisado a mi confesor, me aconsejó no fuese con él ni con el padre Roque Arbildo, dándome algunos motivos, que omito.] [díjele tal y tal cosa . . . que no quiero referir en éste por haberle dado mi palabra lo callaría.] [Irá a acusarme.]

53. In works that address the antagonism between men and women, Maravall notes a marked lack of love and even aggressiveness that unleashes between them an "irreconcilable hostility" (*Literatura picaresca* 656), an appropriate description for Úrsula's tempestuous relation with Alemán.

54. [Creo está algo de esto en los otros cuadernos, y si no, quédese en el tintero, por no molestar a vuestra paternidad.] Alemán is not mentioned in any of the earlier notebooks that have survived.

55. Although Úrsula characterizes María de Gamboa as a weak leader, in reality

she seems to have been a woman with substantial political aptitude. Admitted the same time as Úrsula, she was the first of the newly professed nuns to be elected abbess and held the post for three consecutive terms: from 1695 to 1704, and again in 1710 (Guernica 51).

56. Moreover, when, after several years of being denied this position of leadership, Úrsula finally is elected abbess in 1721, it is under a new bishop.

57. [soy tan atrevida que me enojé con su ilustrísima por la plática del *capítulo culpis,* tratándonos como a unas rameras. . . . Aseguro a vuestra paternidad, estuve de las mujeres más avergonzadas y todas lo estaban, y aun los mismos clérigos se tapaban los rostros con los sombreros: no hay palabras para referir esto.] ["¿Qué te pareció la plática?"; yo, muy entera y medio torcida, respondí: "Buena, pero tuvo pero"; dijo: "Ellas tienen peros y peras, y con su mayor"; díjele: "Por lo mismo lo omito." Los demás que estaban en la [ventanilla] miraron, y volvió a ellos y les dijo: "Tan gran filósofa." Acabé la nómina, y a la votación me preguntó: "¿Para quién?" No se votó por cédulas, sino de palabra—díjele–"al mayor honor de esta religión"; dijo: "Nombre del sujeto"; díjele: "Ya vuestra santísima señoría lo tiene dispuesto"; díjome: "¡Diga!"; respondíle: "¿No dice vuestra santísima señoría que a la madre doña María?" y salí de la ventanilla.] The expression used by the bishop is difficult to translate. However, his reference to "peros" and "peras"—or Úrsula's memory of it—seems to suggest a play on words based on popular sayings that encouraged silence and obedience from subordinates and women, such as: "La mujer y la pera, la que calla es buena" [With women and pears, the silent ones are best] and "Ni en burlas, ni en veras, con tu amo no partas peras" [Not in jest, nor in truth, with your master should you share fruit]. Úrsula's response, that for that very reason she will keep her objections (her "peros") to herself, seems to support this interpretation.

58. Another possibly important factor in the mystery is that in 1730 the convent was severely damaged by an earthquake (Guernica 116).

59. Ramón de Córdoba was actually a distant relative but frequently visited Úrsula in the convent. He was a deputy for the Inquisition in Santiago.

60. This is confusing because it apparently conflates the events of 1710 with those of 1715 with little distinguishing transition.

61. [que nadie . . . sepa lo que tantos años he callado.]

62. This is also in line with the seventeenth-century definition of comedy by Covarrubias: "Comedy typically begins with disputes, disagreements, conflict and despair, and ends in peace, harmony, friendship and happiness. The opposite is tragedy, which ends in some great disaster." [Suele la comedia empezar por riñas, cuestiones, desavenencias, despechos, y rematarse en paz, concordia, amistad y contento. Lo contrario es en la tragedia, que tiene fin en algún gran desastre.] In this way we might suggest that Úrsula attempts to script her life story as comedy but ends it as tragedy.

63. [¿Cómo reina, comedianta o farsanta?]

64. [Díjome no dijese lo que dijo San Pablo, sino lo que Samuel, también las palabras de la Virgen Santísima.] ["Cuando estés callada." "Mucho me falta, que no puedo estar callada."]

65. [Hija, todo lo que he hecho contigo ha sido por tu bien; no me hables en latín ni me nombres a San Pablo ni me tomes en la boca la Biblia.] Paul had said: "Am I not an apostle? Did I not see Jesus our Lord?" (1 Corinthians 9.1).

66. Also recall the belief in early medicine that menstruation was a purgative process that could occur in any part of the female body, including the mouth (Laqueur 105).

67. The dream must have occurred before 1718, since Viñas died that year.

Epilogue

1. Among the many fine critical treatments of this essay I have found particularly useful are Asunción Lavrin's "Sor Juana: Obediencia y Autoridad"; "Las tretas del debil" [Tricks of the Weak] by Josefina Ludmer; Kathleen Myers's "Sor Juana's *Respuesta*: Rewriting the *vitae*" and "Sor Juana: Monstruo de su laberinto" by José Pascual Buxó. Octavio Paz's controversial *Sor Juana Inés de la Cruz o las trampas de la fe* is an indispensable starting point for the study of the Mexican author and her times; Stephanie Merrim's collection of essays, *Feminist Perspectives on Sor Juana Ines de la Cruz*, is also excellent. There is at least one other text in which Sor Juana discusses her life, *Autodefensa Espiritual* [Spiritual Self-Defense], believed to have been written around 1681 (*Carta de Sor Juana Inés de la Cruz a su confesor*). See also the *Carta de Serafina de Cristo*, which has been attributed to Sor Juana.

2. *Inundación castálida* was published in Madrid in 1689; however, the expanded two volume collection *Poemas de la única poetisa americana* had a far greater impact on her fame as well as on her misfortune. The first volume was published in Madrid in 1690, in Barcelona in 1691, and in Zaragoza in 1691; the second volume appeared in Sevilla in 1691 and in Barcelona in 1693.

3. As Sor Juana notes in the beginning of her "Reply," although the bishop's reprimand "comes in the guise of counsel, it will be for me be equivalent to a precept. . . . I well recognize that your very sage advice does not apply to *it* [the letter], but to all those writings of mine which you will have seen on human subjects" (462/208) [aunque viene en traje de consejo, tendrá para mí sustancia de precepto. . . . Bien conozco que no cae sobre ella [la carta] vuestra cuerdísima advertencia, sino sobre lo mucho que habréis visto de asuntos humanos que he escrito.]

Bibliography

Achury Valenzuela, Darío. Introducción. *Obras completas de la Madre Francisca Josefa de la Concepción de Castillo.* Vol. 1. Ed. Darío Achury Valenzuela. Bogotá: Banco de la República, 1968.
Adorno, Rolena. "Nuevas perspectivas en los estudios literarios coloniales." *Revista de Crítica Literaria Latinoamericana* 14, no. 28 (1988): 11–27.
———. "El sujeto colonial y la construcción cultural de la alteridad." *Revista de Crítica Literaria Latinoamericana* 14, no. 28 (1988): 55–68.
Agustín de la Madre de Dios. *Tesoro Escondido en el Santo Carmelo Mexicano: Mina Rica de Ejemplos y Virtudes en la Historia de los Carmelitas Descalzos de la Provincia de la Nueva España* [1649]. Mexico City: PROBURSA/Universidad Iberoamericana, 1984.
Ahlgren, Gillian. *Teresa of Ávila and the Politics of Sanctity.* Ithaca, N.Y.: Cornell University Press, 1996.
Alonso de Madrid. *Arte para servir a Dios* [1526]. *Místicos franciscanos españoles.* Vol. 1. Ed. Juan Bautista Gomis. Madrid: Biblioteca de Autores Cristianos, 1958. 85–182.
Althusser, Louis. *Lenin and Philosophy and Other Essays.* New York: Monthly Review Press, 1971.
Antonopoulos, Anna. "Writing the Mystic Body: Sexuality and Textuality in the *écriture-féminine* of Saint Catherine of Genoa." *Hypatia* 6, no. 3 (1991): 185–207.
Arbiol y Díaz, Antonio. *La familia regulada: Con doctrina de la sagrada escritura, y santos padres de la Iglesia Católica.* Madrid: Ibarra, 1783.
Ardener, Shirley. "Ground Rules and Social Maps for Women: An Introduction." *Women and Space: Ground Rules and Social Maps.* Ed. Shirley Ardener. New York: St. Martin's Press, 1981.
Arellano, Ignacio. "La generalización del agente cómico en la comedia de capa y espada." *Criticón* 60 (1994): 103–28.
Arenal, Electa, and Stacey Schlau. "'Leyendo yo y escribiendo ella': The Convent as Intellectual Community." *Journal of Hispanic Philology* 13, no. 3 (1989): 214–29.
———. "Stratagems of the Strong, Stratagems of the Weak: Autobiographical Prose of the Seventeenth-Century Hispanic Convent." *Tulsa Studies in Women's Literature* 9, no. 1 (1990): 25–42.

———. *Untold Sisters: Hispanic Nuns in their Own Works*. Albuquerque: University of New Mexico Press, 1989.
Armacanqui-Tipacti, Elia Juliana. *Sor María Manuela de Santa Ana: Una Teresina peruana*. Ph.D. diss., University of Wisconsin, 1995.
Arte y mística del barroco. Mexico City: Consejo Nacional para la Cultura y las Artes, 1994.
Astell, Ann. *The Song of Songs in the Middle Ages*. Ithaca, N.Y.: Cornell University Press, 1990.
Bakhtin, Mikhail. *The Dialogic Imagination: Four Essays*. Ed. Michael Holquist. Trans. Caryl Emerson and Michael Holquist. Austin: University of Texas Press, 1981.
———. *Problems of Dostoevsky's Poetics*. Trans. Caryl Emerson. Minneapolis: University of Minnesota Press, 1984.
Bargellini, Clara. "Cristo en el arte barroco." *Arte y mística del barroco*. Mexico City: Consejo Nacional para la Cultura y las Artes, 1994. 43–47.
Barros Araña, Diego. *Historia General de Chile*. Vol. 6. Santiago: Jove, 1886.
Barthes, Roland. *Sade Fourier Loyola*. Trans. Richard Miller. New York: Hill and Wang, 1976.
Bellido, Joseph. *Vida de la v.m.r.m. María Anna Águeda de San Ignacio*. Puebla, Mexico: Biblioteca Mexicana, 1758.
Benassy-Berling, Marie-Cécile. *Humanismo y religión en Sor Juana Inés de la Cruz*. Trans. Laura López de Blair. Mexico City: Universidad Nacional Autónoma de México, 1983.
Benjamin, Jessica. "Master and Slave: The Fantasy of Erotic Domination." *Powers of Desire: The Politics of Sexuality*. Ed. Ann Snitow, Christine Stansell, and Sharon Thompson. New York: Monthly Review Press, 1983. 280–99.
Berger, Peter L. "Christian Faith and the Social Comedy." *Holy Laughter: Essays on Religion in the Comic Perspective*. Ed. M. Conrad Hyers. New York: Seabury, 1969. 123–33.
Beristain de Souza, José Mariano. *Biblioteca Hispanoamericana Septentrional* [1816]. 3 vols. Mexico City: Universidad Nacional Autónoma de México, 1980.
Bernard of Clairvaux. *Sermones sobre El Cantar de los cantares. Obras completas de San Bernardo*. Vol. 2. Madrid: Biblioteca de Autores Cristianos, 1953.
Bernstein, Susan David. *Confessional Subjects: Revelations of Gender and Power in Victorian Literature and Culture*. Chapel Hill: University of North Carolina Press, 1997.
Bilinkoff, Jodi. "Confessors, Penitents and the Construction of Identity in Early Modern Ávila." *Culture and Identity in Early Modern Europe (1500–1800): Essays in Honor of Natalie Zemon Davis*. Ed. Barbara B. Diefendorf and Carla Hesse. Ann Arbor: University of Michigan Press, 1993. 83–100.
Blanco, Lourdes. "Poder y pasión: Espíritus entretejidos." *El monacato femenino en el imperio español: Monasterios, beaterios, recogimientos y colegios*. Ed. Manuel Ramos Medina. Mexico City: CONDUMEX, 1995. 369–78.
Bonaventure. *Meditaciones de San Buenaventura sobre la pasión de nuestro salvador Jesucristo*. Brussels: Francisco Foppens, 1659.

Bordo, Susan. "The Body and the Reproduction of Femininity." *Writing on the Body: Female Embodiment and Feminist Theory.* Ed. Katie Conboy et al. New York: Columbia University Press, 1997. 90–110.

Bravo Arriaga, María Dolores. "El 'Costumbrero' del convento de Jesús María de México o del lenguaje ritual." *Mujer y cultura en la colonia hispanoamericana.* Ed. Mabel Moraña. Pittsburgh, Pa.: Biblioteca de América, 1996. 161–70.

Burns, Kathryn Jane. *Convents, Culture and Society in Cuzco, Peru, 1550–1865.* Ph.D. diss., Harvard University, 1993.

Bynum, Carolyn Walker. *Holy Feast and Holy Fast: The Religious Significance of Food to Medieval Women.* Berkeley: University of California Press, 1987.

Calancha, Antonio de la, and Bernardo de Torres. *Crónicas agustinianas del Perú* [1638–1653]. 2 vols. Madrid: C.S.I.C., 1972.

Cánovas, Rodrigo. "Úrsula Suárez (monja chilena, 1666–1749): La autobiografía como penitencia." *Revista Chilena de Literatura* 35 (1990): 97–118.

Carducho, Vicente [Vicenzo Carducci]. *Diálogos de la pintura: Su defensa, origen, esencia, definición, modos y diferencias* [1633]. Ed. Francisco Calvo Serraller. Madrid: Turner, 1974.

Carta de Serafina de Cristo, 1691. Ed. Elías Trabulse. Toluca, Mexico: Instituto Mexiquense de Cultura, 1996.

Caskey, Noelle. "Interpreting Anorexia Nervosa." *The Female Body in Western Culture: Contemporary Perspectives.* Ed. Susan Rubin Suleiman. Cambridge, Mass.: Harvard University Press, 1986. 175–89.

Castillo y Guevara, Francisca Josefa. *Obras completas de la Madre Francisca Josefa de la Concepción de Castillo.* Vol. 1: *Su vida.* Vol. 2: *Afectos espirituales* [1721]. Ed. Darío Achury Valenzuela. Bogotá: Banco de la República, 1968.

Catherine of Siena. *Passion for the Truth, Compassion for Humanity: Selected Spiritual Writings.* Ed. Mary O'Driscoll. Trans. Suzanne Noffke. Hyde Park, N.Y.: New City Press, 1993.

Cerda, Juan Luis de. *Vida política de todos los estados de las mujeres.* Alcalá de Henares: Juan Gracián, 1599.

Certeau, Michel de. *Heterologies: Discourse on the Other.* Trans. Brian Massumi. Minneapolis: University of Minnesota Press, 1985.

———. *The Mystic Fable.* Vol. 1. Trans. Michael B. Smith. Chicago: University of Chicago Press, 1992.

———. *The Writing of History.* Trans. Tom Conley. New York: Columbia University Press, 1988.

Cesareo, Mario. *Cruzados, mártires y beatos: Emplazamientos del cuerpo colonial.* West Lafayette, Ind.: Purdue University Press, 1995.

Chazal, Gilles. "Arte y mística del barroco." *Arte y mística del barroco.* Mexico City: Consejo Nacional para la Cultura y las Artes, 1994. 17–28.

Colmenares, Germán. *Historia económica y social de Colombia, 1537–1719.* Medellín: La Carreta, 1975.

Cross, F. L., and E. A. Livingstone, eds. *The Oxford Dictionary of the Christian Church*, 3d. ed. Oxford: Oxford University Press, 1997.

Cruz, Anne. "Studying Gender in the Spanish Golden Age." *Cultural and Historical*

Grounding for Hispanic and Luso-Brazilian Feminist Literary Criticism. Ed. Hernán Vidal. Minneapolis, Minn.: Institute for the Study of Ideologies and Literature, 1989. 193–222.

Curran, Patricia. *Grace Before Meals: Food Ritual and Body Discipline in Convent Culture.* Urbana: University of Illinois Press, 1989.

Curtius, Ernst Robert. *European Literature and the Latin Middle Ages.* Trans. Willard R. Trask. Princeton, N.J.: Princeton University Press, 1953.

"Declaración de Doña María Francisca González Carrillo Guerra y Vertiz para su ingreso de religiosa de coro, y velo negro, con la dote correspondiente en el Sagrado Convento de Santa Brígida de esta Capital" [Mexico City, 1778]. *Documents Relating to Catholic Convents.* Berkeley: Bancroft Library, University of California, Ms. M-M 521.

De Lauretis, Teresa. *Technologies of Gender: Essays on Theory, Film, and Fiction.* Bloomington: Indiana University Press, 1987.

Doane, Mary Ann. "The Clinical Eye: Medical Discourses in the 'Woman's Film' of the 1940s." *The Female Body in Western Culture: Contemporary Perspectives.* Ed. Susan Rubin Suleiman. Cambridge, Mass.: Harvard University Press, 1986. 152–74.

Domínguez Urregolabeitia, Francisco, and Antonio María de Castillo y Alarcón. "Breve noticia de la patria y padres de la v.m. y observante religiosa Francisca Josefa de la Concepción" [1817]. In Castillo *Obras completas,* vol. 1: 217–22.

Donahue, Darcy. "Writing Lives: Nuns and Confessors as Auto/biographers in Early Modern Spain." *Journal of Hispanic Philology* 13, no. 3 (1989): 230–39.

Dunn, Peter N. *Spanish Picaresque Fiction: A New Literary History.* Ithaca, N.Y.: Cornell University Press, 1993.

Eckenstein, Lina. *Woman under Monasticism, Chapters on Saint-Lore and Convent Life between* A.D. *500 and* A.D. *1500* [1896]. New York: Russell and Russell, 1963.

Eguiara y Egurén, Juan José de. *Vida del venerable padre Don Pedro Arellano y Sossa.* Mexico City: Imprenta Real del Superior Gobierno, 1735.

Eich, Jennifer L. "Giving the Devil His Due: A Man's Place in Women's Spiritual Narratives." *Confluencia* 14, no. 1 (1998): 67–81.

Espinosa, Isidro Félix de. *El peregrino septentrional Atlante: Delineado en la exemplaríssima vida del venerable padre Fray Antonio Margil de Jesús.* Mexico City: Joseph Hogal, 1737.

Faria, Francisco Xavier. *Vida y heroycas virtudes del venerable padre Pedro de Velasco.* Mexico City: María de Ribera, 1753.

Ferguson, George. *Signs and Symbols in Christian Art* [1959]. London: Oxford University Press, 1980.

Ferrando, Miguel Ángel. "Ver a Jesús, un aspecto fundamental de la cristología del Cuarto Evangelio." *Cristología en la perspectiva del corazón de Jesús.* Ed. Roger Vekemans. Bogotá: Instituto Internacional del Corazón de Jesús, 1982. 88–101.

Ferreccio Podestá, Mario. Prólogo. *Relación autobiográfica* [1730]. Ed. Mario Ferreccio Podestá. Santiago: Academia Chilena de la Historia, 1984. 9–31.

Florencia, Francisco de. *Relación de la exemplar, y Religiosa vida del Padre Nicolás de Guadalajara*. Mexico City: Juan de Ribera, 1684.
Foster, Dennis A. *Confession and Complicity in Narrative*. Cambridge: Cambridge University Press, 1987.
Foucault, Michel. *Discipline and Punish: The Birth of the Prison*. Trans. Alan Sheridan. New York: Pantheon, 1977.
———. *The History of Sexuality*. Vol. 1. Trans. Robert Hurley. New York: Pantheon, 1978.
Francis de Sales. *The Love of God: A Treatise* [1616]. Westminster: Newman, 1962.
Franco, Jean. *Plotting Women: Gender and Representation in Mexico*. New York: Columbia University Press, 1989.
Franco Salamanca, Germán. *Templo de Santa Clara Bogotá*. Bogotá: Instituto Colombiano de Cultura, 1987.
Fraschina, Alicia. "Los conventos de monjas en Buenos Aires." *Todo es Historia* 29, no. 340 (1995): 8–25.
Freedberg, David. *The Power of Images: Studies in the History and Theory of Response*. Chicago: University of Chicago Press, 1989.
Freedman, Barbara. *Staging the Gaze: Postmodernism, Psychoanalysis, and Shakespearean Comedy*. Ithaca, N.Y.: Cornell University Press, 1991.
Friedman, Edward H. "The Picaresque as Autobiography: Story and History." *Autobiography in Early Modern Spain. Hispanic Issues*. Vol. 2. Ed. Nicholas Spadaccini and Jenaro Talens. Minneapolis, Minn.: Prisma Institute, 1988. 119–27.
Gallagher, Ann Miriam. "The Indian Nuns of Mexico City's Monasterio of Corpus Christi, 1724–1821." *Latin American Women: Historical Perspectives*. Ed. Asunción Lavrin. Westport, Conn.: Greenwood Press, 1978. 150–72.
Gallego, Julián. *Visión y símbolos en la pintura española del siglo de oro*. Madrid: Aguilar, 1972.
Gallop, Jane. *The Daughter's Seduction: Feminism and Psychoanalysis*. Ithaca, N.Y.: Cornell University Press, 1982.
García de la Concepción, Joseph. *Historia belemítica. Vida ejemplar y admirable del venerable siervo de Dios, y padre Pedro de San José Betancur; Vida del Rmo. Padre Fray Rodrigo de la Cruz* [1723]. Guatemala City: Biblioteca "Goathemala," 1956.
García de la Concha, Víctor. *El arte literario de Santa Teresa*. Barcelona: Ariel, 1978.
Gerónima del Espíritu Santo. See Nava y Saavedra.
Gilbert, Sandra M., and Susan Gubar. *The Madwoman in the Attic: The Woman Writer and the Nineteenth-Century Literary Imagination*. New Haven, Conn.: Yale University Press, 1979.
Giles, Mary E. "The Discourse of Ecstasy: Late Medieval Spanish Women and Their Texts." *Gender and Text in the Later Middle Ages*. Ed. Jane Chance. Gainesville: University Press of Florida, 1996. 306–30.
Gilmore, Leigh. *Autobiographics: A Feminist Theory of Women's Self-Representation*. Ithaca, N.Y.: Cornell University Press, 1993.

Glantz, Margo. "El cuerpo monacal y sus vestiduras." *Mujer y cultura en la colonia hispanoamericana*. Ed. Mabel Moraña. Pittsburgh, Pa.: Biblioteca de América, 1996. 171–82.

———. *Sor Juana Inés de la Cruz: ¿Hagiografía o autobiografía?* Mexico City: Grijalbo/Universidad Nacional Autónoma de México, 1995.

Glave, Luis Miguel. "Santa Rosa de Lima y sus espinas: la emergencia de mentalidades urbanas de crisis y la sociedad andina (1600–1630)." *Manifestaciones religiosas en el mundo colonial americano*. Vol 1. Ed. Clara García Ayluardo and Manuel Ramos Medina. Mexico City: UIA/INAH/CONDUMEX, 1991. 53–70.

Gómez de la Parra, José. *Fundación y primero siglo del muy religioso convento de Sr. San Joseph de religiosas carmelitas descalzas de la ciudad de la Puebla de los Ángeles* [1732]. Mexico City: Universidad Iberoamericana, 1992.

Gómez Moriana, Antonio. "Autobiografía y discurso ritual: Problemática de la confesión autobiográfica destinada al tribunal inquisitorial." *L'autobiographie en Espagne*. Université de Provence, 1982. 69–94.

González Marmolejo, Jorge René. "Clérigos solicitantes, perversos de la confesión." *De la santidad a la perversión: O de por qué no se cumplía la ley de Dios en la sociedad novohispana*. Ed. Sergio Ortega. Mexico City: Grijalbo, 1986. 239–54.

Greenspan, Kate. "The Autohagiographical Tradition in Medieval Women's Devotional Writing." *Auto/biography Studies* 6, no. 2 (1991): 157–68.

Guernica, Juan de. *Historia y evolución del Monasterio de Clarisas de N[ues]tra S[eño]ra de la Victoria en sus cuatro períodos*. Santiago: Sagrado Corazón de Jesús, 1944.

Gutiérrez, Ramón, and Ernesto J. A. Maeder. "El convento urbano: Una función clave en la vida colonial." *Iberoamérica Siglos XVI-XVIII: Tradiciones, utopías y novedad cristiana*. Ed. Graciela María Viñuales et al. Madrid: Encuentro, 1992. 108–31.

Gutiérrez Dávila, Julián. *Vida y virtudes de el siervo de Dios, el venerable Padre Don Domingo Pérez de Barcia*. Madrid: Rodríguez Francos, 1720.

Heffernan, Thomas. *Sacred Biography: Saints and their Biographers in the Middle Ages*. New York: Oxford University Press, 1988.

Ignacio de Loyola. *The Autobiography of St. Ignatius Loyola*. Trans. Joseph F. O'Callaghan. Ed. John C. Olin. New York: Harper and Row, 1974.

———. *Los ejercicios espirituales de San Ignacio de Loyola* [1522]. 3d. ed. Ed. Juan Roothaan. Zaragoza: Hechos y Dichos, 1959. [In English: *The Spiritual Exercises of St. Ignatius*. Trans. Anthony Mottola. Garden City, N.Y.: Image Books, 1964.]

———. *The Spiritual Journal of St. Ignatius of Loyola* [1544–45]. Trans. William J. Young. Woodstock, Md.: Woodstock College Press, 1958.

Irigaray, Luce. *Speculum of the Other Woman*. Trans. Gillian C. Gill. Ithaca, N.Y.: Cornell University Press, 1985.

Juana Inés de la Cruz. *The Answer/La Respuesta* [1690]. Ed. Electa Arenal and Amanda Powell. New York: Feminist Press, 1994.

———. *Carta de Sor Juana Inés de la Cruz a su confesor: Autodefensa espiritual.* Ed. Aureliano Tapia Méndez. Monterrey, Mexico: Al Voleo el Troquel, 1993. [In English: Paz 495–502; Scott 433–37.]

———. *Obras completas.* Ed. Francisco Monterde. Mexico City: Porrúa, 1969. [A selection is available in English: *A Sor Juana Anthology.* Trans. Alan S. Trueblood. Cambridge, Mass.: Harvard University Press, 1988.]

Juan de la Cruz. *Súbida del Monte Carmelo* [1578–1585]. *Obras completas.* Madrid: Editorial de la Espiritualidad, 1957. [In English: *John of the Cross: Selected Writings.* Ed. Kieran Kavanaugh. New York: Paulist Press, 1987.]

Juan de la Presentación. *La corona de Madrid: Vida devota de la beata madre María Ana de Jesús* [1673]. 3d ed. Madrid: Hernández Pacheco, 1784.

Kahane, Claire. *Passions of the Voice: Hysteria, Narrative, and the Figure of the Speaking Woman, 1850–1915.* Baltimore, Md.: Johns Hopkins University Press, 1995.

Keller, Catherine. "The Breast, the Apocalypse and the Colonial Journey." *The Year 2000: Essays on the End.* Ed. Charles B. Strozier and Michael Flynn. New York: New York University Press, 1997. 42–58.

King, Margaret L. *Women of the Renaissance.* Chicago: University of Chicago Press, 1991.

Knipping, John B. *Iconography of the Counter Reformation in the Netherlands: Heaven on Earth.* 2 vols. Nieuwkoop: Graaf, 1974.

Kohl, Benjamin, and Ronald G. Witt, eds. *The Earthly Republic: Italian Humanists on Government and Society.* Philadelphia: University of Pennsylvania Press, 1978.

Kristeva, Julia. *Powers of Horror: An Essay on Abjection.* Trans. Leon Roudiez. New York: Columbia University Press, 1982.

Lagos, María Inés. "Confessing to the Father: Marks of Gender and Class in Úrsula Suárez's Relación." *Modern Language Notes* 110, no. 2 (1995): 353–84.

Laqueur, Thomas. *Making Sex: Body and Gender from the Greeks to Freud.* Cambridge, Mass.: Harvard University Press, 1990.

Lavrin, Asunción. "De su puño y letra: epístolas conventuales." *El monacato femenino en el imperio español: Monasterios, beaterios, recogimientos y colegios.* Ed. Manuel Ramos Medina. Mexico City: CONDUMEX, 1995. 43–61.

———. "Espiritualidad en el claustro novohispano del siglo XVII." *Colonial Latin American Review* 4, no. 2 (1995): 155–79.

———. "In Search of the Colonial Woman in Mexico: The Seventeenth and Eighteenth Centuries." *Latin American Women: Historical Perspectives.* Ed. Asunción Lavrin. Westport, Conn.: Greenwood Press, 1978. 23–59.

———. "Sor Juana Inés de la Cruz: Obediencia y autoridad en su entorno religioso." *Revista Iberoamericana* 61, no. 172–73 (1995): 605–22.

———. "Unlike Sor Juana? The Model Nun in the Religious Literature of Colonial Mexico." *Feminist Perspectives on Sor Juana Inés de la Cruz.* Ed. Stephanie Merrim. Detroit: Wayne State University Press, 1991. 61–85.

———. "Vida conventual: rasgos históricos." *Sor Juana y su mundo: Una mirada actual.* Ed. Sara Poot Herrera. Mexico City: Universidad del Claustro de Sor Juana, 1995. 33–91.

———. "La vida femenina como experiencia religiosa: biografía y hagiografía en Hispanoamérica colonial." *Colonial Latin American Review* 2, nos. 1–2 (1993): 27–52.

Lea, Henry Charles. *A History of Auricular Confession and Indulgences in the Latin Church* [1896]. 3 vols. New York: Greenwood, 1968.

Lemus, Diego de. *Vida, virtudes, trabajos, favores y milagros de la venerable madre Sor María de Jesús, angelopolitana religiosa.* León: Anisson y Posuel, 1683.

Leonard, Irving Albert. *Baroque Times in Old Mexico.* Ann Arbor: University of Michigan Press, 1959.

———. *Books of the Brave: Being an Account of Books and of Men in the Spanish Conquest and Settlement of the Sixteenth-Century New World.* Cambridge, Mass.: Harvard University Press, 1949.

Lerner, Gerda. *The Creation of Feminist Consciousness: From the Middle Ages to 1870.* New York: Oxford University Press, 1993.

Letona, Bartolomé de. *Perfecta religiosa: de la vida de la Madre Gerónima de Asunción.* Puebla, Mexico: Viuda Juana de Borja, 1662.

Little, Judy. "Humoring the Sentence: Women's Dialogic Comedy." *Women's Comic Visions.* Ed. June Sochen. Detroit: Wayne State University Press, 1991. 57–81.

Lochrie, Karma. "The Language of Transgression: Body, Flesh and Word in Mystical Discourse." *Speaking Two Languages: Traditional Disciplines and Contemporary Theory in Medieval Studies.* Ed. Allen J. Frantzen. Albany, N.Y.: State University of New York Press, 1991. 115–40.

Loreto López, Rosalva. "La sensibilidad y el cuerpo en el imaginario de las monjas poblanas del siglo XVII." *El monacato femenino en el imperio español: Monasterios, beaterios, recogimientos y colegios.* Ed. Manuel Ramos Medina. Mexico City: CONDUMEX, 1995. 541–55.

Ludmer, Josefina. "Tricks of the Weak." *Feminist Perspectives on Sor Juana Inés de la Cruz.* Ed. Stephanie Merrim. Detroit, MI.: Wayne State University Press, 1991. 86–93. [In Spanish: "Las tretas del débil." *La sartén por el mango.* Ed. Patricia Elena González and Eliana Ortega. San Juan, P.R.: Huracán, 1984.]

Luis de Granada. *Memorial de la vida cristiana* [1572]. Biblioteca de autores españoles. Vol. 8. Ed. José Joaquín Mora. Madrid: Rivadeneyra, 1851.

Luis de León. *La perfecta casada* [1583]. Madrid: Taurus, 1987.

Magnarelli, Sharon. "Staging the Pre-scription of Gender: Manuel Puig's *La traición de Rita Hayworth.*" *Carnal Knowledge: Essays on the Flesh, Sex and Sexuality in Hispanic Letters and Film.* Ed. Pamela Bacarisse. Pittsburgh, Pa.: Tres Ríos, 1993. 199–215.

Maravall, José Antonio. *La cultura del barroco: Análisis de una estructura histórica,* 4th ed. Barcelona: Ariel, 1986. [In English: *Culture of the Baroque: Analysis of a Historical Structure.* Trans. Terry Cochran. Minneapolis: University of Minnesota Press, 1985].

———. *La literatura picaresca desde la historia social*. Madrid: Taurus, 1986.

———. "Relaciones de dependencia e integración social: criados, graciosos y pícaros." *Ideologies and Literature* 1, no. 4 (1977): 3–32.

María Ana de la Encarnación. *Relación de la fundación del Convento Antiguo de Santa Teresa* [1641?]. Austin: University of Texas Benson Latin American Collection.

María Coleta de San Joseph. *Acusación contra Sor María Coleta, religiosa capuchina por tener pacto con el demonio y relaciones ilícitas con su confesor (1774). Cartas dirigidas a su padre confesor* [Oaxaca, 1751–1775]. Archivo General de la Nación (Mexico City), vol. 1172, expediente 7.

María de San José. *Word from New Spain: The Spiritual Autobiography of Madre María de San José (1656–1719)*. Ed. Kathleen Myers. Liverpool: Liverpool University Press, 1993.

María Magdalena. *Libro en que se contiene la vida de la Madre María Magdalena* [1636?]. Austin: University of Texas Benson Latin American Collection. [There is another copy at the Bancroft Library, Berkeley, California.]

María Manuela de Santa Ana. *Esquelas originales de correspondencia espiritual.* Archivo Convento Santa Rosa de Lima de Santa María, Lima, Perú. In Armancanqui 231–70.

———. *Su vida*. Archivo Convento Santa Rosa de Lima de Santa María, Lima, Perú. In Armancanqui 160–90.

María Marcela. *Vida de la Madre María Marcela, Religiosa Capuchina del Convento de Querétaro* [1757]. Copy made in 1844. Biblioteca Nacional, Mexico City.

María Zeraphina de Nazareth. *Cartas de amor a Fray Blas de Placencia de Santa María* [Manila, 1745]. Archivo General de la Nación, Mexico City, vol. 863, expediente s/n.

Mariscal, George. "A Clown at Court: Francesillo de Zúñiga's Crónica burlesca." *Autobiography in Early Modern Spain*. Hispanic Issues. Vol. 2. Eds. Nicholas Spadaccini and Jenaro Talens. Minneapolis, Minn: Prisma Institute, 1988. 59–75.

———. *Contradictory Subjects: Quevedo, Cervantes, and Seventeenth-Century Spanish Culture*. Ithaca, N.Y.: Cornell University Press, 1991.

Márquez, Antonio. *Literatura e Inquisición en España (1478–1834)*. Madrid: Taurus, 1980.

Martín, Luis. *Daughters of the Conquistadors: Women of the Viceroyalty of Peru*. Albuquerque: University of New Mexico Press, 1983.

Massé, Michelle A. *In the Name of Love: Women, Masochism, and the Gothic*. Ithaca, N.Y.: Cornell University Press, 1992.

Mayora, Juan. *Relación de la vida y virtudes del Padre Antonio Herdoñana*. Mexico City: Bibliotheca Mexicana, 1758.

Maza, Francisco de la. *Arquitectura de los coros de monjas en México*. Mexico City: Imprenta Universitaria, 1956.

Mazzoni, Cristina. *Saint Hysteria: Neurosis, Mysticism and Gender in European Culture*. Ithaca, N.Y.: Cornell University Press, 1996.

McKendrick, Melveena. *Woman and Society in the Spanish Drama of the Golden Age. A Study of the Mujer Varonil.* Cambridge: Cambridge University Press, 1974.

McKnight, Kathryn Joy. *The Mystic of Tunja: The Writings of Madre Castillo (1671–1742).* Amherst: University of Massachusetts Press, 1997.

Medina, José Toribio. *Biblioteca hispanoamericana, 1493–1810.* 7 vols. Amsterdam: N. Israel, 1962.

———. *Historia del Tribunal del Santo Oficio de la inquisición en Chile.* Santiago: Medina, 1952.

———. *Historia del Tribunal del Santo Oficio de la inquisición en Lima.* 2 vols. Santiago: Gutenberg, 1887.

———. *Historia del Tribunal del Santo Oficio de la inquisición en México.* Mexico City: Consejo Nacional para la Cultura y las Artes, 1991.

———. *La imprenta en Guatemala 1660–1821* [1910]. Amsterdam: N. Israel, 1964.

———. *La imprenta en Lima, 1584–1824.* 4 vols. Santiago: Medina, 1907.

———. *La imprenta en México, 1539–1821.* 8 vols. [1909]. Amsterdam: N. Israel, 1965.

———. *La imprenta en la Puebla de los Ángeles.* [1898]. Amsterdam: N. Israel, 1964.

Mercado, Pedro de. *Historia de la Provincia del Nuevo Reino y Quito de la Compañía de Jesús* [1682–1685]. Bogotá: Empresa Nacional de Publicaciones, 1957.

Merrim, Stephanie, ed. *Feminist Perspectives on Sor Juana Inés de la Cruz.* Detroit, Mich.: Wayne State University Press, 1991.

Mignolo, Walter D. *The Darker Side of the Renaissance: Literacy, Territoriality, and Colonization.* Ann Arbor: University of Michigan Press, 1995.

Miqueorena, Agustín de. *Vida de la Venerable Madre Micaela Josepha de la Purificación.* Puebla, Mexico: Viuda Miguel de Ortega y Bonilla, 1755.

Moore, Henrietta L. *Space, text and gender: An anthropological study of the Marakwet of Kenya.* Cambridge: Cambridge University Press, 1986.

Moraña, Mabel. "Barroco y conciencia criolla en Hispanoamérica." *Revista de Crítica Literaria Latinoamericana* 14, no. 28 (1988): 229–51.

Morrison, Robert. "Graciosos con breviarios: The Comic Element in the *Comedia de Santos* of Lope de Vega." *Crítica Hispánica* 12, nos. 1–2: 33–46.

Muriel, Josefina. *Conventos de monjas en la Nueva España.* Mexico City: Santiago, 1946.

———. "Los conventos de monjas en la sociedad virreinal." *Artes de México,* 198, n.d., 7–23.

———. *Cultura femenina novohispana.* Mexico City: Universidad Nacional Autónoma de México, 1982.

———. *Las indias caciques de Corpus Christi.* Mexico City: Universidad Nacional Autónoma de México, 1963.

———. "Lo que leían las mujeres en la Nueva España." *La literatura novohispana:*

revisión crítica y propuestas metodológicas. Ed. José Pascual Buxó and Arnulfo Herrera. Mexico City: Universidad Nacional Autónoma de México, 1994. 159–73.

———. *Las mujeres de Hispanoamérica: Época colonial.* Madrid: MAPFRE, 1992.

———. *Los recogimientos de mujeres: respuesta a una problemática social novohispana.* Mexico City: Universidad Nacional Autónoma de México, 1974.

Muriel, Josefina, and Manuel Romero de Terreros. *Retratos de monjas.* Mexico City: Jus, 1952.

Myers, Kathleen. Introduction. *Word from New Spain: The Spiritual Autobiography of Madre María de San José (1656–1719).* Liverpool, England: Liverpool University Press, 1993. 5–76.

———. "'Miraba las cosas que desía': Convent Writing, Picaresque Tales, and the Relación autobiográfica by Úrsula Suárez." *Romance Quarterly* 40, no. 3 (1993): 156–72.

———. "Sor Juana's Respuesta: Rewriting the vitae." *Revista Canadiense de Estudios Hispánicos* 14, no. 3 (1990): 459–69.

Nava y Saavedra, Jerónima. *Autobiografía de una monja venerable* [1727]. Ed. Angela Inés Robledo. Cali, Colombia: Universidad del Valle, 1994.

Nuñez de Miranda, Antonio. *Cartilla de la doctrina religiosa.* Mexico City: Viuda Calderón, 1672.

———. *Distribución de las obras ordinarias y extraordinarias del día.* Mexico City: Viuda Calderón, 1712.

———. *Plática doctrinal que hizo el Padre de la Compañía de Jesús.* Mexico City: Viuda Calderón, 1679.

Olmos, Juan de. "Elogio de la autora." *Autobiografía de una monja venerable.* Ed. Angela Inés Robledo. Cali, Colombia: Universidad del Valle, 1994. 29–51.

Orozco Díaz, Emilio. *El teatro y la teatralidad del barroco: Ensayo de introducción al tema.* Barcelona: Planeta, 1969.

Pacheco, Juan Manuel. *Los jesuitas en Colombia.* Vol. 2. Bogotá: San Juan Eudes, 1954.

Pagden, Anthony. "Identity Formation in Spanish America." *Colonial Identity in The Atlantic World, 1500–1800.* Ed. Nicholas Canny and Anthony Pagden. Princeton, N.J.: Princeton University Press, 1987. 51–93.

Pardo, Francisco. *Vida y virtudes heroycas de la madre María de Jesús.* Mexico City: Viuda Calderón, 1676.

Pascal, Roy. *Design and Truth in Autobiography.* Cambridge, Mass.: Harvard University Press, 1960.

Pascual Buxó, José. "Sor Juana: Monstruo de su laberinto." *Y diversa de mí misma entre plumas ando: Homenaje internacional a Sor Juana Inés de la Cruz.* Ed. Sara Poot Herrera. Mexico City: Colegio de México, 1993. 43–70.

Pastor Bodmer, Beatriz. *El jardín y el peregrino: Ensayos sobre el pensamiento utópico latinoamericano, 1492–1695.* Amsterdam: Rodopi, 1996.

Paz, Octavio. *Sor Juana Inés de la Cruz o las trampas de la fe,* 2d ed. Mexico City: Fondo de Cultura Económica, 1983. [In English: *Sor Juana or, The traps of faith.*

Trans. Margaret Sayers Peden. Cambridge, Mass.: Belknap/Harvard University Press, 1988.]

Pedro de Alcántara. *Tratado de la oración y meditación* [1587]. Buenos Aires: Cursos de Cultura Católica, 1938.

Peña, Margarita. "La vejación del cuerpo en biografías de monjas y santas." "Sábado," suppl. of *Unomásuno,* 875, July 9, 1994, 1-3.

Perry, Mary Elizabeth. "Subversion and Seduction: Perceptions of the Body in Writings of Religious Women in Counter-Reformation Spain." *Religion, Body and Gender in Early Modern Spain.* Ed. Alain Saint-Saens. San Francisco: Mellen Research University Press, 1991. 67-78.

Petroff, Elizabeth Alvilda. *Medieval Women's Visionary Literature.* New York: Oxford University Press, 1986.

Praz, Mario. *Studies in Seventeenth-Century Imagery.* London: Warburg Institute, 1939.

Procesos de beatificación y canonización de Sta. Teresa de Jesús. Ed. Silverio de Santa Teresa. Burgos, Spain: Monte Carmelo, 1935.

Puccini, Vicenzo. *The Life of the Holy and Venerable Mother Suor Maria Maddalena de Patsi* [1619]. Menston, England: Scolar Press, 1970.

Quiroga, Domingo de. *Compendio breve de la vida y virtudes de la Venerable Francisca de San Joseph.* Mexico City: Joseph Bernardo de Hogal, 1729.

Rama, Ángel. *La ciudad letrada.* Hanover, N.H.: Ediciones del Norte, 1984. [In English: *The Lettered City.* Trans. John Charles Chasteen. Durham, N.C.: Duke University Press, 1996.]

Ramón, Armando de. Estudio preliminar. *Relación autobiográfica.* Ed. Mario Ferreccio Podestá. Santiago: Academia Chilena de Historia, 1984. 33-80.

Ramos Medina, Manuel. "Esplendor del culto carmelita." *El monacato femenino en el imperio español: Monasterios, beaterios, recogimientos y colegios.* Ed. Manuel Ramos Medina. Mexico City: CONDUMEX, 1995. 497-509.

———. "Isabel de la Encarnación: monja posesa del siglo XVII." *Manifestaciones religiosas en el mundo colonial americano.* Vol 1. Ed. Clara García Ayluardo and Manuel Ramos Medina. Mexico City: UIA/INAH/CONDUMEX, 1991. 41-52.

Régnier-Bohler, Danielle. "Imagining the Self: Exploring Literature." *A History of Private Life.* Vol. 2: *Revelations of the Medieval World.* Ed. Philippe Ariès and Georges Duby. Cambridge, Mass.: Belknap/Harvard University Press, 1988. 311-93.

Restrepo, José Manuel. *Historia de la Nueva Granada.* Bogotá: Cromos, 1952-1963.

Reyna, María del Carmen. *El convento de San Jerónimo: Vida conventual y finanzas.* Mexico City: INAH, 1990.

Ribadeneyra [Rivadeneira], Pedro de. *Flos Sanctorum o Libro de las vidas de los Santos* [1599], 2d ed. Rev. Juan Eusebio Nieremberg and Francisco García. Madrid: Ibarra, 1761. [In English: *Lives of the Saints with Other Feasts of the Year According to the Roman Calendar.* Trans. William Petre. St. Omers: Ioachim Carlier, 1669.]

Ripa, Cesare. *Iconologie* [1593]. New York: Garland, 1976.

Rivero, Juan J. *Historia de las Misiones de los Llanos de Casanare y los ríos Orinoco y Meta* [1736]. Bogotá: Silvestre, 1956.

Ross, Kathleen. *The Baroque Narrative of Carlos de Sigüenza y Góngora: A New World Paradise*. Cambridge: Cambridge University Press, 1993.

Ruiz Gomar, Rogelio. "La penitencia." *Arte y mística del barroco*. Mexico City: Consejo Nacional para la Cultura y las Artes, 1994. 183–89.

———. "Retratos de monjas." *Artes de México*, 198, n.d., 24–51.

Saldaña, Ignacio. *Penitente paloma, o gemebunda Maya. Sermón fúnebre, en las exequias que el observantíssimo Convento de San Juan de la Penitencia de México hizo a su muy amada hija la venerable madre sor Sebastiana Josepha de la Santíssima Trinidad*. Mexico City: Imprenta Bibliotheca, 1758.

Salmerón, Pedro. *Vida de la Venerable Madre Isabel de la Encarnación*. Mexico City: Francisco Rodríguez Lupercio, 1675.

Sánchez de Castro, Joseph Gerónimo. *Vida de la V.M. Sor Antonia de la Madre de Dios*. Mexico City: Viuda Hogal, 1747.

Sánchez Lora, José L. *Mujeres, conventos y formas de la religiosidad barroca*. Madrid: Fundación Universatria Española, 1988.

Santander y Torres, Sebastián de. *Vida de la venerable madre María de San Joseph*. Mexico City: Viuda Miguel de Rivera, 1723.

Scaramelli, Giovanni Battista. *Directorio ascético: en que se enseña el modo de conducir las almas por el camino ordinario de la gracias a la perfección christiana, dirigido a los directores de las almas* [1752]. Madrid: Ramón Ruiz, 1761. [In English: see Stockman.]

Scarry, Elaine. *The Body in Pain: The Making and Unmaking of the World*. New York: Oxford University Press, 1985.

Scott, Joan Wallach. *Gender and the Politics of History*. New York: Columbia University Press, 1988.

Scott, Nina. "'If you are not pleased to favor me, put me out of your mind . . .': Gender and Authority in Sor Juana Inés de la Cruz." *Women's Studies International Forum* 11, no.5 (1988): 429–38.

Sebastián, Santiago. *El barroco iberoamericano: Mensaje iconográfico*. Madrid: Ediciones Encuentro, 1990.

Sebastiana Josefa de la Santíssima Trinidad. *Cartas en las quales manifiesta a su Confesor las cosas interiores y exteriores de su vida la v.m. Sebastiana Josepha de la Santíssima Trinidad, Religiosa de Velo negro del Convento de San Juan de la Penitencia de la Ciudad de México* [1756]. Ms. 1793, Biblioteca Nacional, Mexico City.

Showalter, Elaine. *The Female Malady: Women, Madness and English Culture, 1830–1980*. New York: Pantheon Books, 1985.

———. *The New Feminist Criticism: Essays on Women, Literature and Theory*. New York: Pantheon Books, 1985.

Sigüenza y Góngora, Carlos. *Parayso occidental: Plantado y cultivado por la liberal benéfica mano de los muy católicos y poderosos reyes de España* [1683]. Mexico City: Universidad Nacional Autónoma de México/CONDUMEX, 1995.

Silva Cotapos, Carlos. *Historia Eclesiástica de Chile*. Santiago: San José, 1925.

Siria, Antonio de. *Vida admirable y prodigiosas virtudes de la v. sierva de Dios doña Anna Guerra de Jesús*. Guatemala City: Antonio de Velasco, 1716.

Slade, Carole. *St. Teresa of Ávila: Author of a Heroic Life*. Berkeley: University of California Press, 1995.

Smith, Sidonie. *A Poetics of Women's Autobiography: Marginality and the Fictions of Self- Representation*. Bloomington: Indiana University Press, 1987.

Spender, Stephen. "Confessions and Autobiography." *Autobiography: Essays Theoretical and Critical*. Ed. James Olney. Princeton: Princeton University Press, 1980. 115–22.

Stallybrass, Peter. "Patriarchal Territories: The Body Enclosed." *Rewriting the Renaissance: The Discourses of Sexual Difference in Early Modern Europe*. Ed. Margaret W. Ferguson, Maureen Quilligan, and Nancy J. Vickers. Chicago: University of Chicago Press, 1986. 123–44.

Stanbury, Sarah. "Regimes of the Visual in Premodern England: Gaze, Body and Chaucer's Clerk's Tale." *New Literary History* 28, no. 2 (1997): 261–89.

Stockman, P. J. *Manual of Christian Perfection*. Los Angeles: Immaculate Heart College, 1921. [English translation of Scaramelli.]

Stoller, Robert. *Observing the Erotic Imagination*. New Haven, Conn.: Yale University Press, 1985.

Suárez, Úrsula. *Relación autobiográfica* [1730]. Ed. Mario Ferreccio Podestá. Santiago: Academia Chilena de la Historia, 1984.

Surtz, Ronald E. *Writing Women in Late Medieval and Early Modern Spain: The Mothers of Santa Teresa of Ávila*. Philadelphia: University of Pennsylvania Press, 1995.

Tambling, Jeremy. *Confession: Sexuality, Sin, the Subject*. Manchester, England: Manchester University Press, 1990.

Taylor, William B. *Magistrates of the Sacred: Priests and Parishioners in Eighteenth-Century Mexico*. Stanford, Calif.: Stanford University Press, 1996.

Tentler, Thomas N. *Sin and Confession on the Eve of the Reformation*. Princeton, N.J.: Princeton University Press, 1977.

Teresa de Jesús. *Camino de perfección* [1583]. Madrid, Espasa-Calpe, 1942. [In English: *The Way of Perfection*. Trans. E. Allison Peers. New York: Image Books, 1991.]

———. *El libro de la vida* [1588]. Madrid: Cátedra, 1982. [In English: *The Complete Works of Saint Teresa of Jesus*. Vol 1. Trans. E. Allison Peers. London: Sheed and Ward, 1946.]

———. *El libro de las fundaciones* [1610]. Madrid: Espasa-Calpe, 1991. [In English: *The Book of the Foundations*. Trans. David Lewis. London: Baker, 1913.]

———. *Las moradas* [1578]. Mexico City: Porrúa, 1979. [In English: *Interior Castle*. Trans. E. Allison Peers. New York: Image Books, 1961.]

Thomas à Kempis. *The Imitation of Christ* [1441]. Trans. Aloysius Croft and Harold Bolton. Milwaukee, Minn.: Bruce, 1952.

Thomas de Cantimpré. *The Life of Lutgard of Aywières*. Trans. and ed. Margot H. King. Saskatoon, Sask.: Peregrina, 1987.

Torre Revello, José. "Lecturas indianas." *Thesaurus* 17, no. 1 (1962): 1–29.

Torres, Miguel de. *Vida ejemplar y muerte preciosa de la Madre Bárbara Josepha de San Francisco.* Mexico City: Herederos de la Viuda de Francisco Rodríguez Lupercio, 1725.

Valdés, Joseph Eugenio. *Vida admirable y penitente de la V.M. Sor Sebastiana Josepha de la SS. Trinidad.* Mexico City: Bibliotheca Mexicana, 1765.

Vargaslugo, Elisa. "Mística y pintura barroca en la Nueva España." *Arte y mística del barroco.* Mexico City: Consejo Nacional para la Cultura y las Artes, 1994. 31–41.

———. "La obra de arte como móvil de la experiencia mística." *Arte y mística del barroco.* Mexico City: Consejo Nacional para la Cultura y las Artes, 1994. 117–24.

Vega, Lope Félix de. *Obras escogidas.* Ed. Federico Carlos Sainz de Robles. Vol. 1. Madrid: Aguilar, 1966.

Velasco, Sherry M. *Demons, Nausea, and Resistance in the Autobiography of Isabel de Jesús, 1611–1682.* Albuquerque: University of New Mexico Press, 1996.

Vetancourt, Agustín de. *Crónica de la Provincia del Santo Evangelio de México.* Teatro mexicano. Vol. 4. Mexico City: María de Benavides, 1697.

Villavencio, Juan José de. *Vida y virtudes de el venerable, y apostólico padre Juan de Ugarte de la Compañía de Jesús.* Mexico City: Colegio de San Ildefonso, 1752.

Viñuales, Graciela María. "Aislamiento y contemplación: Los monasterios de monjas y el papel de la mujer en la sociedad colonial." *Iberoamérica Siglos XVI-XVIII: Tradiciones, utopías y novedad cristiana.* Ed. Graciela María Viñuales et al. Madrid: Encuentro, 1992. 196–214.

Vives, Juan Luis. *Instrucción de la mujer cristiana* [1524–1528]. Buenos Aires: Espasa-Calpe, 1940. [In English: *A very fruteful and pleasant booke called the Instruction of a Christen woman.* Trans. Rycharde Hyrde. London: Henry Wykes, 1557.]

Warren, James. "What's important? Ask Sister Rose Marie." *Chicago Tribune*, September 19, 1997, sec. 5: 3.

Weber, Alison. "The Paradoxes of Humility: Santa Teresa's *Libro de la vida* as Double Bind." *Journal of Hispanic Philology* 9, no. 3 (1985): 211–30.

———. *Teresa of Ávila and the Rhetoric of Femininity.* Princeton, N.J.: Princeton University Press, 1990.

Weinstein, Donald, and Rudolph M. Bell. *Saints and Society: The Two Worlds of Western Christendom, 1000–1700.* Chicago: University of Chicago Press, 1982.

Williams, Drid. "The Brides of Christ." *Perceiving Women.* Ed. Shirley Ardener. New York: Wiley, 1975.

Woolf, Virginia. *A Room of One's Own.* New York: Harcourt Brace, 1957.

Ximénez Samaniego, José. *Prólogo galeato. Relación de la vida de la venerable madre sor María de Jesús.* Madrid: Imprenta de la Causa de la Venerable Madre, 1759.

Zimmerman, T. C. Price. "Confession and Autobiography in the Early Renaissance." *Renaissance Studies in Honor of Hans Baron.* Ed. Anthony Molho and John Tedeschi. Dekalb, Ill.: Northern Illinois University Press, 1971. 121–40.

Index

Abstinence, 7, 81–83, 90–92, 166nn.24, 32. *See also* Ascetism
Aguiar y Seijas, Francisco de (Archbishop of Mexico), 93, 138, 147n.4
Anna Guerra de Jesús, 65
Anxiety of authorship, 21–27, 87, 148n.22. *See also* Rhetoric of humility
Antonia de la Madre de Dios, 21, 65
Art, baroque, 101–8, 169nn.24–27
Ascetism, 64–65, 69–70, 73, 81–84, 88–92, 94, 162n.61, 166n.29. *See also* Abstinence, Penitence
Augustine, Saint, 147n.9, 172nn.63, 67

Bárbara Josefa de San Francisco, 65
Benites, Luisa, 74, 77
Bernard of Clairvaux, 107, 113
Berruecos Palacios, Juana. *See* María de San José

Carducci, Vicenzo, 103–4, 169n.26
Castillo, Francisca Josefa de, 6, 25, 48–61, 64–68, 72, 76–78, 99–100, 112–13, 115–16, 125, 135, 143n.28, 145n.44, 146n.48, 147n.1, 152n.70, 153n.74, 155n.5, 10, 156nn.20, 22, 158nn.6, 36, 168n.13; background of, 48–49, 53–54, 60, 66–67, 70; relation to confessors, 29, 40–43, 49–51, 53, 57–59, 61, 145n.44, 152n.70, 153n.74, 155n.4; and writing, 27, 49–53, 156n.13.
—*Works: Afectos espirituales*, 40, 49, 51–52, 112–13, 155n.10; *Su vida*, 49–61
Catherine of Siena, Saint, 64, 66, 74, 79, 80, 89, 94, 114–15, 158n.2, 160n.28, 165n.12, 171n.43, 172n.57

Chile. *See* Peru, viceroyalty of
Christ. *See* Jesus Christ
Church: position of women in, 1–6, 15–16, 19, 21–22, 97
Claire of Assisi, Saint, 91
Class relations, 3–8, 11–12, 76
Colombia. *See* New Granada, viceroyalty of
Comedies, 125–7, 134–5, 177nn.24–26, 180n.62. *See also* Theatricality
Communion, 2, 19, 41, 82–83
Confession, 2, 19–47, 147n.2, 149nn.30, 36; as communicative act, 39–42, 98, 112; handbooks for, 28–29, 98, 149n.32; as instrument of social control, 19–22, 73–74, 83, 149n.32
Confessors: antagonism of, 23, 29–30, 40–44, 147n.5; dependency on, 24, 28, 39–40, 44–45; role of, 21–47, 53, 57–59, 147nn.2–3, 5, 8–9, 151n.50; solicitation of, 32–39, 147n.3, 151nn.51–54, 56; support of, 39–40, 44–45
Convent life, 3–9, 55–58, 70–71, 97–98, 156nn.21–22, 167nn.2–3
Criollos. *See* Race relations

Devil, 26–27, 57–58, 75–77, 114, 162n.59
Dowries, 3, 5–9, 86, 142n.12. *See also* Marriage

Escobar, Marina, 64, 122, 174n.5
Eucharist. *See* Communion

Fasting. *See* Abstinence
Fernández de Santa Cruz, Manuel (Bishop of Puebla), 10, 12, 23, 38, 138

Flos sanctorum, 62, 64, 74, 94, 158n.4, 170n.37. *See also* Hagiography
Food. *See* Abstinence
Francisca de San Joseph, 64, 65
Francisca Josefa de la Concepción. *See* Castillo, Francisca Josefa de
Francis de Sales, Saint, 112, 113, 115–16, 173n.69
Francis of Assisi, Saint, 107

Gerónima de la Asunción, 65
Gerónima del Espíritu Santo, 7–8, 10, 68, 78–79, 83, 99, 105–6, 110–11, 114–18, 137; relation to her confessor, 24, 44–45; visionary authority, 117, 119
God. *See* Jesus Christ
González, María Marcela. *See* María Marcela

Hagiography, 53, 55, 62–84, 94, 98, 122, 158nn.2, 4, 159n.10, 180n.37. *See also Flos sanctorum*
Hurtado de Mendoza, María Manuela. *See* María Manuela de Santa Ana

Ignacio de Loyola, 3, 13, 62–63, 94, 98–102, 108, 110, 145n.44, 158n.4, 161n.46, 164nn.3, 8, 169n.22. *See also* Jesuits
Illness narrative, 77–82, 89, 162n.61
Imitatio Christi. See Jesus Christ
Indigenous community, 5, 145nn.39, 43, 165n.22. *See also* Race relations
Isabel de la Encarnación, 72, 79–80, 163nn.67, 69

Jesuits, 13, 35, 54–55, 73, 90, 102, 145nn.38, 44, 156n.19, 169nn.22–23. *See also* Ignacio de Loyola
Jesus Christ, 39, 43, 46–47, 71–73, 83–84, 88, 98–99, 101–16, 118–19, 129–32, 161n.42; body of, 83, 102–3, 105, 108; as bridegroom, 113–16, 131, 159n.17, 171n.43; *imitatio Christi*, 66, 72–73, 83–84, 99, 161n.40; mystical union with, 75, 110–16; pain of, 71–72, 103, 108, 115–16; representations of, 103–8
Juana Inés de la Cruz, Sor, 14, 21, 128, 137–40, 143n.27, 145n.44, 146n.46, 147n.5, 177nn.31–32, 181nn.2–3
Juan de la Cruz, 3, 31, 58, 111; and writing, 22, 25, 38, 47, 66, 144n.30, 161n.46

Limpieza de sangre, 4–5. *See also* Race relations
Lope de Vega Carpio, Félix, 125, 129, 172n.19
Lutgard of Aywières, 105, 107, 115, 167n.11, 174n.78

Madre Castillo. *See* Castillo, Francisca Josefa de
María Ana de la Encarnación, 7, 64
María Anna Agueda de San Ignacio, 6, 64, 65, 80
María Coleta de San José, 10, 14–15, 79, 137, 149n.29; relation to her confessor, 30, 35–36, 45
María de Jesús Agreda, 14, 76, 146n.47, 170n.40
María de la Antigua, 14, 64, 122, 174n.5
María de San José, 6, 12, 20–22, 25, 64, 66–68, 71, 76, 81, 99, 105–6, 111, 116–17, 127, 137, 143n.28, 144n.30, 146n.48; relation to her confessors, 21–22, 29–30, 32, 41–42, 149n.37; visionary authority, 32, 46–47; and writing, 22, 25, 38, 47, 66
María Magdalena, 64–65, 78, 81, 163n.65
María Manuela de Santa Ana, 24–26, 82–83, 113–14, 137; relation to her confessor, 24, 32, 39–40, 45–46, 152n.68; visionary authority, 32, 45–46, 67–68, 110, 118–19; and writing, 25–26, 45
María Marcela, 6, 24, 34, 36–37, 66–67, 69, 70–72, 78, 81, 107, 114–15, 117, 137, 170n.38, 177n.24; relation to her confessors, 31–32, 150n.45; and writing, 28
Mariana de la Encarnación. *See* María Ana de la Encarnación
María Zeraphina de Nazareth, 34
Marriage, 5–6, 53, 124–25
Martyrdom, 54–55, 72, 159n.21, 161n.41, 171n.48
Mary Magdalene, Saint, 66, 72, 93, 99, 158n.2, 167n.9

Mary Magdalene of Pazzi, Saint, 59, 66, 74, 79, 110, 114–15, 158n.2, 162n.51, 163n.68, 172nn.57, 63
Mary, Virgin. *See* Virgin Mary
Maya Marín, Sebastiana Josefa. *See* Sebastiana Josefa de la Santísima Trinidad
Mestizos. *See* Race relations
Mexico. *See* New Spain, viceroyalty of
Micaela Josefa de la Purificación, 64
Mortification. *See* Pain; Penitence
Mysticism, 2, 58, 101–5, 120, 126. *See also* Visionary experience

Nava y Saavedra, Gerónima. *See* Gerónima del Espíritu Santo
New Granada, viceroyalty of, 3, 33, 48, 54–55, 142nn.11, 13, 143nn.22, 26, 155nn.1, 3
New Spain, viceroyalty of, 3–6, 12–13, 33–34, 144n.35, 145nn.38, 40
Núñez de Miranda, Antonio, 21, 94, 145n.44, 147nn.4–5

Obedience, 20–22, 26, 29, 71, 85, 147n.8

Pain, 71, 73–84, 88–90, 93–96, 115–16. *See also* Penitence
Paula, Saint, 96, 166n.33
Pedro de Alcántara, Saint, 2, 73, 100, 144n.30, 161n.46, 168n.17
Penitence, 53, 64–65, 71–74, 88–90, 93–95, 103, 161nn.47, 50, 162n.61, 165n.12. *See also* Ascetism, Pain
Persecution motif, 55–58, 72, 161n.42. *See also* Martyrdom
Peru, viceroyalty of, 3, 5–6, 8–9, 12, 143nn.17, 26, 144n.35
Picaresque, 123–4, 175nn.10–11

Race relations 4–5, 12–13, 76, 86, 142nn.13–14, 143n.17, 145nn.38–40, 162n.57
Reading, 9–10, 63–64, 66–67, 144nn.29–30, 158n.4, 161n.40
Rhetoric of humility, 22–25, 27, 85. *See also* Anxiety of authorship; Obedience
Rosa of Lima, Saint, 12, 53, 64, 65, 76, 80, 145n.38, 158n.2, 160n.28

Saints, lives of. *See* Hagiography
Scaramelli, Giovanni Battista, 35, 73, 90, 147n.9, 164n.7
Sebastiana Josefa de la Santísima Trinidad, 12, 64, 72, 75–77, 79, 85–96, 103–5, 107, 111, 115, 126–7, 137, 170n.38; ascetism of, 69, 87–91, 93–95; background of, 86–87; relation to her confessors, 30, 35, 45; and writing, 26–27, 66, 85, 87
Sigüenza y Góngora, Carlos de, 12, 74, 145n.39, 161n.50
Silence, 15–16, 30–31, 84, 88, 137–40
Song of Songs, 10, 42–43, 111–14, 131, 170n.35
Sor Juana Inés de la Cruz. *See* Juana Inés de la Cruz
Suárez, Úrsula, 6–8, 20, 64, 66–68, 76, 82, 99, 110–11, 117–18, 121–36, 137, 142n.12, 143nn.23, 28, 147n.1, 174nn.1–4, 175nn.12–14, 178nn.34, 42–43, 179nn.51, 53, 55, 180nn.56–60, 62; background, 66–67, 70, 72, 121–23, 175nn.12–13; relation to her confessors, 30–32, 36, 122, 128, 130–32, 135–36, 145n.44, 179nn.51, 53; relation with the bishop, 130–31, 133–36, 179n.46; sense of humor, 127–31, 135, 178nn.39, 43; visionary authority, 68, 110–11, 117–18, 130; and writing, 26, 121–22, 129–30, 133–34, 174nn.3–4

Teresa de Jesús, Saint, 10, 14–15, 27, 53, 62–64, 66–68, 72–74, 77, 94, 105, 108–12, 114–16, 128–29, 142n.10, 144nn.32, 44, 146nn.48, 50, 148n.15, 157n.24, 158nn.4, 6, 170n.35, 172n.58, 67, 175nn.9–10, 176n.19, 177n.28; relation to confessors, 29, 31, 41, 145n.44, 152n.71; visionary authority, 24, 101, 108, 118.
—Works: *Camino de perfección*, 105, 114, 157n.24; *El libro de las fundaciones*, 53, 66, 158n.6, 163n.68, 175nn.9–10, 176n.19; *El libro de la vida*, 15, 24, 29, 66–68, 77, 101, 105, 110, 112, 116, 118, 158n.6, 163n.68; *Las moradas*, 72, 94, 108–9, 148n.15, 172n.58

Theatricality, 17, 98–99, 123, 125–8. *See also* Comedies
Torture. *See* Pain; Penitence

Vega, Lope de. *See* Lope de Vega Carpio, Félix.
Virgin Mary, 32, 43, 106–7, 111, 118, 135, 146n.48, 164n.76
Visionary experience, 14, 24–25, 27–29, 32, 45–46, 105–20. *See also* Mysticism
Voyeurism, 37–39

Writing, women and, 6, 9–11, 14–18, 25–29, 137–40, 141n.2, 144n.35; as confession, 22, 28; justification of, 14–15, 22, 25–29, 52; as obedience, 25–27. *See also* Reading, Visionary experience

Kristine Ibsen is an associate professor in the Department of Romance Languages and Literatures at the University of Notre Dame. She is the author of *Author, Text and Reader in the Novels of Carlos Fuentes* (1993) and editor of *The Other Mirror: Women's Narrative in Mexico, 1980–1995* (1997).